Chicken Soup
for the Soul®

inspiration for Writers

Chicken Soup for the Soul: Inspiration for Writers
101 Motivational Stories for Writers—Budding or Bestselling—from Books to Blogs
Jack Canfield, Mark Victor Hansen, Amy Newmark, Susan M. Heim

Published by Chicken Soup for the Soul Publishing, LLC www.chickensoup.com
Copyright © 2013 by Chicken Soup for the Soul Publishing, LLC. All Rights Reserved.

The publisher gratefully acknowledges the many publishers and individuals who granted Chicken Soup for the Soul permission to reprint the cited material.

Front cover photo courtesy of iStockPhoto.com/Maica (@ Carmen Martínez Banús).
Back cover photo courtesy of iStockPhoto.com/nyul. Interior photo courtesy of Photos.com

Cover and Interior Design & Layout by Brian Taylor, Pneuma Books, LLC

Distributed to the booktrade by Simon & Schuster. SAN: 200-2442

Publisher's Cataloging-in-Publication Data
(Prepared by The Donohue Group)

Chicken soup for the soul : inspiration for writers : 101 motivational
  stories for writers--budding or bestselling--from books to blogs /
  [compiled by] Jack Canfield ... [et al.].

    p. ; cm.

  ISBN: 978-1-61159-909-1

  1. Authors--Literary collections. 2. Authorship--Literary collections. 3. Authors--Anecdotes. 4. Authorship--Anecdotes. 5. Anecdotes. I. Canfield, Jack, 1944- II. Title:
Inspiration for writers : 101 motivational stories for writers--budding or bestselling--from books to blogs

PN6071.A9 C45 2013
810.8/02/0357   2013933526

PRINTED IN THE UNITED STATES OF AMERICA
on acid∞free paper
22 21 20 19 18 17 16 15 14 13   01 02 03 04 05 06 07 08 09 10

Chicken Soup for the Soul®

inspiration for Writers

101 Motivational Stories for Writers—
Budding or Bestselling—
from Books to Blogs

Jack Canfield, Mark Victor Hansen,
Amy Newmark, Susan M. Heim

Chicken Soup for the Soul Publishing, LLC
Cos Cob, CT

www.chickensoup.com

Contents

❸

~Making Time to Write~

❹

~Take My Advice~

❺

~Wrestling with Writer's Block~

❻

∼The Healing Power of Words∼

❼

∼Mentors Who Mattered∼

8

~Reflections on Rejection~

9

~Finding Inspiration~

10

~Try, Try Again~

⑪

~Writing Changes Lives~

Introduction

I got twenty-four rejection letters on my first novel. To be clear, there were only twenty publishers at the time — and I got twenty-four rejection letters, which means some people were writing me twice to make sure I got the point.

That book is still sitting on my shelf, published by Kinko's. But I had twenty-four people tell me to give it up — that I couldn't write. Does that make everyone who sent me objections wrong? Not a chance.

The best and worst part of publishing is that it's a subjective industry. All it takes is one person to say "Yes." You just have to find that person.

So let me just say this: No matter what kind of book you're writing, don't let anyone tell you "No."

~Brad Meltzer

Brad Meltzer is the #1 New York Times bestselling author of *The Inner Circle*, as well as the bestsellers *The Tenth Justice, Dead Even, The First Counsel, The Millionaires, The Zero Game, The Book of Fate* and *The Book of Lies*. His newest thriller is *The Fifth Assassin*.

He is also the host of *Brad Meltzer's Decoded* on the History network. His bestselling non-fiction books, *Heroes for My Son* and *Heroes for My Daughter*, are collections of heroes — from

Jim Henson to Rosa Parks—that he's been working on since the day his kids were born. He's also one of the co-creators of the TV show, *Jack & Bobby*—and is the Eisner Award-winning author of the critically acclaimed comic book, *Justice League of America*.

He also wrote the first story in *Chicken Soup for the Soul: Thanks Mom*, about his mother, Teri Meltzer, who was his biggest fan.

inspiration *for* Writers

Facing My Fears

*You block your dream when you allow your fear
to grow bigger than your faith.*

~Mary Manin Morrissey

Celine and Me

Who makes the rules? We make the rules.
I want to be the conductor of my own life.
~Celine Dion

When an editor wrote to offer me an assignment writing Celine Dion's authorized biography, I did not reply, "Me? Are you sure you have the right writer?" But that's just what I was thinking.

At that point in my career, although I'd written many magazine articles, I had just a few small books to my name... children's educational books, mostly. I had sent this editor my resume and writing samples more than a year prior and never heard anything other than, "Thanks. We'll keep you on file."

They actually did!

It was such an unassuming little e-mail, too. Just a polite little, "Would you be interested in writing this?" As if I'd have to consider it. "Hmm, gee, write a book with the top-selling female artist of all time? I'll check my schedule."

Of course, I said yes, and out of a fear of exposing my anemic credentials, I didn't ask why they chose me until well after contracts were signed.

"Because of your warmth," the editor told me. One of my writing samples was an article I'd written for a local newspaper about a man who rows a boat around Long Island every year to raise money for breast cancer research. She liked the tone of the article and thought my style would be a good fit for Celine. So that's what did it—a local newspaper article. You never know where one little thing may lead.

I spoke to one of my writer-friends who had also worked on celebrity biographies, and she warned me, "Just understand that celebrities will treat you like poo. They all seem nice on television, but you are nothing but a peon to them." I accepted that and stored that helpful info in my brain. It was okay, I figured. I pretty much felt like a peon anyway, and I was sure the tradeoff would be worth it. I was going to write a Really Big Book and get paid Really Big Money. If she made me fetch her slippers and call her "Your Majesty," so be it.

After the initial excitement wore off, the fear set in: I was going to fly to Las Vegas to meet Celine. For me, getting on a plane was roughly the same as being chased by hungry gorillas. The reason I became a writer in the first place was that I had a crippling panic disorder that left me housebound with agoraphobia for about four years. I had to find a way to make a living from home, and writing was the natural option. By then, I was past the worst of the panic disorder, but there were many things I hadn't yet conquered—like plane travel.

I'd tried getting on a plane once, and spent the entire ride home clutching the armrests with a kind stewardess by my side. Seriously, she spent the whole flight just trying to keep me from melting down. When I signed on to write Celine's book, I conveniently left out this little detail. I don't know why, but I thought I'd manage to get over my fear in the two whole weeks before the flight.

Didn't happen.

The night before the flight, I cried and cried. "WHY did I ever agree to do this? I'm not ready for this! I can't get on a plane! And I can't get on a plane to MEET CELINE DION! She's a superstar, and I'm an amoeba! I'm probably going to start hiccupping and developing facial tics if I even make it off the plane. What was I thinking? I have to cancel this!"

I didn't sleep at all. I paced and cried and flung myself dramatically on couches and tried to remember to breathe. How I convinced myself to get on that plane after all is a mystery, but I did it, and there was a surprising lack of freaking out once we were in the air.

That night, I met Celine. If there were any leftover panicky feelings, they dissipated within minutes of meeting her. My friend was wrong; Celine was an absolute sweetheart. Humble, down-to-earth, funny, silly, and very caring. She talked to me about my life and shared cookies with me. She sat on the floor with me and chatted into the middle of the night like we were old school buddies.

I went back to Vegas several times over the next few months. Celine met my family, and members of a Celine fan website brought me beautiful cards and drawings because I had involved them in the book. To make it a great book for the fans, I figured, I should find out what the fans wanted to know! Their appreciation was beautiful, and when my post office box overflowed with requests for signed bookplates, the postal worker refused to believe me when I said they were fan letters. From my fans.

Hmph. What did he think I was, a peon?

My experience with Celine was life changing in so many ways. She cried in my arms once when talking about the pressures of fame at such a young age, and it made me see her—and myself—in a new light. When I was younger, I had wanted that kind of fame. I had hoped to be a professional actress or singer, but in that moment, I knew I was doing the work I was supposed to do. It might have taken a strange path to get me there, but I loved being a writer.

"Never in my life have I wanted a journalist, a writer, to talk to me again," Celine told me. "It's hard for me to open up and trust. This is the first time I called to say, 'I want to see her. Ask her if she wants to see me again.' There's something about you."

When I was finished with the book, Celine's husband, René, called to tell me how well I had captured Celine, and that he felt very emotional and proud reading the manuscript.

The editor was right, I thought. She could have had any number of writers with stacks of celebrity books to their name, but the writer who was right for Celine was… me. Before I left Vegas for the last time, we hugged and said "I love you" to each other, and I knew that I'd just met one of the nicest and most inspiring people I'd ever encounter. She deserves every bit of her success.

Getting on that plane opened up my world again and made me see that anything was possible. My limitations had no hold over me anymore. Since that time, I've traveled many times, met fascinating people, and helped to write their stories. It's an exciting and meaningful career, but in a larger sense, it's a wonderful life. And it's exactly where I'm meant to be.

~Jenna Glatzer

Queries, Agents, and Insomnia

A ruffled mind makes a restless pillow.
~Charlotte Brontë

Three terrors kept giving me sleepless nights: the economy, my parents' health, and querying literary agents.

The first two things—well, I knew I had no control over those. All I could do was hope and pray. But the third? I wanted to control that by writing an awesome book that made agents squeal with joy. I wanted to experience that magic moment that writers dub The Call, when agents phone them and utter the words, "I'd love to represent you and your book."

My past querying efforts hadn't gone well. I had already given up on two books. I sent out a few queries only to receive form rejections in return or no reply at all. In the end, I just didn't have enough faith in my books to continue.

To me, it felt like literary agents lived in grandeur at the top of some high tower far away in New York City. From their high vantage points on gilded thrones, I was as significant as an ant. I understood that a single agent might receive thousands of queries a year, and out of that choose only two or three new authors to represent.

Basically, the odds really stank.

I was terrified of trying at all, but I knew my new novel was something special, something different. Unlike my past books, this one had been worth rewriting again and again. I mean that in the most severe sense—the last rewrite involved cutting out 80,000 words and keeping only 20,000, and completely rearranging the plot. I sent several versions through a critique group and absorbed their scary feedback. I couldn't even count the hundreds of hours I spent writing and polishing.

But now my insomnia stemmed from one big problem: My novel was done. I could have probably continued to edit for all eternity—there would always be more typos to catch, more words to fiddle with—but, deep down, I knew I was procrastinating.

I needed to start sending out query letters.

Query letters were terrifying unto themselves. A good query letter entices agents to read the enclosed pages. From reading agent blogs, I knew most query letters didn't do their job. I labored over my letter, had it critiqued, rewrote it, and rewrote it again. As I stretched out sleepless in my bed, I knew the words of my query letter from memory, and parts of my novel as well. When I closed my eyes, I could even see where the words landed on the page.

Finally, enough was enough. I had to conquer my fear. I needed sleep. I needed my sanity.

I gave myself a deadline: I had to start querying by the end of January. I only had one real shot with these agents; most of the time, a rejection means an author can't query that agency again with the same book. There were probably a hundred agents in my genre. My plan was to send out queries in batches of five. That way, if I didn't get any positive responses right away, I wouldn't have burned up all my opportunities. I could revise and then send out more letters.

I had to do this. I had to try. I had worked on my book for two years to get to this point. I couldn't stop now.

I read over my query letter and my novel. I stared down agency guidelines. I scarfed down chocolate. I read more. I ate more chocolate. My hands trembling, I prepared that first e-mail. I clicked Send.

I almost threw up.

I sent out several more e-mails in quick sequence. I stared at the screen and ate more chocolate. There. The journey had begun.

Within a few hours, I had a reply: a request for sample pages, a partial request! I screamed and danced around the house. A request, on my first query! I quickly sent off a reply, visions of contracts and hardcover books dancing in my head.

The dancing stopped the very next day as rejections trickled in, including a swift "no" on my partial. I told myself that this was all okay. This was part of the querying cycle. So, I sent out more. I had met an agent at a conference the year before, so I sent her a query. Within an hour, I was stunned at her request for the full manuscript.

I almost threw up again.

More rejections arrived. Every time I had notification of more e-mail, I was filled with dread. Some agents offered pleasantly positive feedback, even as they passed on my project, but the result was the same: no. It became harder and harder for me to muster energy to send out more queries.

Out of this quagmire of negativity, I had a surprise e-mail: a second request for my full manuscript. I hadn't heard anything from the first agent with my full book. Instead of feeling joy, though, I felt numb as I sent out my novel again. How long would it be till I heard back with yet another "no"?

A week later, that agent mailed me again. "Well, that was fast," I muttered out loud, bracing myself for the worst. Instead, I read, "I'm loving your novel. Can I call you later this week?"

I screamed, and then I broke into hysterical sobs. An agent loved my book. She wanted to give me The Call.

The agent called me. I was awed by how passionate she was about my characters, and tickled to pieces that she was so enthralled with reading that she missed a subway stop. She wasn't some snob on a gilded throne. She was a book lover, and she found a book she loved: mine.

Things became even more surreal days later when the first agent with my full novel also offered me representation. I deliberated and made my choice.

It took me years of writing to get to that high point. Months of working up the nerve to send out that first query. Weeks of frustration and tears as those rejections filled my inbox, but it was all worthwhile.

I had an agent.

And after all that, I was sleepless again, but for a very different reason: pure happiness.

~Beth Cato

Poopy Pants and Butterflies

Nerves and butterflies are fine — they're a physical sign that you're mentally ready and eager. You have to get the butterflies to fly in formation, that's the trick.

~Steve Bull

"Of course, I'd love to come!" I lied to my son's teacher when she asked if I'd speak to her second-grade class about writing. I always dreaded speaking opportunities. I am a writer, not a speaker — an introvert who deliberately chose a solitary profession. I hated to speak in public. Besides, what could I say to a bunch of kids about my career?

It got worse. The teacher called the next week to say they wanted me to speak to *all* of the second-grade classes. They would divide the six classes into two groups, so I'd have to give my presentation twice. Double torture.

I called my sister, Karen, an elementary school teacher. She'd had her share of authors in her classroom. How did they keep the kids' attention? What could I possibly say that would interest children? Fortunately, Karen's memory was better than mine.

"Do you remember when you wrote your first book in second grade, and it was the most popular book in your classroom library?" she asked.

How could I have forgotten? The title of my "bestseller" was *The Girl Who Pooped Her Pants*. Fortunately, my mother had saved my masterpiece, and it still contained the library card filled with kids' signatures. They'd all laughed at my tale about the girl who got in trouble with her mom for her lack of toilet training. It definitely wasn't brilliant writing, but I had learned the first lesson of children's writing: Meet kids at their level.

To my children, all boys, poop, boogers, cooties and farts were their favorite topics! They loved my book when I dug it out of storage and read it to them. "Read it again!" they told me over and over. I knew I'd found the perfect icebreaker for my presentation!

The day of the classroom visits finally arrived. My stomach was churning, but I felt fairly confident that I'd prepared well. I'd brought a bag filled with some of the books I'd written and showed them to the kids. "Is that really your name on that book?" They were definitely impressed.

My story about the incontinent girl was a big hit! I followed it up with several poems I'd written for my boys. One was about leaving a tooth under my pillow for the tooth fairy. Another was about chocolate cake that caused a bellyache. A third poem described my fat cat that fell off the chair. "As you can see from my silly poems," I told them, "you can write a poem or story about anything! Write about your baby brother, a baseball game, or even a peanut-butter sandwich!" I could see the light bulbs go on in their heads. They, too, could be writers.

The next day, my son's backpack was bulging with thank-you notes from second-graders.

"I loved your story about the girl who pooped her pants!"

"You inspired us to write!"

"I think I will be an author when I grow up."

Many of the notes contained short poems and stories the children had written for me.

I'm sure I'll still have butterflies in my stomach when I get the call for another classroom visit. But I'll pull out the letters from the children and remember the joy I saw in their eyes when they were inspired by a writer.

~Susan M. Heim

The Day I Turned Scarlett

Always be a first-rate version of yourself,
instead of a second-rate version of somebody else.
~Judy Garland

I t had to be a hundred degrees in my dorm room that night, and by two o'clock in the morning, I was hot and tired and spent. Sweat literally dripped off me. It smeared the ink on all the pages, and I had yet to create something that I felt confident about sharing with eleven talented writers with whom I was studying at a summer writers' intensive.

I never dreamed that I would be accepted into such an esteemed program in the first place. The workshop leader was an accomplished author whose work I had greatly admired. I wished I could write the way she did—deep, rich, evocative details spun around immensely profound literary stories. I had always aspired to become the next Edith Wharton or Willa Cather. But no matter how hard I tried, in the end my work somehow managed to veer more toward the style of Erma Bombeck, and my characters were more like Bridget Jones. I wanted to expand my horizons and break away from the comic and absurd. I wanted my work to be taken seriously.

"Send a writing sample. What have you got to lose?" my boyfriend suggested when I told him my doubts about applying to the program.

"I'm too old," I said.

"Old? Forty is the new thirty. You'll fit right in."

I smirked at him. "I'm afraid they'll laugh when they read my stuff. I hardly write serious literature."

"Why can't there be room for everyone — all types of writing?"

I just stared at him, deadpan. He didn't understand.

When I received a letter of acceptance in the mail weeks later, I feared it was the result of a clerical error. But when I showed up at the university on a hot day in June and found my name on the registration list, I knew it was for real.

On the first day of the program, my heart pounded while I listened to introductions from the eleven other writers. We were all seated at a table around the workshop leader. I swallowed hard as my much younger peers rattled off litanies of Ivy League institutions and publishing credits from esteemed academic literary journals. I, too, was a college graduate — from a very small, state school — and while I was a published author, my work had found its way into magazines and anthologies that I was sure none of the other writers seated around that table had ever heard of or read.

When it came time for me to introduce myself, all I managed to say was, "Hi. I think I am going to learn a lot just by breathing the same air as you people."

My peers, along with the workshop leader, physically leaned in my direction, as though waiting to hear the rest of my credentials. But all I could do was sit there and force a smile. I was too petrified to speak another word.

Intimidated. Insecure. Out of my league. Those words describe my feelings for four hours each day as part of the group. The writers were not only more gifted and talented than me, but also much more ambitious. When I called my boyfriend each night, I'd give him a daily update.

"More I-R-S," I'd say, using the acronym I devised for the plethora of stories that were written about incest, rape and suicide. They were recurrent themes, and it amazed me how courageous some were to read aloud pieces that addressed those issues — some of them, I learned, were deeply personal. I didn't dare volunteer to read my stories, which seemed like insignificant little ditties in comparison.

The main thrust of the workshop delved into what makes characters unforgettable, and we dissected the traits of strong archetypes in fiction. For example, the essence of lasting and memorable characters can often be evoked simply by conjuring a name. Take Ebenezer Scrooge—a miser; Peter Pan—someone unwilling to grow up; Hester Prynne—an adulteress.

During the workshop, we were all given an assignment to be completed over the course of the program. We were to take a literary archetype of our own choosing and create a story that would put that character into a situation that would specifically test his or her main trait. On the last day of the workshop, we would share our stories with the group.

With that in mind, I was inspired by one of my favorite fictional heroines, Scarlett O'Hara from Gone with the Wind. I found her fascinating—colorful, headstrong, a real drama queen. She'd be perfect.

For a whole week after class, I went straight to my dorm room, intent on fashioning a serious and profound short story. I decided to focus on Scarlett being a manipulative woman-in-distress who insisted on getting—and having—her own way. But when I sat down to write, nothing jelled. I brought her back to Tara and the Civil War, but I found it immensely hard to cover new ground on the page. Even setting her in a scene of conflict with Rhett Butler, her one true love, somehow seemed tired. I tried to plug her into the I-R-S model, but that certainly didn't feel right for Miss Scarlett.

Day after day, I wrote pages upon pages—but they were merely false starts filled with cross-outs. Nothing I wrote held my interest. At 2:00 A.M. on the night before the deadline, I knew I had come up short, and I finally succumbed to the pressure and wept. There I was—a woman creeping toward middle age, sobbing in a dorm room at 2:00 A.M., sweating both literally and figuratively, over homework. Even working my hardest and trying my best, I felt beaten by inescapable mediocrity. Not knowing what else to do or where to turn, I plucked out a few more tissues, then picked up the phone and dialed my boyfriend. I knew he was flying out on business early the next day, but I was desperate for his moral support.

"Don't you see? What you're doing is going against the grain," he told me, his gravelly voice filled with sleep. "Why don't you stop trying to be someone you're not and write the way that feels natural for you? Just have fun with it."

Fun? The word sounded completely foreign to me.

The minute I hung up the phone, I sucked back my tears. I took a deep breath, along with his advice, and began to free-write in the voice of Scarlett O'Hara herself. I took snippets of all the drama that swirled inside my own mind and decided to channel it comically through Scarlett's voice. Suddenly, things started to take shape. I updated Scarlett O'Hara for the new millennium—made her over in the throes of midlife, harried and hot, and put her in the same airport my boyfriend would be departing from the next day. Scarlett's conflict would be that she'd be denied a first-class seat on the airplane—oh, tragedies of tragedies! What was a Southern belle to do?

While the rest of the college slept, I wrote nonstop, stifling my giggles while the story poured onto the page. Then, I read and re-read the piece—tweaking it along the way—until the sky finally brightened outside my window, and I hurried off to the workshop at 8:00 A.M.

Each participant's story was more seriously moving and profound than the next, and a sense of doom and dread overwhelmed me. How could the entertaining nature of my own story possibly measure up?

When I was finally called on to share my work, I stared down at my own handwriting on the page and broke out into a sick, clammy sweat. But I pushed through my fear and started to read. Everyone at the table sat perfectly still as I began to tell Scarlett O'Hara's story. When my words were met with eruptions of laughter, it felt like cool breezes were suddenly rising up all around me, lifting my spirits and boosting my confidence, word by word. When I finished reading, the room burst into applause and cheering.

"Well, I think Kathleen's story was just the thing we all needed to cool off," the workshop leader announced after I was nominated by my peers to read the story aloud at the final reception, which would be attended by industry agents and editors. It seemed even more unbelievable than my getting into the program in the first place.

Still on a high after the workshop, I was anxious to call my boyfriend with the news. When my cell phone proved out of range, I found a pay phone in the lobby of the dorm and immediately sat down in the booth and dialed him.

"How wonderful! I can hear you smiling," he said, thrilled to share my victory.

When I finally slipped the receiver back on the cradle, I was beaming. I had no idea that weeks afterward, the director of the writing intensive would nominate my story for Best New American Voices (a national prize in literature), or that I would later adapt the story into a play that would be showcased off-Broadway in New York City.

At that moment, I just sat in the phone booth, stunned, listening to all the coins I had inserted register down into the pay phone. Ca-ching. Ca-ching. Ca-ching. The clinking sound didn't stop. It chimed on and on until almost ten dollars in quarters poured out of the change return into my lap. Running my fingers through all the coins, I stared at the reflected image of myself in the glass that encased me in that phone booth and burst out laughing. I had hit the jackpot—in more ways than one.

~Kathleen Gerard

The Hard Truth

The truth brings with it a great measure of absolution, always.

~R. D. Laing

"Y ou must be SO excited about your story!" My friend grinned enthusiastically and squeezed my arm. "I can't wait to read it. Think of all the people who will see it!"

I managed a feeble smile as my stomach twisted into a knot. "Yeah... I can't wait."

Any fledgling writer would have been thrilled with my achievement—my first byline in a major magazine. The story had attracted attention all right. Chosen from thousands of entries, it was the ticket to a thrilling, all-expenses paid trip to New York to learn to write for a magazine with a circulation of millions. Nearly overnight, my dream of becoming a real writer had come true. There was only one small problem. No, it was a big problem. The story I had written was true and intensely personal. It was even embarrassing—a chronicle of major failure in my life and marriage and the journey to healing. So why had I chosen to write about it?

Weeks away from publication, I couldn't remember why, exactly, I had chosen this story. It certainly wasn't because it was something I was proud of. No, it was almost like God had spoken to my heart when I entered the writing contest, on a whim, and instructed me to write and submit the story. After all, the magazine wanted true, unpublished stories of personal change. Mine certainly qualified.

After the workshop, my story was given a publication date. I was excited... for a little while. Then came the task of rewriting... and more rewriting. With the rewrites came the realization that the story was, in fact, going to appear in print. Fear began to replace my excitement. One day, after a long conversation with my editor, I hung up the phone and burst into tears. We had been shaping the story together, and each change cut closer and closer to my heart. I hadn't expected to feel this way. Writing so personally was hard. It was painful. Still, I gave my approval and waited for the day the magazine would appear.

During the last days before publication time, I was ambivalent, one minute filled with proud anticipation, the next considering a stake-out at all major booksellers and buying every copy of the magazine. And what about the friends and relatives who would receive copies in their mailboxes? Most of them didn't know about my experience. Would they be disgusted? Lose all respect for me? Some days, I felt physically ill with worry.

Then, a few days after I knew the issue was in stores, my worst fear came true. I was invited to a friend's home for Easter dinner along with some relatives, my sister, and a couple of her friends. All the way there, I thought about the story and wondered who might have read it. And, sure enough, when I entered the house, I spied a copy of the magazine prominently displayed on a side table. Nonchalantly, I sat down next to the table and covered the magazine with another publication when no one was looking. Perhaps everybody would just forget about it.

"Hey, Cath, don't we have a copy of your story around here somewhere?" My sister gestured toward a dinner guest. "Sara wants to read it."

"Really?" I felt my face grow hot as I wished the couch I was sitting on would swallow me whole.

"Of course. We're so proud of you!" My sister got up from her chair and rummaged through the stack of magazines. "Here it is, Sara. Cath's first big story."

At that moment, I excused myself and fled to the kitchen. A

bottle of Chardonnay sat on the counter, and I poured myself a glass and gulped it down. Briefly, I considered disappearing into the back bedroom with the entire bottle.

When I reentered the room, Sara laid down the magazine.

"Uhhh, congratulations." She shifted in her seat. The look on her face said it all.

Quickly, I shifted the conversation to another topic, but the damage had been done. I contemplated my dismal future as a writer. I had been too real, and people were disgusted with me. Maybe I would be better off making up stories for the many celebrity tell-all magazines common at grocery store checkouts.

Later that night, I lay in bed, knees pulled to my chest. Was it the money, the attention that prompted me to tell that story? Would people think I was willing to air "dirty laundry" in exchange for a few hundred bucks? Would they judge me, think I had no talent?

Then I remembered one of the magazine editors who had approached me one night at the workshop.

"I was the first one to read your story, Catherine. It stood out immediately; it had emotional honesty."

Emotional honesty?

I had never considered it. I'd only written as much from my heart as possible in hopes that someone else would benefit somehow—perhaps a reader who had gone through a similar experience. I hadn't thought of the people who might not understand why I chose to write about my experience.

When I thought about it, that editor wasn't the only one who was touched by the story. There was the woman who approached me privately after reading it and shared her own experience—one that very few people knew about.

"I want you to know I admire you for your courage and honesty," she had told me. Remembering her words brought instant comfort.

As I lay in bed, new thoughts strengthened my resolve. This was what writing was about: telling the truth. The sometimes hard truth. Sure, some people might not understand; they might even judge me. Certainly, not every true story is one that needs to be told. But when

I thought about it, the authors and books I admired most shared a common quality: They had a transparency, an honesty, that touched me. And that was the kind of writer I wanted to be.

~Catherine Madera

Write from the Start

Everything becomes a little different
as soon as it is spoken out loud.
~Hermann Hesse

It was my wife who'd gotten me into this mess. She'd been encouraging me to "take up writing" for several years. I didn't pay her much mind at first. I didn't know much about writing, but I knew you didn't "take it up" like one might take up golf or string art. Besides, she'd led me down the garden path before. This is the same woman who insisted I buy a Betamax, promised I'd love the movie *Kung Fu Panda*, and swore to me that vasectomies didn't hurt.

One day, she brought home an adult-education schedule and tossed it on my lap. One class caught my eye: "Write from the Start." Cork Millner — Instructor. Clever title, I thought, but I didn't know how much I could learn from a guy named Cork. I already knew how to drink.

I showed up that Thursday night carrying a full load of excitement and trepidation. The registrar came by and took my twenty dollars. Then Mr. Millner handed out the syllabus.

"You'll notice that this class normally takes ten weeks," he explained. "But the spring semester is shorter by three weeks, and I can't be here for another week, so we're going to condense it into six weeks. Don't worry, it won't be a problem."

No problem at all, I thought, as I looked around for the registrar. I might not have known how to write, but I knew how to add, and someone owed me eight bucks!

When the first class was over, Cork had done his job. Properly motivated, I couldn't wait to start the assignment—a 500-word humorous essay describing an event in my life. After shoveling down dinner, I turned on our new computer and stared at the keyboard. Rats! Writer's block already?

At approximately 4:30 in the morning, I leapt out of bed with an idea and pecked at the keys like a stuttering rooster. Ten minutes before I had to be at work, I turned off the computer and ran out the door.

After work, I raced home to review my masterpiece but found zip... nothing. Following an hour of panicked exasperation, I surmised that I forgot to save and swore I'd never write again.

Thirty minutes later, I was rewriting my previous tour de force from memory. When I finished, I checked the word count—556 words. I had to cut fifty-six words, so I went back in. One hour later, I checked the count again—678 words.

On Thursday night, I tossed my assignment on Mr. Millner's desk and watched student after student place theirs on top of mine, burying my work of genius.

Thirsty for writing knowledge, I listened intently to Coach Millner's lecture. Then he stretched and said, "Okay, let's take a little break. Afterward, we'll read some of your assignments."

"What did he say?" I croaked. Sweat poured out of my body. Searching for the best escape route, I tried to calm down between gulps of coffee.

Cork returned to the head of the classroom. "Okay, Susie, would you like to come up here and read your piece?"

Damn, he was going to make us read. Aloud!

My brain was so cluttered with terror-stricken thoughts that I couldn't hear Susie, but when her lips stopped moving, I echoed the class: "Very good."

Mr. Millner snatched another assignment and called out a name, but I was in my own petrified private Idaho. I saw mouths moving, but all I could hear above my pounding heart was my inner voice yelling, "Run! Run!"

I noticed that he was taking assignments off the top of the stack, so I might be safe. Slowly, my hearing returned. I calmed down enough to try and work out a plan in case he called me. Maybe I could start signing like a deaf person. No, that wouldn't work. I'd already opened my big mouth once or twice in class. Maybe I could stand and say, "Instead of reading my piece, I'd like to offer one of my kidneys to science."

I watched the clock like a Dead Man Walking. I noticed it took about three minutes to read the assignment and about two minutes for the class to evaluate it. Fifteen more minutes were left in the class. I'm home free, I thought. There were at least ten pieces ahead of mine. Hell, I might even savagely critique the next person's work with the rest of the class.

Just as the sweat started to evaporate from my brow, Cork shuffled the assignments and randomly took one from the middle. "Okay, let's hear from a man now," Cork said. "Here we go. Jim?"

I sat motionless, conjuring a cloaking device.

"Jim Alexander?" Mr. Millner said.

I looked around the room like the rest of the class, hoping, praying there was another Jim Alexander. Oh, please, God, I'll never write again if there's another Jim Alexander.

Mr. Millner smiled at me knowingly. Before I could protest that I was baptized James, not Jim, he handed me my assignment.

I began to read, but I wasn't sure if anything came out of my mouth. The pages were shaking so badly I had to lay them down on the table. In the background, I heard a chuckle as I read. Then giggling, followed by laughter. I stopped about a minute into the piece, realizing that I hadn't taken a breath since I started. Glancing up, I saw my classmates smiling. I started to read again and heard more laughter, followed by a roar.

They liked me! The worm had turned, and I was a writer.

~Jim Alexander

A Change of Direction

*If one advances confidently in the direction of his dreams and
endeavors to live the life which he has imagined,
he will meet with success unexpected in common hours.*
~Henry David Thoreau

When my first novel was published in 2004, I had so many people asking me for writing and publishing advice that I decided to shape my business around this particular service. I was already a life coach so the change made sense — the issues that keep people from completing their writing are often life issues. Little did I know I was going to learn this lesson myself.

I thought a business helping people to write books would allow me to make money as a writer while still pursuing my own creative work. Ghostwriting projects and book-coaching clients came my way easily, especially after I hired a well-known Internet entrepreneur to teach me how to develop and market my business. I devoted many hours to our work, and it involved a lot of writing: newsletters, e-mails, sales letters, website copy, manuals. When I wasn't writing client projects, I was writing business materials. My writing — my next novel specifically — received my attention only once or twice a month, if at all.

As I shifted my business to work with entrepreneurs who wanted to write books, I began joining networking and mastermind groups to meet potential clients and to learn more marketing tactics. One group in particular, called Peak Performers, included many talented entrepreneurial minds. We met several times a year, and at each meeting I felt the same way: I was a first-grader in a room full of college students.

At the end of one meeting, we received an assignment from one of our mentors. We had spent the day learning about the power of our personal stories, and how to use them to create persuasive marketing pieces. We had to write such a piece and submit it for competition. The winners would be announced at the next meeting. I looked around the room (there were about eighty of us in all) and picked out the people I figured would win. "Fabienne, Beth and probably Adam," I said to myself. Though I raised my hand along with everyone else when our mentor asked who would complete the assignment, I was already thinking, "What's the point?" By the time I got home, I'd forgotten all about it.

A few days before the contest deadline, I received an e-mail from our group's administrator reminding us of the assignment and the commitment we made during the meeting. I realized it did mean something to me to keep that promise, so I decided to write a sales letter. When I had sent it in, I patted myself on the back and gave myself credit for completion—that would be my prize.

Not long after the deadline passed, our mentor sent out a fax with a list of names in connection with the assignment. It said again that the winners would be announced at our upcoming meeting. I looked over the names and saw mine wasn't on it, just as I expected. I was okay with that.

On the day when the time came to announce the winners of the contest, our mentor talked about how much he had been affected by the work of the top three entries. He felt connected to the writers, as if he were emotionally invested in each one. The pieces moved him, and he wanted to read them again and again. He thought we could all learn a lot from this work, and he said he wanted each of the top three to read their pieces out loud.

I was looking around the room to see who would get up when I heard him call my name. Me. I put my hand over my mouth and stared at him in shock. As it turned out, I had misread the list I'd seen: It included the people who had completed the assignment, leaving out the top entries. I fought hard to swallow my tears. I didn't want to cry in front of everyone because they would totally misunderstand what I was crying about.

I wasn't crying because I was happy to learn I was in the top three. I was crying in disappointment because I realized how much I had discounted myself. I had been writing since I was a girl. When I knew nothing else in the world, I always knew I was a writer, and a good one at that. But there I was, swimming in a place where I was not only not honoring my talent, I was also devaluing it.

My mastermind group was a good one. I learned a lot, but what my mentors didn't realize that day was that they had inadvertently coached me right out of the group. I didn't want to be surrounded by entrepreneurs anymore. I wanted to be surrounded by other writers—literary writers. I made a decision to change direction. I would find a way to make my writing the focus of my life. Now I had a new problem to address, and at the heart of it was this question: *How do I make it happen?*

The funny thing is, I'd had the answer for a while: enroll in a master's program and get an MFA in creative writing. However, I didn't do it for years because whenever I spoke about the idea, someone would say, "You don't need to do that. You've already published a novel." Or they would talk about the endeavor being a waste of money. I would listen to these thoughts, put aside the idea, and keep floundering on my own.

Then, just as I was beginning to gain confidence in thinking about a master's program, my sister Theo died. She was barely a year younger than me. I fell into a confusing mix of emotions: I was paralyzed with grief, but I also had a stunning awareness that time was not guaranteed to me. Suddenly, I had no patience for all the reasons I didn't need an MFA. I could only focus on why I did, because I have so much to say as a writer. I also needed a supportive community of writers/friends/teachers, and I wanted them to inspire, encourage, and challenge me to write what I've never written before.

By the end of the year, I had applied, been accepted to, and begun my first semester at the Vermont College of Fine Arts, one of the top writing programs in the country. As of this writing, I'm in my second semester, and already I've grown more and produced more as a writer (short stories, essays and a novel-in-progress) than I have in my previous eight years. I love the people around me — the teachers and the students — and they continually marvel at how happy I am and totally willing to soak up everything they have to offer. They don't realize how big a role they are playing in my life or how different things are for me because of them. But another friend, after seeing a photo on Facebook of me writing at a VCFA residency, understood it all.

"I love it," she wrote in the comments. "You are in your joy!"

Yes. She is absolutely correct.

~Sophfronia Scott

The Secret Life of a Teenage Author

Find out the reason that commands you to write;
see whether it has spread its roots into the very depth of your heart;
confess to yourself you would have to die if you were forbidden to write.
~Rainer Maria Rilke

Growing up, writing was something I'd been taught to scoff at. I was going to be a biochemical engineer. I was going to be a genetic pathologist. I was going to be an aeronautical physicist or a neuropsychologist or an architectural historian. I wanted to be something that came with a long, fancy title after my name and a Ph.D. in front of it, like my dad, the nuclear physicist, or my mom, the actuary scientist. Not an author.

Yes, I loved to read. Yes, sometimes I wrote a poem that was featured in the school's newspaper. But I had grown up in an environment that valued intelligence above creativity, and to me, writing was a joke. An English major? Please. I was meant to go into pre-med or pre-law... wasn't I? That's what I had been told growing up, and my parents had drilled it into me so deeply that I had never considered anything else.

In eighth grade, I moved from St. Louis, Missouri (population: 4 million) to Sheboygan Falls, Wisconsin (population: 7,000... barely). The culture shock was too much for me to handle. I became moody, angry, and rather unpredictable. I didn't like my new friends because they weren't my old ones. I hated Wisconsin because it wasn't Missouri (also, it had cows… and no decent malls). My transcripts had gotten messed up during the move, so I ended up taking algebra twice and being put in an eighth-grade level science instead of biology. Also, my new school didn't offer any of the honors courses I was supposed to take. Suddenly, I was an angst-ridden teenager with too much time on her hands and no idea what to do with it.

So I escaped into writing. My first story was written in a blue notebook fondly named Ricardo. Sometime while I drafted that first novel, I realized that I was not, in fact, a terrible writer. (Looking through Ricardo now, though, I find this was a rather mistaken realization.) More than that, I realized that I liked writing. I liked the way the words poured out of me and turned my frustrations into lengthy paragraphs about characters I'd grown to love. For the first time in my life, I'd found something that I was both good at and enjoyed doing—not like studying for SATs (which I'd started in seventh grade, at my parents' insistence), or playing piano for six hours.

My search for publication, on the other hand, began as my personal rebellion. My genius parents, naturally, did not approve of the hours I spent huddled over my laptop, hours I should have been using to read *Les Misérables* or learn calculus. I wanted to be published, not because I wanted to share my story with the world, but because I wanted to prove that I could.

I began querying my second novel, a YA fantasy, on my fifteenth birthday. With little knowledge about the industry, I contacted more than forty agents, receiving only about seven requests for partial or full manuscripts. I was a teenager—I thought I was prepared for rejection.

I wasn't.

After taking my SAT during the winter of freshman year and failing to score as high as my parents expected (having changed "studying time" to "WIP editing time" on my schedule), I was beginning to have doubts. After all, what were my odds? I was fifteen. I was a fangirl, not an author. I had seen the rates of success in the publishing industry, and they didn't point in my favor. Thousands and thousands of people were better than me and had more experience than me and had just as much unrelenting passion. And then there was still the small fact that I was fifteen. I needed to get into a good college; I needed to major in a useful subject; I needed to get a good job that could support my normal, two-story suburban future home and my normal, 2.36 future children. Writing wasn't the path to reaching these goals; neuropsychology was. Or genetic pathology. Or biochemical engineering.

Also, at the time, I had absolutely no one to support me. My parents were wonderful and loving and (painfully) intelligent, but they had never taken my writing seriously. At best, they indulged me. At worst, they told me to forget "this writing thing" and study for upcoming ACTs. I had never told anyone outside of my immediate family about my passion (obsession) for writing, much less admitted that I was looking for publication. The snarky voice in my head, in addition to the traditional lines ("You're not pretty enough, skinny enough, athletic enough, smart enough"), began to whisper that I would never be good enough. In a classic teenage identity crisis, I was beginning to lose faith in myself and my writing abilities. Being starved for encouragement, I was starting to think that this dream would likely soon join the rest in my graveyard of memories.

Three months after I had started querying, though, I got the most wonderful rejection of my life. The agent decided to pass on my partial, but said that she would be willing to look at revisions. Admittedly, I was discouraged at first. At that point, I had already rewritten my novel seven times. Revisions would be a huge time commitment, and my parents would be far from pleased. On top of that, I had at least some semblance of a social life. I was involved in clubs, extracurriculars, and sports, and my inner teenage girl wanted to flirt and go shopping and spend my Saturdays somewhere other than my room, with someone other than my laptop.

But that rejection gave me hope that maybe I could do it. Maybe I really could get that frustrating, demanding, annoyingly beloved manuscript published. So I got to work, locking myself in my room again with my laptop balanced on my knees. I emerged a month later with essentially a new novel, a new understanding of the industry, and a new faith in myself.

I began looking for representation again in late January. In two weeks, I sent out nine queries, received four full requests, and received an offer from the same agent who had suggested I revise my novel. I got her e-mail in Global Studies class on February tenth and promptly proceeded to fall out of my chair.

I realized that day that I didn't want to be a biochemical engineer, or a doctor, or a lawyer. At all. Those had never been my dreams. I wanted to write.

So I went home. I wrote. And I haven't stopped.

~Amy Zhang

Seeing My Way to Success

The art of living lies less in eliminating our troubles
than in growing with them.
~Bernard M. Baruch

y husband burst into my office. "We got to number one, honey!" He hugged me and twirled me around.

"I can't believe it!" I gasped. "We have to celebrate."

I wasn't just celebrating the fact that my latest release reached the #1 spot on Amazon in its category. Rather, I was cheering the triumph over impossibilities.

Initially, a muffled voice, mocking and sort of unkind, threatened to drown my dream to write. It reminded me of the impossibility—me, write? How ridiculous. Being blind, how in the world would I write?

But in my own world of physical darkness, a light shined when I installed a software program on my computer. This tool allowed me to hear the letters I keyed on the keyboard, to read them back, to navigate through Word documents, and read and write e-mails.

"I love you," I wrote my husband. And I could hardly contain my glee when I heard the robotic voice of the screen reader pronounce his response.

That was the beginning. God had given me this tool that opened a new world to me. I sifted through the insights I had stored in my heart. One by one, I wrote stories. I detailed episodes of the time I clung to the hope of keeping the little eyesight I had left. The time I woke up and saw nothing, as the progressing retinal disease had finally robbed my sight completely. I related how my world turned upside down with sorrow as I entered the world of the blind.

But when I saw the other side of adversity, I began my first book. On its pages, I strung words that painted the colorful world I learned to see with my heart. I described new possibilities and traced insights to reveal hope. With each line, I savored the privilege of taking my readers from the messy mud of trials to the green meadows of joy.

I never stopped. Words strung together effortlessly, bringing each chapter to a close. And finally, when I'd written the end to the book, I put it out for the world to read. The response glowed with hues of victory and shimmered with the beauty of satisfaction. Readers found inspiration and courage for their own troubles.

But the real test was yet to come. Magazine articles and stories which I'd crafted with passion and diligence came back with a "Your story doesn't fit our publication." Simple words to them, but to me, they were swords of rejection that pierced deep.

But silencing the voice of discouragement, I kept my fingers dancing on the keyboard. And my mind kept soaking in lessons about the writing craft. Eventually, one by one, my stories appeared in hundreds of publications, including a featured story in *Guideposts* magazine.

The next level was to get an agent. And that step came easier than expected. She represented me as she tried to find a publisher for my novel. The novel went nowhere. And months later, the agent ended the contract with me.

I went to bed with disappointment, rejection and discouragement on my pillow. But in the morning, I gave a deep sigh. Then I navigated to the special file where I kept sweet words: all the encouraging comments, all the testimonials of my first book, and all the stories about how lives were changed. Then I grinned silently and wrote myself a short to-do list: Never give up.

I followed that list and decided to search for another agent. With bags packed and a heart filled with hope, I grabbed my white cane and headed to the next writers' conference. My goal was defined: to find another agent.

I scheduled a meeting with various agents. One of them was a gentleman who possessed decades of experience. Seated before him, I handed him a book proposal I had worked on for months. And while he turned one page after another, my stomach turned and churned. I braced myself. Would he choose to represent me, or would he not?

"Hmmm," he said. "I'm going to do something I seldom do…" I held my breath, waiting. "And that is offer a contract to you."

Should I dance? Should I cheer, or just let my heart sing with joy? I chose the latter. My agent found a publisher for my book, which I titled, *Simply Salsa: Dancing Without Fear at God's Fiesta.*

Sassy title, but the contents described my life—the dance in darkness. The rhythm of challenges, the melody of triumph, and the symphony of a life free from fear.

I didn't fear the bitterness of rejection anymore. Instead, I knew it was a necessary step to the sweetness of victory. The passion I poured into each chapter of *Simply Salsa* equaled the determination to have it dance into the hearts of thousands of readers.

And those readers waited and cheered along with me as I shared quotes and details of *Simply Salsa*'s arrival on Facebook and Twitter. And with my new friends standing by, the glorious day came one week after its release.

Fellow authors and I planned a virtual launch. We chose to hold it on Amazon.com. The preparation took hours and hours. But when the launch day came, the music played. Numbers started at 500,000 out of 7 million books that fill the virtual Amazon bookshelves. But with each hour, the climb was swift. At moments, slow. Then hours of fast moves upward. Until in my category, nearly the last hour, *Simply Salsa* reached 100, then 60, 50, 30, 20, 10… all the way to #1.

Hubby had been monitoring each minute. And when he announced the victory, I jumped up. Then that voice came back again. But this time with a lovely message: Blindness, rejection, setbacks, or even ended contracts can't stop a heart filled with passion.

Nor can they slow down a mind fueled with creativity. But the greatest message that leaps from the lines written on the pages of my life is the value of obstacles. They don't have to stop us, hinder our efforts or block our path. Rather, they are the very things that sharpen our tenacity.

And equipped with that passion and drive, we discover sweet surprises, delight in small victories, and savor big, unexpected triumphs.

~Janet Perez Eckles

Princess of
Procrastination

Procrastination is something best put off until tomorrow.
~Gerald Vaughan

I had been sitting on my manuscript for several years. Dreaming of getting it published—but never acting on it—meant I could wallow in "what ifs." Sitting on it was safe. Never submitting it meant that it would never get rejected. In my mind, it was more comfortable to speculate what response an editor would have, rather than knowing for sure via a rejection letter.

A meaty picture book with just under 3,000 words, *A Home for Always* told the story of a stray dog looking for a forever home, and it had undergone many revisions. When I went to a writing retreat, I took the piece and got it critiqued, which led to yet another draft. I shared the story with my writer friends and got their feedback. After I had made the tale as good as I could, I fantasized about how incredible it would be to walk into a bookstore and find a book—written by me—on one of the shelves. But I continued to keep my words locked in a computer file, protected from any potential publisher. I was well aware that if I used my time to write and submit, instead of making excuses, I might actually get something published. But still I sent out nothing.

During the summer of 2010, I began a blog. As a teacher, I had some time off, so I made a permanent place on the couch for myself—just me and my laptop—and blogged away. Putting up posts resulted in instant gratification: I had an audience—people read what I wrote. Comments trickled in, and I snagged a few followers.

On August fourth, I publicly called myself on my procrastination. For all my readers to see (probably a whopping three at the time), I vowed that by the end of the month, I would send out my manuscript. It was an easy promise to make—because I didn't really intend on following through with it. It was one of those casual claims that I tossed out, shrouded in pseudo-determination, but I figured when September rolled around, no one would connect the dots to discover I was not a woman of my word.

In my post, I got a bit flippant and said that after I sent off my manuscript, I would let everyone know with a coded message like "The eagle has flown," or "The chicken has landed."

One local writer, Donna Volkenannt, jumped on my promise, writing, "I'll check back on September 1st to see if 'the eagle has flown.'"

Oh, no. Now I would have to keep my promise, or at least one person would know I was a liar. Donna would know that I was all talk, and couldn't walk the walk of a writer.

Because I'm the Princess of Procrastination, it wasn't until the last day of the month—August 31st—that I sent off my manuscript. I snapped a picture of the mailing envelope as further "proof."

After I received a rejection letter from a large East Coast publisher (I have it framed in my den), I sent A Home for Always off to a small, independent publishing house. They said yes; an illustrator is now working on the pictures.

If I had stayed on the edge of the cliff, refusing to take even one risky step forward, I would have been safe. Safe from rejection. But I'd never have found out how exciting it is to take that first step into the unknown.

Now the biggest "what ifs" I have are what if I had never opened my big blogging mouth and made a promise I never intended on keeping? And what if Donna had never called my bluff? If those questions remained in the "never" category, I never would have seen a dream of mine come true.

But I did open my mouth, and Donna did hold me to my word. And because of that, I'm now blogging true success....

~Sioux Roslawski

inspiration
for
Writers

A Little Help
from My Friends

In union there is strength.

~Aesop

Coffee and Confidence

As soon as coffee is in your stomach, there is a general commotion.
Ideas begin to move... similes arise, the paper is covered.
Coffee is your ally and writing ceases to be a struggle.
~Honoré de Balzac

The three of us had our first meeting at a funky coffee shop that looked like a fifties breakfast room. We were professional magazine and fiction writers, each with a manuscript that needed help. We were good writers, and we wanted to grow better. During the initial session, we created a template for our critiquing work. We read each other's stories and line-edited. Then we talked through each manuscript, celebrating the phrases and ideas we liked, and analyzing the aspects that didn't work. Each of us listened intently when we were being critiqued. We took notes and asked clarifying questions. When the session ended, we returned to our home offices with renewed confidence, ready to make the recommended changes and send our improved manuscripts off to our editors.

Every Thursday morning at 7:00, we gathered, work in hand, and settled in at the large, square lime-green table. We spent our first moments sharing news of marketing, publishing, writing and life, and then settled into reading and editing. We ate our scones, refilled our coffee, and then carefully critiqued the manuscripts.

"Are you all praying?" a woman once asked us.

"We're editing," I answered, although our time together felt holy.

To do such hard and honest work, we needed a sacred space. For several years, that coffee shop was our cloister. The scones emerged from the oven just as we arrived; the coffee was fair trade, rich and fresh. The staff turned down the rock music when they saw us coming, and the owner was a former writer herself. We were at home there.

Then, the landlord raised the rent, and the owner had to sell. We searched for a new meeting place. One shop was too noisy, another too cold. One place had plastic-tasting coffee and cavernous acoustics. We finally settled on a modern shop with smooth tabletops and matching chairs. They featured lovely white porcelain teapots and an array of exotic loose teas. We began sipping fragrant chamomile and jasmine. The scones were small and dense, so we ate bagels. Week by week, we brought in our chapters, articles, and stories, and doggedly helped each other tighten paragraphs, increase focus, deepen characterizations, and heighten plots. The staff always welcomed us warmly, and the other patrons occasionally dropped by our table to see what we were working on.

After two years, when the price of tea grew too steep and the bagels became too stale to enjoy, we moved. Several coffee shops and many years later, we still meet every Thursday. The magazines, books and publishing markets have radically changed. We work with different editors. Our writing styles, genres and subjects have fluctuated and expanded. But our critique group remains a constant in our lives. We still rely on those early morning moments at the coffee shop, where we give each other exactly what we need: encouragement, honest editing, and a deep sense of possibility and community.

~Deborah Shouse

Will Write for Crab Cakes

Comedy is half music.
~Joan Rivers

Ι'm a humor writer. My work appears in magazines from *The Funny Times* to *The Christian Science Monitor*. My friend Janet is a history professor whose writing was confined to academic journals and the occasional op-ed. Driving back from the Jersey shore one day, we were kibitzing, and Janet had a funny idea.

"That would make a good essay," I told her.

"You can write it," she said.

"Let's write it together," I suggested.

We hatched a plan. We'd turn Janet's funny idea into a humor piece, sell it to *The Funny Times*, and spend the money on crab cakes at our favorite lunch spot the next time we were at the shore.

[Janet: I couldn't turn down Roz—none of my other friends can take off mid-week to go to the beach with me.]

When I got home, I came up with a title and an adequate first draft, and e-mailed them to Janet. Within an hour, she'd punched up some lines, deleted others, added some funny business of her own and shot it back, with a much better title. A writing partnership was born! The essay went back and forth till we couldn't make it funnier. We submitted it to *The Funny Times*. They took it.

Acquiring a partner this late in my writing career was completely unexpected. I felt like the friend who'd had one of those late-in-life babies. You think the pattern of your life is set, then—surprise!

[Janet: At our age, a new writing partner is much better than a newborn.]

Writing with a partner is more fun than writing solo. It's easier, too. You know when you—creatively speaking—hit a wall? With a writing partner, there's always a door in that wall. When you're stumped, you just open the door and lob the mess you've created at her. It comes back fixed! Or, at least, improved. With Janet, I can even place an order. "The third paragraph needs a movie title that's a pun about monetizing nature documentaries," I once requested. Within moments, she came back with "Crouching Tiger, Hidden Profits."

Our brains don't always work together as one. Janet once put a wisecracking baby elephant in an early draft. I didn't think he was funny, so I deleted him when I returned it. When her redraft hit my inbox, he was back. As we sent it back and forth, redrafting and polishing, I kept removing the baby elephant, and Janet kept replacing him. Finally, the piece was done. Except for the elephant. In or out? I figured the piece was strong enough by then that an unfunny elephant wouldn't stop an editor from taking it. Let the editor delete the elephant! I punched up the elephant's lines, and he stayed in. Later, when I read "Gone with the Wildebeest" in print, I thought the baby elephant was hilarious.

[Janet: You're welcome.]

We've encountered a few glitches. Whenever I e-mailed one work-in-progress to Janet, it vanished. Turns out her prudish spam filter kept dumping it in her spam file because it contained the words "erectile dysfunction."

[Janet: My spam filter obviously didn't get the joke.]

We haven't merged into a single Humor Writing Brain yet. We both continue to write solo. But I can count on Janet to add a funny line to whatever I'm working on. For some reason, she hasn't asked me to make any of her academic papers funnier. But I'd be happy to try.

[Janet: My academic papers are hilarious enough already, thanks.]

While we work well together, we don't always think alike. I

love Terry Gross; Janet lunges to change the channel when *Fresh Air* comes on. I spend my evenings reading magazines; Janet prefers movies. She's happily married; I'm happily divorced. But we're both opinionated and fairly clever, and neither of us is afraid to fall on her face when reaching for a joke. And we throw out each other's lines, paragraphs and ideas with impunity because we both recognize that it's not that important—it's humor writing, not brain surgery. It's fun. And there's a big reward: crab cakes.

[Janet: Make that a tasty reward. The crab cakes are actually pretty small. It's not as if we're stuffing our faces like those morons who enter hot-dog-eating contests.]

So we sit at our respective computers, batting our work back and forth until it's done. She's in charge of keeping us moving forward, and I'm in charge of sending out the completed work. We're currently working on a darkly comic mystery novel set in a suburban library. Who knows if it'll sell? But we're having fun writing it.

[Janet: If it sells, we're celebrating with crab cakes at the beach—in Aruba.]

So the next time you're chatting with a friend and she comes up with a Good Idea, don't just grab it. Offer to share. You never know what might happen. Maybe we'll run into you at the shore next summer, enjoying crab cakes.

[Janet: But remember, the left front table is ours!]

~Roz Warren [and Janet Golden]

The Restless Writers

Finding a writing group is a lot like finding a man or a good melon:
you just know when you have your hands around the right one.
~Lori Dyan

For me, it happened with a manuscript. I was working full-time as an environmental specialist, but had spent months writing a novel. I was in need of a copy editor—someone to read it, dissect it, and love it as much as I did—someone with stellar editing ability and an empathetic heart. I didn't know how to find such a person, but after speaking to colleagues at work, I began collecting names. I contacted a woman named Maria, and the magic began.

Maria was a full-time communications advisor, part-time indexer, sometime student, and permanent dreamer. And she liked to write. Thankfully, she liked to read too because she had two hundred pages coming at her! Maria enthusiastically agreed to review my manuscript, and I was anxious to release it to the universe, which Maria represented to me at that point in my literary life. So we began the process of reading, and after a few weeks had passed, we learned that what was meant as an editing gig had turned into a lasting friendship.

We spent evenings poring over pages. The time we spent reviewing manuscripts eventually evolved into brainstorming future writing projects, publication prospects, and even small business ideas. But the idea that stuck was one of a writing group—more officially, a critique group. We envisioned a writing circle where we could engage with other women, whip our manuscripts into shape, and support each other on our journey to publication. However, we couldn't possibly form a writing group with only two members. It was time to solicit a third writer, possibly a fourth. Our list of wants included someone with good writing skills, creative intuition, and a passion for the writing life.

We placed a courageous classified ad in the *Quick Brown Fox*, a popular creative-writing newsletter compiled by Toronto book editor Brian Henry. It went something like this: "Desperately seeking Susan, if Susan were a fanciful writer oozing of unmistakable talent, of course." And she totally was—but her name was Lori.

Lori responded to our classified ad, and we all agreed to a meet-and-greet at a local restaurant. A public place seemed like a suitable choice because we suspected that finding a group member might be a bit like online dating, except with a greater chance of hooking up with a sociopath. Our preliminary meeting was a monumental success. Not only did Lori meet our list of wants, she was literary (and sassy) perfection—a corporate communications writer by day and writer of women's fiction by night. She was a shoo-in. We quickly learned that the three of us shared something similar: the burning desire to write. And, let's face it, an equally burning desire to escape the familiar. Our writing group was born, and we called ourselves The Restless Writers.

The real work soon began as the three of us perfected manuscripts and submitted pages after pages for critique. We trusted each other with our words, our secrets, and our dreams. We also functioned as a sounding board for new ideas while also kvetching about our lives, sharing tears and triumphs—and drinking wine. We started a blog to document our literary adventures together. The journey to publication had officially begun.

It's been three years since our writing group has been together, and we continue to meet on a regular basis. We're not a formal group with rules and rigidity; we agreed this would likely make us irritating as hell. Our lives were overly structured as it was. We are a group that has fun yet still manages to keep each other accountable with deliverables such as pages, word counts, and submissions. We continue to build our platform and maintain social media commitments: website, Twitter, and our restlesswriters.ca blog, which recently welcomed its 26,000th visitor. We have earned a readership and a respect amongst the online writing community, while at the same time, discovered other writers who wanted to take the journey with us.

As a writing group and as individuals, we have celebrated many successes. We have traveled to international conferences, completed novels, screenplays, and short stories—some published, some still stashed away in drawers. One of us recently landed a literary agent after months of queries and rejections. We have published heaps of blog posts, the most popular being "Permission to Proceed Imperfectly," "How to Write Naked," "Taking a Vacation from Myself," and "Your Life in Six Words."

Writing can be painstaking work, yet incredibly rewarding—and what better way to share the experience than with exceptional like-minded women. If you want to become a successful writer, you too could benefit from a super-supportive group that helps you be the best writer you can be—a group that provides the discipline and motivation you need to keep your dreams alive.

When it comes to meeting new friends, it can happen in the strangest of ways. I found mine in my writing group. These women know me better than anyone. They make me a better writer and a better person. They have become my best friends.

As Lori often says, "Finding a writing group is a lot like finding a man or a good melon: you just know when you have your hands around the right one."

~Beckie Jas

Fishing Buddies

When they go fishing, it is not really fish they are after.
It is a philosophic meditation.
~E.T. Brown

The soothing cadence of the train created the perfect ambiance to allow me to drift into my own world of excitement and anticipation. Despite the warnings about meeting people on the Internet, I was on a two-hour train ride to meet someone with whom I had shared my thoughts, life and friendship through e-mail. It was a short ride from San Diego to Fullerton, but it provided ample time to reflect on the possibilities of this adventure.

Two years earlier, I had written an online article outlining the challenges of our youth today, and some insight into why I believe they are heading down the wrong path. In response, I received an e-mail from a woman in Oregon named JoAnne.

"I enjoyed your article, 'Ask Me Why.' I am working on a book proposal for a major publishing house. I would like permission to include your story in a chapter of the book. Your article fits perfectly with the theme of this project. It would be a welcome addition."

Over the next year, we had a few brief contacts sharing what was going on with her book proposal and our writing in general. A few months later, I received a message regarding a change of plans for her project.

"I received a letter from the publisher stating they are not interested in my book at this time. I have considered resubmitting to another publisher, but I think I'll just put it on the shelf for a while."

The project was on hold, but not our friendship. We began to write more often about our daily lives, our work, and our families. We discussed our most recent writing projects, the successes and the disappointments. It became increasingly more comfortable to share the desires of our hearts, our hopes for the future, as well as a few ghosts from the past. As this friendship developed, it amazed me how much we had in common.

When I was ten years old, my biological father left. After forty years, I still wondered what happened to him. My writing buddy, JoAnne, is adopted and has spent many hours gathering information on her birth parents and siblings. We were both dealing with loss and rejection in our early years, and an honest assessment of our lives revealed that issues can follow us into our adult relationships.

It intrigues me that with our history, we both chose to pursue writing. There is probably nothing more discouraging than form letters rejecting your manuscripts. Despite the writers' workshops you attend or books and magazines you read telling you to expect a multitude of rejection letters, each one still hurts. It's comforting to have someone who knows how you feel and can share your disappointments and your successes.

When her daughter graduated from a college about two hours from my house, JoAnne traveled to California with her husband and her younger children to attend the graduation. One afternoon, I received an e-mail message.

"Hi, Val. I'm not sure if it would be possible, but I would love to see you while I am in California if there is some way we can get together. It would be great if we could meet for lunch."

The train ride passed quickly, and before I knew it, I was exiting toward the waiting area. I descended the stairs and scanned the crowd, where I saw a woman with brown curly hair and a medium build, wearing a soft summer dress and the kindest smile I'd ever seen. Yep, that's her, I thought smugly. I'd know her anywhere. She looks just like I thought she would. She was waiting at the bottom of the stairs, and as soon as we walked up to each other, I knew we would be friends for life.

We sat in a quiet corner at lunch, and the more we talked, the more obvious it became how much we had in common. JoAnne lives in Oregon, the last known residence of my father. I love fishing, and so does she. And we have both written stories about our childhood fishing memories.

"You need to come to Oregon so we can go fishing. Just remember, I don't do worms!" she said. I'm okay with worms, so we make a good team.

I have a hard time expressing my feelings, but I love to listen to JoAnne talk about her experiences. She is blessed with an open heart, the willingness to sacrifice for those she loves, and the ability to share her life with others not only through her writing, but by the way she lives each day. We even discovered our birthdays are just one day apart.

The time passed so quickly that we were shocked when I looked at my watch to find my return train would leave in twenty minutes. During those few hours, we watered the seeds of friendship that were planted months earlier by what some people might call a "chance" meeting. Our adventure has taught me that there are times when it's necessary to take a risk and step out in faith to write that story, or to find an unexpected treasure in a new friend.

I'll never again think of my childhood, see a train or hear a fish story without thinking of my writing friend. I'm a little sad that we can't spend much time together, but that's okay, because we have a plan. We have e-mail, and we have telephones—and we have decided that we're going fishing! I can see it now, a cool flowing stream with green grass on the banks and two comfy chairs sitting next to a stringer full of fish. I'll be there baiting the hooks. JoAnne will be the one with the kind smile and the tender heart, and most likely the biggest fish! It's the perfect picture—a container of worms, two fishing poles, two cups of tea, and, of course… my fishing buddy and me.

~Valerie J. Frost

Complementary Attraction

A critic can only review the book he has read,
not the one which the writer wrote.
~Mignon McLaughlin,
The Neurotic's Notebook

"That was so bad, I had to turn my hearing aid off," the older woman said after I finished reading aloud a scene from my novel. She tapped her red pen on the printed handout as an exclamation point.

I suppressed the urge to correct her split infinitive and, instead, giggled, believing the hearing aid comment a group initiation prank. But I spied others nodding.

Another woman said, "You know, this will never be published." And yet another suggested I seek mental-health counseling since the plot was too depressing for a writer with a healthy psyche.

I thought back to the eye-catching flyer posted at the recreation center, claiming the critique group provided positive feedback in a supportive environment. As my chest and neck flushed, I controlled the desire to stand and rip my manuscript in half, to yell "never mind" and flee the building. Instead, I waited for someone to give me a reason not to quit this writing gig while I still retained a sliver of pride.

Having recently moved to town, I envisioned the evening as an opportunity to make new friends who shared the same passion and to bond with those who understood the difficulties of writing a novel. Unfortunately, the stern-faced writers meeting my gaze didn't care about my need for camaraderie or support.

After the group expressed their overall displeasure with my prose, the founder of the group announced it was time to critique my work page by page. "Time to nitpick," he warned.

Flipping through my handout, I cursed myself for bringing an entire chapter rather than an excerpt. The group exuberantly discovered missing commas, unnecessary adjectives, and missing end quotes, as if unearthing golden treasures.

Soon, a "can you top this?" attitude surfaced, and they began critiquing each other's critiques, pointing out one another's inadequacies in perfecting the craft. While they battled for the Best Editor of an Edit Award, I sat quietly, summoning enough strength to endure the rest of the evening. The reprieve didn't last long, and the group refocused its assault on my self-esteem. What made me think I could effectively write my name, let alone a book? Whatever possessed me to call that number on the flyer? Why did I move to this stinking town? I offered an occasional "uh-huh" and "I see" as not to appear ungrateful to them for revealing my grave oversights.

Once the meeting adjourned, the leader invited everyone out for drinks. I politely declined, believing the drinks would have been more effective before the meeting. Besides, I couldn't imagine what they'd say to me with a few drinks in them. As the members shuffled out, patting each other on the back for such an insightful critique, I stumbled to my car.

"Hey, Cathi," the leader called before I reached safety. I turned, bracing for one last discouraging word. "I hope they didn't scare you."

I waved off his concern, and a member named Michael made his way over. "They can be a little rough, especially with new members."

Did he actually think I'd become a member? "Rough? I hadn't noticed," I said.

We all laughed.

"You held up well tonight," Michael said. "We've had others

leave in tears right in the middle of a critique. I was sure they'd break you."

And there it glimmered — the gauntlet — lying at my feet. Never one to turn down a challenge, I announced, "I'll see you both next Wednesday then."

The following week, as I listened to Michael get a tongue-lashing from the group, I realized why he wanted me to return. Why he needed me to return. Self-preservation. My writing served as a temporary distraction to the group's larger plan to thwart his chances at publication.

After the meeting, Michael and I stood in the parking lot. I said, "Wow, you took a beating tonight. I was certain they'd break you." I smiled. "They can be a bit rough, especially with the old members."

"Yeah. They've never liked my writing."

"Then why do you still come?"

"The same reason you came back, I suppose. Searching for that elusive praise from someone… anyone. Writers are good at beating themselves up, you know. Besides, it's become a game of sorts."

"A game?"

"I'll score a compliment from them before the end of the book." He smiled. "In fact, before you get one."

"Oh, really?" Yet another challenge I couldn't pass up. "Game on."

For my next critique, I set out to dazzle the group with my deft prose. I offered a killer simile. Not exactly a cliché but too close, they thought. A line of alliteration. Too sing-songy, like a nursery rhyme. I added symbolism. Too transparent, some believed. Too unclear for others.

"I thought you had it," Michael said after the meeting.

"Well, technically the word 'okay' can be viewed as a compliment," I said.

"Come on. Everyone knows that's code talk for 'not so good.' Merely adequate."

We watched the others pull from the lot. "Hey, how about dinner?" he asked.

Ah, an opening. I smirked and said, "Okay."

He paused. "Good one."

We found a new reason to stay in the group—each other. Over the course of numerous rewrites and months of laughter and compassion, Michael proved himself not only a keen editor, but also a soul mate. While the group continued to whittle away at each other's self-esteem, they hadn't noticed Michael and I helping one another along the path to publication.

Then one day, Michael asked, "Have you considered dropping the first fifteen pages of your novel? The story actually starts with the second chapter."

What? Had he been a spy for the enemy all along? Stunned, I went home that night, betrayed by my confidant, my only fan. Then I reread the first chapter, and he was right. I cut it, trusting Michael acted in my best interest. What were a mere fifteen pages of writing besides days of work and a chunk of my ego? I learned to listen to Michael and improved my novel.

Our relationship inside and outside the group flourished as we shared our love of literature and writing. Besides, any man who could convince me to drop the first chapter of my beloved novel could certainly convince me to say "yes" to marriage. And with this simple word, we not only gained a loving partner for life, but we also acquired an in-house editor: a major bonus for any writer.

These days, I say, "Hey, honey, what's a synonym for lethargy?"

"Somnolence," Michael tosses over his shoulder.

We no longer search for that elusive compliment. We complement each other just fine.

~Cathi LaMarche

Stretching Forward, Reaching Back

There is magic in long-distance friendships. They let you relate to other human beings in a way that goes beyond being physically together and is often more profound.
~Diana Cortes

"I'd love to look at your story," my friend Peggy said. I could tell from her voice that she meant it. And I was blessed. By her time. By her heart. By her willingness to read my words and help me grow.

Peggy was a wonderful friend, and she was a gifted and successful writer, too. I'd followed her stories well before we'd met at a writers' workshop and became soul sisters. Now we wrote for some of the same publications, and she was always willing to peek at my pre-submission drafts.

"Are you sure you have time?" I asked.

"Yes," she said. "I love to help and encourage you. It's a pleasure."

For the millionth time, I wished I could give her a hug. But she lived in New York, and I lived in Illinois. Our conversations were on the phone, but it felt like she was next door.

"Thanks, friend," I said. "I'll e-mail it in the morning."

Peggy and I talked about a hundred other things, and then said goodbye. I set the phone back on the charger and thought about my friend. I knew that she was over-the-top busy with her own writing endeavors, yet she always took time for me. And she never, ever made me feel inadequate.

What made her want to give? It was a sacrifice of time, for sure. But Peggy always was thorough, taking time to read the manuscript to the end. She'd remind me of structure; she'd show me where I wandered off track; she'd bring my attention to things like red herrings and bunny trails and holes in my plots. She saw things I just couldn't see. And she was honest. The first thing a writer needs to grow is thick skin, and Peggy always spoke the truth. But she did it in such a kind, encouraging way, though we lived thousands of miles apart, I could imagine the care and concern in her green eyes.

One day, she asked me to read through one of her drafts.

"I'd love to," I said. But inside I was trembling. Who was I to critique someone more advanced and accomplished than me? But I read through the manuscript anyway, held my breath, and offered up just a few thoughts.

"I agree completely with your comments" came the e-mail later in the afternoon. "You have an instinct for this, and you helped me. Thank you." While I was shaking in my writing boots, trying to help her, she encouraged me.

Peggy and I grew in friendship while I grew in the craft. If I e-mailed her and told her I was stuck or needed some fresh thoughts, she'd write back: "Give me a call. Let's brainstorm." If I didn't know how to handle a professional situation, she'd offer sweet advice from her experience. If I felt discouraged and wanted to slip my laptop under my four-poster bed forever, she'd pull me back to my passion. "You have a gift," she'd say. "You're going to be fine." And when a rejection from an editor came, she'd be fast to remind me, "It's part of the business. The sooner you understand that, the better off you'll be."

That was Peggy. And with Peggy's gentle, kind encouragement, I became more experienced, too. My manuscripts were selling regularly, and though I couldn't see it, I believed that my writing must have been getting stronger. My confidence grew a smidgen, too. So when another gal, my local friend Sarah, expressed a hidden desire to write and quietly delivered her first manuscript to my inbox, my heart filled with joy. "Why don't you come on over?" I said when I called her up. "We'll look at your story together."

That was the bud of a new aspect of writing, too. Helping someone who's just getting started. Sarah and I sat at my dining-room table, her printed sheets fanned out on the old, worn oak. More than a half-dozen kids, hers and mine, swarmed around us, but we took care of words while we took care of them. And at the end of the afternoon, Sarah hugged me, firm and warm. "Thank you," she said. "I'm so grateful."

And I understood that gratitude.

Sarah continued to write, to learn, to create and carve and shape written words. And it's been my blessing to help, to see her grow. I loved seeing a spark in her warm brown eyes. It brought me pleasure. The investment gave me joy.

It would seem that writing is a solitary thing. One beating heart, full of words, full of passion, hunkered over a keyboard alone. But I've found that it's not really a solitary thing at all. Writers need one another. For encouragement. For sharpening. For help and hope. Peggy reaches her hand back to help me, and I stretch up to her. I reach back my other hand to help Sarah, and she stretches up to me.

After all, we're on the same sweet ladder.

And I'd be missing a crazy amount of blessing if I were climbing all alone.

~Shawnelle Eliasen

Secrets... to Success

The nice thing about teamwork is that you always have others on your side.
~Margaret Carty

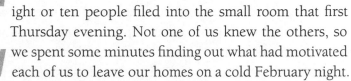

Eight or ten people filed into the small room that first Thursday evening. Not one of us knew the others, so we spent some minutes finding out what had motivated each of us to leave our homes on a cold February night. Craig served as a pastor. Barb was a military spouse from a nearby army base. Kathy stayed at home with her kids. What we all shared was a secret passion for writing.

This first meeting had brought us together despite our different ages, diverse church denominations, and our wide variety of literary genres. Cindy confessed her love for script writing. Barb wanted to write books for children, while Kathy wrote devotionals. Craig preferred fantasy. Chip had a flair for poetry. And I specialized in non-fiction. Each of us had written for years, but hidden our efforts in file cabinets and desk drawers.

In the months and years that followed, the group's membership expanded. John, who wrote Gothic horror, couldn't have been more different from ninety-year-old Wilma with her whimsical poetry, but they became fast friends. In truth, we discovered that our strength lay in the very diversity of the group. As we hesitantly read our pieces aloud to the group, we realized that each person had a unique perspective to offer during the critique.

One evening, Chip read one of his poems to the group. The lines were exquisite, drawing us in with images of color and sound. Yet I, with no credentials as a poet, ventured a tentative suggestion. "Chip, you've allowed us to see, hear and even taste the scene you describe, but don't you have a nose?"

A smile spread across Chip's face. "You're right!" He recognized that odors can trigger intense emotions and made a note to incorporate that aspect of the senses into his writing in the future. Months later, with Chip's encouragement, I tried writing a poem myself and was surprised when an editor selected it for publication.

Some meetings focused on technical details as Lynne taught appropriate uses of commas or capitalization. Dangling modifiers and unclear referents were all fair game for a red pencil. Editors might reject a manuscript for any number of other reasons, but grammatical mistakes such as these would not be one of them.

Often critiques provoked humor. In a story about a parachutist, a key character dropped from the sky and landed on his son's birthday cake. We laughed until Craig pointed out an earlier description of the cake mentioned that it was decorated with burning Fourth-of-July sparklers. Ouch! When a character in another story finished eating a breakfast of pancakes and sausages, someone noted that the same character moments later was washing a frying pan used for scrambled eggs. Neither author had caught these mismatches, but group members did.

When we first assembled as a writers' group, few of us had ever seen our words in print. But in the following years, Barb received recognition in a national poetry contest. Cindy flew across the country to Los Angeles to receive an award for a video she had scripted; we all sat in the front row when her first play was produced on a local stage. Articles in magazines and journals of all sizes began to appear with the names of members of our group listed at the top.

The group rejoiced with me as I signed my first book contract. A half-dozen members gave up an entire evening when they volunteered to edit the page proofs carefully. One person went through every sheet just focusing on page numbers and running heads. Another looked up each scripture reference to make sure every single one was correctly cited. Another friend went through the manuscript checking that pronouns referring to God were all capitalized. Tasks that would have taken me days to accomplish were completed in a few hours.

On the day my copies of the book arrived from the publisher, I ripped open the package and breathed in the aroma of the freshly inked pages. I proudly left a copy on the dining table where my husband could not miss it when he walked in from work. I dreamed that he might sweep me off my feet and suggest going out to a restaurant to celebrate the occasion. Or he might offer a bouquet of roses to mark the special event.

But, no. Not being a writer himself, he had no idea at that time what a milestone this was in my life. He walked in the front door, noticed the book and said, "Oh, your book arrived." Then as he thumbed through the rest of the mail, he asked, "What's for dinner?"

What's for dinner? My heart missed a beat or three before I was able to answer his question in a normal tone.

The next night, the writers' group gathered for their monthly meeting. What a contrast! I caressed my slim volume as gently as if it were a new baby. Everyone huddled around it, oohing and aahing. Their excitement reminded me of the scene in *Fiddler on the Roof* where the tailor gets his new sewing machine, and the entire town turns out to congratulate him and wish him, "*Mazel tov!*"

Someone had obtained a photo of the book's cover and taken it to the local bakery where the chief baker reproduced it in icing. Another writer in the group brought a camera to capture a picture of me holding my book beside the cake. The group's excitement about my achievement was what I needed. These friends were writers themselves and understood all the effort that had brought me to this moment.

That first book has since gone through multiple printings. During that time, five more of my books have gone to press, and the publisher plans to release another later this year. But none of these landmarks would have come to be without the support of those loyal friends who stood on the sidelines and cheered me on. I look at them

today—each with their own list of publishing credits—and to them
I say, "*Mazel tov!* Congratulations!"

~Emily Parke Chase

The Surprise Party

It is a good thing to be rich, and it is a good thing to be strong, but it is a better thing to be loved by many friends.
~Euripides

The alarm clock buzzed, shooting knives through my brain. I dreaded getting out of bed and facing the day. Three months away from my first book's deadline, I seriously considered packing up my family and moving to the mountains, where the Internet and cell phones didn't exist. I had it all planned out: I'd assume a new identity, ensuring that the publisher could never, ever find me. The editor would eventually forget my existence, and I could forget about bothersome things like manuscript deadlines.

I rolled over with a moan and silently pleaded to the Almighty. "God, I really need a fresh batch of joy if I'm going to survive the next few months."

I imagined God whipping up a set of circumstances as enjoyable and comforting as an apple pie.

Minutes after my desperate plea, my five-year-old walked into the bedroom with glassy eyes and rosy cheeks. Before I touched his forehead, I knew he had a fever. So much for apple-pie joy.

Instead of spending the rest of the week hunched over my computer hammering out paragraphs, I spent the days huddled on the couch with a sick child, offering him Popsicles and cold washcloths and holding him until he fell back to sleep.

While a sick child wasn't the batch of joy I'd hoped for, those few days of tending to my little guy reminded me that the whole of my life wasn't summed up by a book deadline. I had other really great things in my life too, like my family and friends. The book would come, one line at a time, but it didn't need to define me.

By Friday, after a week of snuggling on the couch in sweatpants, I was ripe for a shower and my big-girl clothes. A few friends and I headed out to dinner. My friend Jenna had relocated six months prior, and her husband flew her home to celebrate her birthday with friends.

My husband, Kedron, shooed me out the door, saying, "Don't worry about the kids or the book. Just enjoy this evening. It's been a long week. You need to get out."

I met up with my girlfriends, and we headed to a restaurant. As we walked to our table in the back, I turned the corner and saw Kedron sitting at a table with my friends Susie, Jennifer and Cindy. I stopped, confused as to why my husband was having dinner with my friends. And then I wondered who had the kids. He was supposed to be at home with the kids!

I frowned as the group at the table waved at me. My mouth opened, but I couldn't formulate words. I looked back at Jenna, and before I could ask what was going on, I knew by the smirk on her face that I had just been fooled.

Susie stood up, nearly knocking over her water glass, and shouted, "Surprise!"

I looked at Kedron and the three friends at the table, and back to the group that I came to the restaurant with. The two groups of friends didn't know each other. At least, I didn't think they did.

Everyone started laughing. I finally asked, "What are you all doing here? We're here to celebrate Jenna's birthday."

Susie flashed a satisfied smile and replied, "Well, yes, it is her birthday, but this is a surprise party for you!"

"Umm… it's not my birthday."

Susie looked to the others at the table and laughed. That's when I noticed there was also a cake on the table that said, "Congratulations, Amelia!"

"This is a surprise party to congratulate you on your book contract!"

"That's really old news!" I replied.

"Yeah, do you have any idea how hard you are to plan a surprise party for? This is the third date we've tried!" Susie said.

Apparently, the girls' nights out that Jennifer and Susie had tried to plan over the past couple of months had really been surprise parties. I had conflicts each time.

I started shaking, and tears began to well up in my eyes.

"No one has ever, ever surprised me with a party before!"

Jenna patted me on the shoulder and said, "And after the week you just had, the timing couldn't be more perfect."

I sat down at the table, and Susie handed me a red scrapbook filled with letters and e-mails that she had collected from my parents, out-of-state friends, and others who couldn't make it to the party—including a couple of my writing mentors. I wiped tears from my eyes as I read their incredible notes of encouragement:

I have amazing faith in you, Amelia. I know you can do this. I am so proud of the work you are doing and privileged to step in on occasion and offer tidbits of my life to help you through those dreaded moments of writer's block. —Cindy

Ever since you were a baby, you have been fascinated with books! Whether it was one that we read to you or one that someone else was trying to read. It has been amazing to see how God has directed your life in such a way to prepare you for what you are doing now with the talents and gifts He has given you. —Mom and Dad

Continue to write from your heart. You have a gift, an amazing gift. The things that you write about hit home on so many levels. —Jennifer

I thumbed through page after page, looking at pictures and words from some of the people who mean the most to me. No one had ever done anything quite so thoughtful or unexpected for me.

Ever. And never had I needed that level of support and encouragement more.

I had asked God for a new dose of joy to make it through the last few months of writing my book. Turns out, He'd already given me one of the greatest joys ever—a community of family and friends who believed in me even when I didn't, who stood by me, held me up and encouraged me every step of the journey.

~Amelia Rhodes

Why I Love
My Writers' Group

Only your real friends will tell you when your face is dirty.
~Sicilian Proverb

I can't speak for others, but for me a writers' group is invaluable. I'd sooner do without my thesaurus or—perish the thought—spell check than without the support of my group. We've been together about five years, through several incarnations and a few times when our collective schedules got so crazy it seemed the group would fizzle. But the times when it's cooking—like it is now—make all the rest worthwhile.

Our group consists of Bert, a forty-something appraiser who, for the past three years, has been writing a "book about people and horses, not necessarily in that order"; Ellen, a retired nurse who hasn't quite settled on a genre; Anna Marie, a bookstore manager and old soul in a twenty-five-year-old body who's crafting a fantasy novel; Ron, a middle-aged salesman who writes side-splitting humor; and me. I'm the Erma Bombeck of the group, specializing in humorous essays about my four kids.

Our eclectic group meets every two weeks, usually in a coffee shop. Each writer brings something he's working on, one copy for each member, and then reads his selection out loud while the rest of us take notes. Next, we proceed around the table one by one, offering our opinion, asking for clarification, and making suggestions. The operative word is "suggestions." Each critique is just one person's opinion and should be looked on as nothing more. Take it or leave it. The writer always has final say.

That's the first rule. The second is simple. No one is allowed to defend his work. You can't say, "Well, I didn't introduce my main character until the second page because..." You won't be there to defend your work when it's published, so you can't defend it during group.

One thing that happens a lot is a writer will write one word and then—without realizing it—read another. Usually, what he reads sounds more natural. We'll make a note and let the writer know, "In the middle of the third paragraph, you wrote, 'She was still alive,' but you said, 'She was alive.' I think the second is stronger." We discuss the big things, then make notes of typos, spelling boo-boos, incorrect tenses, and punctuation, and give the writer back his work with these more minor suggestions written in.

Part of what makes our group work is that we all genuinely enjoy each other's writing. Our styles are different enough to keep things interesting, and there are no prima donnas. We let Bert know when one of his horse terms goes over our heads or tell Anna Marie if her dialogue doesn't sound authentic for her time period. We share calls for submissions and info on writing contests, celebrate each other's publishing successes, and help keep the parade of rejection letters in perspective.

The last thing I love about our group (and some months this would be first) is that, when I know there's a meeting coming up, I'm forced to write something. During the weeks when the muses are giving me the cold shoulder, it's a help to know I have to put something down on paper before the meeting.

Some weeks, I desperately scour my computer in search of something old I can rework and present to the group, then stumble upon a gem I'd forgotten about. More than once, I've unearthed one of those golden oldies, brought it to group, given it a spit shine, then turned around and sold it. I love that!

I hope this group stays together until I'm an old woman writing about my grandkids. I want to attend Bert's first book signing and buy a dozen copies of Anna Marie's novel. I want to be around when people are laughing at Ron's literary skullduggery and wrapping themselves in the warmth of Ellen's prose. The time we've spent together has taught me more than any book or class on writing ever could.

~Mimi Greenwood Knight

inspiration for Writers

Making Time to Write

It is not enough to be busy; so are the ants.
The question is: What are we busy about?

~Henry David Thoreau

The Man in the Green Pickup

Everyone has his own specific vocation or mission in life;
everyone must carry out a concrete assignment that demands fulfillment.
~Viktor Frankl

I didn't know the man. I didn't even know his name. But he changed my life as a writer, and over the years I often felt as though I sat with him in his green Forest Service pickup every day at noon. Each day, he ate a baloney-and-processed-cheese sandwich on white bread with mayo. After he took his last bite, he brushed the crumbs off his lap and swiped the mayo from the corners of his mouth. He poured a plastic cup of instant coffee from his Stanley thermos and set the cup on the dash.

Then he did the truly important thing. He pulled out his yellow legal pad and took a ballpoint pen from his khaki uniform pocket. Only fifteen minutes of his half-hour lunch break remained. He used those fifteen minutes to write. Two years of fifteen-minute segments, and he had written a book. The book was published, but I don't even know its title.

When I heard the story of the man in the green truck, I was a single mother, working full-time as a school counselor. I wanted to write. I'd had a few short articles, essays, stories and poems published, but I wanted to write a book. I just couldn't find the time. I thought I needed big chunks of free time when I could sit at a desk completely undisturbed.

For years, I'd thought about writing a Young Adult biography of Viktor E. Frankl. His book, *Man's Search for Meaning*, is the most hopeful story I know to be written by a Holocaust survivor and has been named one of the most influential books of the twentieth century. I thought Frankl's story could inspire the high-risk kids I'd worked with for years, kids who were trying to survive multiple traumas and poverty.

On a gorgeous spring day, near the end of the school year, I had to put Tommy, a thirteen-year-old boy, into an ambulance. He was in the process of overdosing on inhalants. The reason he gave me? He felt hopeless about his life and his future. When I walked back into the school, it was with newfound determination to begin writing Viktor Frankl's story for teens like Tommy.

As it turned out, I spent the summer teaching writing in a fast-paced program on a university campus. I did not start writing Viktor Frankl's story, but I did get a significant amount of research done. Before I knew it, I was back at my full-time job. I thought I would have to put off writing the book yet again.

That's when I met up with the man in the green pickup. When I heard his story, I thought, "If he could do it, I can do it." Every morning, I fixed and ate breakfast, packed my lunch, drove my daughter to school, then sat at the computer. For twenty minutes. How fortunate I was. I was able to give myself five more precious minutes every day than the man in the pickup ever had.

Those twenty minutes a day turned me into the writer I am today. They taught me that it's wonderful to have big chunks of undisturbed time for writing, but it's not necessary. A book can be written in twenty-minute segments. Or even in fifteen-minute interludes. You make time, and it doesn't have to be much. As with my role model, it took me two years to complete my book, *Viktor Frankl: A Life Worth Living*, which was published by Clarion Books.

~Anna S. Redsand

It Worked for Me

Nowhere can man find a quieter or more untroubled retreat
than in his own soul.
~Marcus Aurelius

The shrill sound of a phone interrupts my concentration. As a journalist, I'm used to this, but a few years ago I added fiction to my writing career. Quite unlike reporting, I soon realized fiction requires thoughtful, unleashed fabrication, and when this mood is interrupted, it's difficult to regroup very quickly. This particular day, I am absorbed in the antics of five women headed to France. The novel is almost complete, but needs serious editing.

Clearly annoyed, I stare at the phone, tempted to let the machine get it. No, I'd better answer. I check the Caller ID. Ugh, my editor from the newspaper.

"Hello."

Helen speaks cheerfully. "Can you meet me for coffee in thirty minutes? I need a brainstorming session."

"Sure." No matter how much I want to say no, my practical mind says yes. My day job always comes first, as it pays the rent. I look at my watch and scowl. Reluctantly, I save the manuscript, put on something more appropriate, and hurry to Starbucks. Fiction must wait.

Later that day, the novel again has my full attention until Yahoo Messenger flashes across my computer screen. It is yet another editor wanting a fact check on my previous assignment ASAP. Again the novel must wait.

It doesn't take long and things go swimmingly on my novel until my concentration is jarred by the doorbell. My neighbor stands outside, ready for some chat time. By now, I'm downright irritated and decide to brush her off. I'll be polite, but firm.

"Sorry," I say in my sweetest voice. "This is not a good time. Maybe another day we can catch up." I cringe. Just because I work at home—and as a writer at that, which no one takes as serious work—doesn't mean my days are empty.

The woman smiles, says she understands, and waves a half good-bye. I scratch my head. Now, where was I going with that scene?

I heave a huge sigh and stare out the window. Something has to give or I'll never complete the novel. Intrusions are breeding redundant phrases, not to speak of details already mentioned in previous chapters.

If I could only find a place without phones, editors, friends, and even family, I could do wonders. A getaway, I think. Why not isolate myself somewhere and whip this thing into shape?

The more I think about it, the more excited I become. I call a fellow fiction writer, whom I know is having her own struggles with peripheral concentration, and present the idea.

"Brilliant," she says. "Plan it."

We discuss rules. To accommodate my work schedule, it has to be a Friday and Saturday event, and since it makes little sense to spend all our time in the car, it has to be no more than two hours away from home.

We choose a remote ranch in the Kansas Flint Hills and reserve a private cottage on the grounds. I load my fiction project onto a flash drive (one can never be too safe), along with a short story that has lain dormant almost two years. I check off a list of essentials: laptop, *The Chicago Manual of Style*, portable printer, red pen, USB cord, the flash drive, and a few items to set the mood. We will need candles to awaken the spiritual senses, fresh flowers for ambiance, chocolate (just because), snacks for fuel, lots of coffee, and wine to shut off our brains at night.

The ranch is seven miles from nowhere and sports a spectacular view of the Kansas prairie. We are bursting with enthusiasm. At check-in, I notice the receptionist keeps glancing out the window. There is a pronounced look of confusion on her face.

"So, you'll be riding?"

I suppress a giggle. "No. We'll be writing, with a W." In calling ahead for reservations, I mentioned we were writers, looking for a quiet spot, and since it was a ranch… well, an honest mistake.

"Ah," she says, smiling. "That explains no horse trailer."

It is quiet. Real quiet. Our cell phones don't even work. The weekend flies while we edit reworked chapters of prose, take walks to loosen stiff joints, and drive twenty miles into town for a barbeque carry-out. The next day, we write more, walk less, snack often and drink the wine. We barely speak.

It works. By the end of the weekend, I have rewritten a solid hundred pages, edited several chapters, and polished the synopsis.

Four months later, in the dead of winter, we go on retreat again, but this time, due to the frequent ice storms in our area, we simply check into a local hotel and choose a two-bedroom suite with a living room. We add a critique session to our weekend, which allows us to give each other sound advice, point out weaknesses, and praise strengths. The candles open the creative juices, the flowers provide beauty, and the wine a reward.

I'm lucky in that my writing partner and I have the same dedication to our work. We work out the little things. For instance, I get up early; she starts her day late. I get up in the night and write; she sleeps soundly. I exercise at intervals during the day, while she is prone to avoid this at all cost unless chided into it.

It's been two years since that first retreat, and it's worked so well that we've expanded the days to three, and scheduled them every three months instead of four. Each time, I return rejuvenated, with a satisfied sense of accomplishment. And when I re-enter my house, with its phone calls, doorbell, Yahoo Messenger, and other unexplained noises, I calmly mark my calendar. It's only three months until my next retreat.

~Arlene Rains Graber

A Few Short Minutes

*Much may be done in those little shreds and patches of time
which every day produces, and which most men throw away.*
~Charles Caleb Colton

"So, what are your plans for today?" my husband, Eric,
asked me when we returned home from church one
Sunday.

"I have so much to do that I don't even know
where to start," I said. "The sink is full of dishes, the laundry hampers
are overflowing, and I need to bake cupcakes for the school bake sale.
Oh, and one of the boys has a birthday party to go to this afternoon."
I sighed and added, "Plus, I really need to get some writing done."

Eric nodded. "What time is the party?"

My eyes lit up. "Are you offering to take care of that one?"

"I was hoping to watch some football this afternoon, but I'm sure
I can squeeze that in."

I thanked him, wishing I felt more optimistic about my chances
of squeezing in some writing time. Lately, it seemed that everything
else was squeezing out my time at the computer. It bothered me that
I hadn't been writing very much, but I was a mom first and a writer
second.

Eric made lunch while I threw a load of clothes into the washing
machine. While we ate, our daughter Julia said, "Can we go out for
ice cream tonight?"

Eric and I looked at one another and smiled. "Sure, that sounds good," he said. "We'll hit Baskin-Robbins tonight, but only if the Colts win."

"Daddy, stop teasing," she said. "I know we'll get ice cream even if your team loses."

Eric smiled. "You're right, but it's double scoops if they win."

An hour later, Eric had returned from birthday party drop-off and settled in front of his football game. I was still working in the kitchen, but I could feel my computer calling me. I sighed, knowing the odds of getting any writing time were slim. There was simply too much to do to sit down at the computer for any length of time.

From the kitchen, I could hear Julia pestering Eric about the ice cream.

"We'll go when the game is over, honey," he answered, not taking his eyes from the TV.

"But can't we just go now?"

"There's six minutes left in the game."

"Six minutes? What can happen in six minutes? Can't we just get the ice cream now?" she asked. "The Colts are winning by fourteen points. There's no way the other guys can catch up in just six minutes."

Eric sighed and shook his head. "Honey, a few short minutes can change everything."

I finished the dishes and plopped down on the couch beside Eric. "Are you done already?" he asked.

"No, but there's no point in starting anything else if we're going to be leaving soon."

Eric shrugged. "Six minutes in football time is like a half-hour in regular time. Get out your computer and see what happens."

I sighed. "I don't think I'll really accomplish anything, but I'll try." I fired up my computer and began working on a story I'd started several days before but hadn't had time to complete.

As I typed, I could hear Eric clapping and yelling at the TV. Then I heard Julia say, "Is it over, Daddy? Is it time to get the ice cream now?"

"Soon, Julia. There's two minutes left."

"Two minutes? Why can't we just leave now? The game is over anyway."

"This game is far from over. Just a few short minutes can change everything."

Eric's statement caught my attention. Of course, he was right. In football, two minutes can change the entire game. But his words were true about more than just sports.

I'd been at the computer for less than thirty minutes, but I'd managed to complete a solid first draft of my story.

Just those few short minutes had made a difference.

I thought about all the other little blocks of time in my life that I thought were too short to use. Now I realized they were too long to waste.

Not to beat a dead horse, but the football analogy really appealed to me. A touchdown is nothing more than getting the ball across the field, yard by precious yard. Sometimes it happens in one amazing, record-setting pass. Other times, it occurs more slowly—and more painfully, with the running back pounding out just a few yards at a time. Either way, seven points is seven points.

I realized my writing was the same way. Occasionally, fabulously, my stories get done in one long burst of inspiration. As a writer, there's nothing better than those precious hours when my muse visits and I have nothing more to do than enjoy the creative process. But since my family insists on eating and wearing clean clothes every day, those times are few and far between.

My life circumstances don't provide me with many big chunks of time to write. So I needed to use the small chunks productively.

And that's where my new motto came in: A few short minutes can change everything.

I bought one of those tiny netbook computers and left it on my kitchen counter. I began writing while I waited for water to boil and frozen pizzas to bake. It wasn't always super-productive, but I usually got a paragraph or two written. After a week or so, those little blocks of time would add up to a first draft.

It was a whole lot more than I would have had. I thought again about my football analogy. Sure, it's more exciting when the touch-down happens with a deep pass downfield, but the points add up the same, no matter how the team gets into the end zone.

Finally, minute by minute, word by word, I was writing. I was submitting my work and getting it accepted. It was my own personal end zone, and it felt nothing less than amazing. No matter how I got there.

A few short minutes were indeed changing everything.

~Diane Stark

Putting Together the Pieces

Nothing is a waste of time if you use the experience wisely.
~Auguste Rodin

The phone rings, and I check the Caller ID. For a split second, I consider letting the machine get it: It's Amanda, and a mutual friend has already warned me she needs a babysitter for her dog while she and her new beau go away for the weekend.

I answer it anyway, and after a few pleasantries, she gets right to the point: "I need you to watch Brutus for me."

"I'm sorry," I say. "There's just no way I can."

"Aw, come on. You're the only one who can. Everybody else works."

I clench my jaw, and I'm sure I hear a tooth crack. I work, too: I'm a writer. Just because I work at home and don't punch a clock doesn't mean I don't have a job.

"I have a deadline," I say.

"What kind of a deadline?" she scoffs.

"There's an anthology," I mumble. "I'm halfway through a story for it."

"Oh, so it's not like a real deadline. And you probably won't even make it in, anyway. What's the statistic? Only one percent of stories sent in are accepted, or something like that?"

I sigh. I wish I hadn't shared the cruel realities of the writing life so liberally with my non-writing friends. "Yeah, but the statistic is zero if I don't at least try."

"Come on. I really need you."

I swallow my guilt. "I'm sorry. I just can't."

"What, is the world going to end if you don't get this story done?"

"No, but I really need to do this. I set this goal, and I need to follow through."

"Fine," she says icily, and hangs up.

I hang up and turn on my computer, shaking my head. I shouldn't feel so guilty; I know I have to stick to my guns. My writing career is never going to take off if I keep letting other things get in the way. It's hard enough to find time to write with all my normal day-to-day tasks, I certainly don't need to take on more!

As it is, I practically live in my car: carting the kids to school, to their jobs, and to their extracurricular activities. And let's not forget the endless housework. The laundry hamper magically refills overnight, and my cats seem to be in perpetual shedding season. If I don't vacuum twice a day, the carpet looks like it has been doused in Rogaine.

A glance out the window reminds me that I have outdoor work waiting for me, too. In a moment of utter insanity, I started a garden to save on our food budget. Instead, I've got a small patch of pitiful plants that wilt if I'm not out there watering them every two hours. I should have known better: Inside, I've got a bay window full of stems that were once lovely houseplants.

And once I've taken care of all that, there's still the dishwasher, the mopping, the dusting, the windows… Exactly when am I supposed to find the time to write?

Just thinking about it all is exhausting. What I need is a minute to clear my head. I only have twenty minutes before I need to pick up my daughter from work, so how much could I accomplish right now, anyway?

I surf to the website of one of my favorite diversions, an online jigsaw puzzle, and spend the next fifteen minutes piecing together a moose. After I complete the puzzle, the "congratulations" screen appears, and the statistics catch my eye: Over the past year, I've played 1,564 games.

"That can't be right," I mutter. "How did I find time to play 1,564 games?"

"What?" my husband asks, coming into the room.

"This thing says I've played 1,500 games."

He leans down and looks at the screen, then turns and arches an eyebrow at me. "Wow. Think of how many words that would be."

I shoot him a look, but he's right.

I average four jigsaws every day, ten to fifteen minutes each, between errands or household tasks. That's 15,640 minutes, give or take a few, or almost 261 hours.

When I get on a roll, I can write 3,000 words per hour. A slow day is 1,000 words an hour. So, even if they were all slow days, that's 261,000 words, or almost three novels, just in those "jigsaw" moments over the course of a year!

So who doesn't have time to write?

"Oh, my," I say, staring at the screen. "I have wasted so much writing time."

My husband gives me a look.

After I throw a pencil at him, and he deftly ducks, I tell him, "Call me in twenty minutes. I'm going to write."

~Brenda Kezar

The Magic Wand

An idea can turn to dust or magic,
depending on the talent that rubs against it.
~William Bernbach

My friend Cath and I were having our weekly phone conversation. "So, how's the magic book coming along?" she asked. "Does J.K. Rowling have anything to fear?"

"Well," I hedged, "it's kind of stalled. Since I've gone back to teaching, I haven't really had the energy to write. I did change the main character's name. Oh, and I worked out a fairly detailed plot line. But as for writing..." My voice trailed off.

For my birthday that year, Cath gave me a beautiful desk set and a package of yellow paper. "This is special paper," she said. "You can only use it to print your book."

I smiled and later printed out the first five chapters of my manuscript. I promised myself I would work on it during the summer break. But the summer came and went with little added to the book and no additional chapters printed.

Five summers passed, but something else always seemed to take priority. I needed the time to de-stress and relax. The house needed painting, a new roof, or a bathroom remodel, and I'd schedule the work for summer when I was around to talk to the workmen. If those excuses didn't work, it was too hot to toil over a keyboard in a house without air conditioning.

During the sixth summer, Cath called with an invitation. "The Harry Potter exhibit is here. Do you want to go? Maybe it will give you the impetus to get back to your book."

Two days later, Cath, her daughter Casey and I spent the morning strolling through scenes and props from the movies. As we exited the exhibit into the gift store featuring Harry Potter memorabilia, Cath said, "I know it's not your birthday for months, but I want you to choose something that will get you back into writing. Casey was so excited when she read your first five chapters, but that was years ago."

I walked around, trying to find the perfect present. Within minutes, I was drawn to the magic wands. I tried one, then a second. When I picked up the third one, the world tilted. Although the logical part of my brain told me it was just overpriced molded plastic, the creative part heard the words: "Magic seeks a willing heart." "This one," I said. "I'll take this one."

For weeks afterward, I'd hold the wand in my hands, letting it work its magic on me. I taped poster-sized sheets of paper on the wall and worked out an intricate plotline. I started a notebook, writing down ideas and bits of dialogue. I bought books on castle construction, medieval customs, and herbal lore. Gradually, the manuscript grew from five chapters to seven and, finally, to thirteen.

September came, and I was back teaching school. Each week, I held the wand less and less as handouts and homework to correct took up my time. Eventually, I placed the wand back in its box and tucked it away in my linen closet. The reality of earning a living took precedence, and I deafened my ears and barricaded my heart against its soft murmurs.

By the time the next summer came, and the ones after it, the magic was muted, and I had lost the thread of the story. Cath hadn't.

"Whatever happened to the book?" she said during one of our weekly phone calls. "You started writing it when Casey was about eleven or twelve. She was really excited when she read the first few chapters. Do you realize she's now twenty-one? At this rate, she'll be able to read it to her own kids."

I sighed, thinking of the magic wand for the first time in years. After our conversation, I dug it out of the linen closet and placed it on my lap as I sat in front of the computer. I opened the box and stared at the lifeless piece of plastic. After a few moments, I ran my fingers along its carved surface, picking out the details of the intertwining vines.

For a second, I could have sworn the wand shimmered. My imagination, I told myself. Or, more likely, my guilt. Still, I cradled the wand in my hands for a few more minutes before carefully placing it back in its box. But this time, rather than hide it, I placed the box on the bookshelf behind my office chair.

The next year was difficult. After two previous occurrences of cancer, my friend Susan was diagnosed with terminal cancer. I spent that summer helping her get her house in order and then sat with her on her last journey. Any thoughts of reviving my book died with her.

The next September, I returned to school, teaching even more hours. But a particularly difficult class had me considering early retirement. "So what are you waiting for?" I asked myself. "Now's your chance to devote yourself to the book. If not now, when?" But thoughts of my puny pension scared me off.

Toward the end of the school year, after a disturbing incident in class one Friday afternoon, I decided I needed a break. Luckily, we were heading into a long weekend. For two days, I simply sat on the couch and read. On the third day, I e-mailed my principal that I needed the rest of the week off. I had barely hit the Send key when I got an idea for the book and scribbled some notes. On the fourth day, I began thinking about reworking the first chapter. On the fifth day, I called my principal and said I wouldn't be coming back for the last six weeks of term. Since she knew how much I had been struggling with the class, she wasn't surprised.

After the phone call, I cleared my desk of all the handouts I had been working on, picked the textbooks off the floor and stuffed them in a cabinet. Then I reached for the wand. My hand hovered over it, not quite steady. I took a few deep breaths. When I picked it up, the wand felt as if it had been made for my hand. Once more, I heard the words: "Magic seeks a willing heart."

I sat there for a few moments, letting ideas for the book wash over me. I figured out how to weave a stubborn subplot into the story. Two additional characters jumped up, begging to be written into the book. I realized I needed to cut out the backstory in chapters 12 and 13 that had ground the action to a halt.

I gently set the wand on my desk, booted up my computer and began to type: Chapter One. Flames danced over Mara's hands...

~Harriet Cooper

Home on the Range

There is nothing to writing.
All you do is sit down at a typewriter and bleed.
~Ernest Hemingway

In 1992, the year my youngest children, twins aged five, started kindergarten, I'd also begun exploring freelance writing after a long hiatus. I couldn't afford daycare, but I needed to work. I opened my own licensed childcare business.

It would be the best of both worlds, I told myself. I'd be there for my own four children, while practicing writing, submitting articles, poems and essays, and earning a paycheck—all while never leaving home. If I required all the children in my care to rest for an hour and a half every day, I'd write during that time. With any luck, I'd be able to publish enough to write full-time. Or so I thought.

Our living room was transformed into a play area, with neat bins filled with blocks, toy cars and dolls arranged on shelves. We set up a play kitchen, shelved lots of books and got a play structure for the yard. I'd lead craft activities on most days. When interviewing potential clients, I had one rule: Parents had to agree that their child would take a ninety-minute nap or rest each afternoon. Some looked puzzled, but all the moms and dads said okay. In no time, I'd enrolled the state limit of five daycare charges, aged two to five. Every day, I looked forward to that rest period and couldn't wait to write. But writing longhand made my fingers ache, and a computer was beyond our means.

Then I remembered—we still had the Royal electric typewriter I'd used in college. I hauled it out of the closet. I was set to launch my writing career, one "rest period" at a time.

Soon, my in-home daycare bustled. The hours were long, but for the most part the children were adorable. And no matter how difficult my day, I would have my writing time. It kept me sane. Besides, with all those kids, I could count on lots of writing material.

The hardest part was figuring out where to station myself while the kids rested or napped. If I tried to sit at the dining table, the kids could see and hear me typing. If I went to another room, I couldn't see or hear them. I loved the children, but I loved writing, too. My plans evaporated like water from a teakettle. I stashed the typewriter in the kitchen, and along with it, my writing dreams.

One afternoon, I bedded down the youngsters, turned on a video for the older kids, and then went around the corner to the kitchen. I stood there at the range, holding back tears, peeking around the corner every few minutes to check on my charges. The urge to write burned in me. I could take criticism, I could take rejection, but I couldn't handle not getting to write at all.

I stared down at the stove burners, splattered with grease and stuck-on macaroni and cheese from lunch. Grabbing a wet sponge, I scrubbed at the mess. The Royal electric still sat in its case in the corner, but I couldn't bear to look at it. In between checks on the kids, I scoured the stovetop until it shone.

Then it dawned on me: Standing at the stove, I only needed to poke my head around the corner to see the children. The wall dampened the sound and shielded me from their curious eyes. I quickly checked to be sure no child had stripped and was running around naked, then lifted the Royal on top of the stove and plugged it in. The typewriter's hum sent my hopes soaring, and I got to work.

Soon, I developed a rhythm—check the kids, type for a couple minutes, and check the kids again. Over the next few weeks, I perfected my routine. Videos were only for rest time, so the kids who didn't sleep looked forward to that part of the day. I trained any rowdy children to calm down immediately if my face appeared around the corner, lest I turn off the entertainment. I kept a timer next to the typewriter to be sure I only made the kids rest for ninety minutes. Best of all, I kept a date with my writing at least five days a week.

I can't say for sure if my crazy routine helped me get published, although I sold my first essay that year. Now I teach writing, and when students complain about their busy schedules, I'm the first to agree that finding time to write is a challenge for most of us. If you want to write, I tell them, you may have to get creative. At the very least, try writing while home on the range.

~Linda S. Clare

So, What Do You Do?

For disappearing acts, it's hard to beat what happens to the eight hours
supposedly left after eight of sleep and eight of work.
~Doug Larson

"So, what do you do?" For years, I was afraid to say it out loud—to use that six-letter word—to reply, "I'm a writer." But after ten years, three hundred articles in print, and essays in a couple dozen anthologies, I'm getting bolder.

The problem with that question is that it's not like you go, "I'm a banker."

And they say, "cool," and leave it at that.

Admit you're "a writer" and be prepared for many questions, the most tactless of which is, "Have you been published?" To this, I always want to answer, "Well, duh."

Then there's the popular "what do you write?"

"Non-fiction... no... creative non-fiction. No wait! Okay, I do write creative non-fiction... I mean, it's what I like to write... but I write some editorial stuff too just to pay the bills. Okay, actually, I'm writing a lot of advertorial lately. It pays better, and I try to make it as creative as I can. So I'm a fiction writer dabbling in non-fiction... okay... ad copy. But, hey, writing is writing. Right?"

But the question I dread most—because I keep asking it myself—is, "When are you gonna write a book?"

It reminds me of those old *Fawlty Towers* episodes where John

Cleese clutches his knee, crying, "Shrapnel. Korean War," when he wants to escape an awkward situation.

Someone asks, "So, when are you gonna write a book?" I grab my wrist, pitch forward with, "Carpal tunnel. Late night deadline," and the conversation moves along.

But if I had a year to do nothing but write, that book would just come tumbling out. Wouldn't it? A publisher would gobble it up. Oprah would love it. Then no one would ask if I'd been published or even what I do for a living. They'd know.

So that's what I need—one year to write. Of course, it would have to come with some fringe benefits. A maid, for one, so I'm not blithely courting the muse when the dryer goes off and I dash to pull the cottons out before they wrinkle. (The muse hates that!)

And I wouldn't need a full-time nanny, just someone to shuttle the kids back and forth to school and do the extracurricular stuff like football and piano and dance and HOMEWORK. And the maid could cook.

I'd have a valid excuse to avoid a half-dozen volunteer commitments to "work on my book," and my husband would hold up on his strategy of slowly delegating all the yard work to me.

With housework, yard work, volunteer stuff and the kids out of the way, I'd have all the time I want to write about—uh—housework, yard work, volunteer stuff, and the kids. Since I write mostly about the day-to-day happenings with kids and house and husband—with life—my creative non-fiction would have to be all the more "creative," I suppose.

When I'm lamenting the sight of Mount Dishmore in my sink, all the while knowing the maid took care of it first thing this morning, when I'm cracking myself up recounting the agility with which I maneuver through the after-school pick-up line while scribbling an essay in a notebook, I'll have to summon the memory of what that was like.

There may be a kink in my reasoning. A year to write uninterrupted would leave me little to write about since the interruptions have been my inspiration—especially those interruptions with

Oreo-smeared faces and their clothes on backwards. Where would I find fodder for my stories if writing was suddenly all I had to do?

If I'm honest with myself, my "writing year" would probably look a lot like the ten that preceded it—frantic, frenzied, but magical. So, when I'm asked what I do, I can honestly say, "I take naps under blanket forts and lament the fact that my daughter suddenly looks so good in her jeans. I dye my hair unnatural colors I found on the sale table and covertly hide the slimy vegetables I forgot to cook at the bottom of the trashcan. I make out with my husband in the driveway, when the kids are asleep, stash the good ice cream in the back of the fridge for myself, and trim the part of the roast the cat gnawed before I serve it to company. On a good day, I get a little of it down on paper."

And, occasionally, somebody prints it.

~Mimi Greenwood Knight

Twins

I write for the same reason I breathe… because if I didn't, I would die.
~Isaac Asimov

Writing and publishing a book is often compared to giving birth. In my case, my first book and my fourth baby had the same birthday.

Like many books, mine started with a germ of an idea about helping women decide on a work-from-home business or at-home employment. I wrote up a proposal and three sample chapters, sending it off with high hopes. A year of rejections from numerous publishers and agents (albeit with several nice notes expressing regret that my book didn't fit their current line-ups) followed my initial foray into publishing. Then I stumbled upon a small press in California that expressed interest.

Nearly twelve months of back-and-forth e-mails resulted in a signed contract and a six-month deadline to complete the manuscript. I was elated yet panicked because I had a three-month-old baby, two preschoolers at home—and no extra money for childcare. With my husband's support, I plowed ahead, knowing it would take determination to research and write a 55,000-word book practically from scratch.

Adding to the challenge, I had to locate and interview women who worked from home to liven up the drier facts and instructional aspect. Thankfully, I already knew several women who had at-home employment. Posting on a few relevant listservs pushed my total number of interviews to fifty.

Researching the book was like a scavenger hunt to uncover the most up-to-date data, and the actual writing was the biggest hurdle of all—not so much the stringing-together-of-sentences part, but the carving-out-time-to-sit-in-front-of-the-computer part. I became adept at snatching every spare moment I had, writing furiously in fifteen- to thirty-minute stretches, which was often the longest period of time I could find during the day. I fit in phone interviews as my children napped. I edited pages sitting on a park bench while my youngsters played on the jungle gym.

Finally, I sent the book off to the publisher for the long wait until publication. Meanwhile, I found out we were expecting baby number four.

The publication date kept getting pushed back until it was smack up against my due date. On June twenty-third, our fourth baby arrived, and when my husband returned home from the hospital, he found a box of books on our doorstep—*Hired@Home* had arrived on the same day as our son.

I felt like the proud parent of two newborns. Having both events happen at the same time brought me more joy than one can imagine.

Along the journey to publication, I learned that it takes more than writing skills to make an author. It takes time management because there are never enough hours in the day in which to write. It takes perseverance because there will be numerous setbacks. It takes optimism that you can write, even when circumstances make it seem impossible.

Today when people ask me how a mother of four children between the ages of four and ten finds time to write, I usually say that I can't not write, that to me, writing is as necessary as eating and breathing. I can't fathom never picking up a pen and writing down my thoughts, my ideas and my stories.

Granted, there are times when life intervenes and my writing has to be put on the back burner for a while. But I've found that you can usually squeeze in a few minutes each day, each week or each month to write—even if it turns out to be only five minutes here or fifteen minutes there.

Like the pregnancy of a first child or a fourth, birthing a book involves careful forethought, followed by patience, and the expectation that the outcome will match all the hopes and dreams that went into its conception.

~Sarah Hamaker

Good Pasta

You have to decide what your highest priorities are
and have the courage—pleasantly, smilingly, nonapologetically—
to say "no" to other things. And the way to do that is
by having a bigger "yes" burning inside.
~Stephen Covey

Discipline is a trait that does not come naturally to me. But as a mother and writer, it's something that I cannot do without.

I purposely push "writing" up a notch or two on my priority list, making sure that it never falls below "walk the dogs." I love my dogs, but there's a perfectly good back yard in which they can run.

Balancing motherhood, family life, and writing is not easy. With the stress and duties of daily life, it's hard to find the time to sit down and write. And I sometimes feel like the world has enough writers. We don't need one more. Nobody needs to hear my words.

Because who am I? Why should my words matter?

Well, my words do matter. All of our words matter. They tell us who we are.

But words will never see the light of day without discipline. Devoting time. Putting the word "write" onto an actual schedule to give it validity.

Your words represent who you are, and sometimes the duties of life can hide that person.

I cleaned out a drawer full of my son's old schoolwork the other day. I hold onto anything with sentimental or artistic value: drawings of George Washington; "What I Did on My Summer Vacation" essays; and, of course, every Mother's Day card.

I came across an essay in which my son had to write about his family, proudly noticing his neat penmanship even in the third grade.

He wrote of his love for baseball and music and *Star Wars*. When the subject of my husband came up, he wrote about his father working for a baseball team and playing awesome guitar in a rock group and worship band.

My heart swelled with the sweetness of it all. Then came my turn.

"My mom makes good pasta."

What? Good pasta?

I'm a writer and a musician, and all he writes is that I make good pasta?

What on earth was going on? Who does he think I am? I thought about this for a while, and it dawned on me that through his eyes, I am the one who makes dinner (the "good pasta"), and picks him up from school. I'm the one who makes sure he practices piano. I'm the one who puts out his clothing the night before so "things match."

I pondered this for a bit, and then made this decision: "He needs to meet his real mother."

The one I know. The one my husband married. And so that's why I now make sure that I make time to write.

I still consider myself a good mother. Okay, maybe my housekeeping skills need some improvement. But it's not fair to my son to not really know who his mother is.

His mother still feeds the dogs and still puts his clothes out and makes a mean pasta, but she also writes. She writes her beliefs and her ideas and her thoughts that become real words.

And his knowing "that mother" will make him a better person in the long run.

~Mary C. M. Phillips

Chapter

4

inspiration
for

Writers

Take My Advice

All of us, at certain moments of our lives,
need to take advice and to receive help from other people.

~Alexis Carrel

Just Tell Them What Happened

A good style should show no signs of effort.
What is written should seem a happy accident.
~W. Somerset Maugham

"You know, this is a for-credit option, Michael," Dr. John Glavin told me sternly. What he meant was clear: if he was going to pass me for three credits at the end of the semester—eight weeks away—I needed to start making progress.

I started my first book—a popular account of the life of Spanish painter Miquel Barceló—in college. I'd been meeting with Dr. Glavin—a strict English professor with a white goatee and a bowtie—for a weekly writing mentorship since the beginning of the fall semester of my senior year at Georgetown University. I had finished the two years of in-depth research by then. Now I had to turn the material into a compelling narrative.

Every Wednesday morning I brought Dr. Glavin two printed copies of what I'd produced in the last week, and read out loud as he followed along. The results had not been good. I'd tried beginning the book by narrating how I'd woken up startled from a dream I'd had about Barceló one night while visiting a friend in England. "Is there a good reason this book about a Spanish painter should begin in Leeds?" Dr. Glavin had deadpanned. Another week, I'd considered rendering a scene from the perspective of a pig Barceló was about to slaughter. This idea was met, mercifully, with silence.

That had been two or three weeks earlier and, since then, I'd basically stalled. I'd hardly ever written anything besides academic papers and I wondered, for the first time, if I just wasn't cut out for writing narrative. But now I had to figure something out. I had one week until my next meeting with Dr. Glavin, who had made it clear that I needed to show him something substantial—at least twenty pages or a complete chapter.

So I was back at my desk, looking at a blank screen and wondering what to do next. What was wrong with what I'd written so far? I'd been trying too hard to make the writing dramatic, I thought. The result had been melodramatic and contrived. Then, for some reason, I remembered an e-mail I'd written a year earlier, the night that I'd first met Barceló. I'd told a journalist friend about the meeting—which had occurred at a private party Barceló threw for his friends—and she'd asked me to tell her everything about it. Late one night I wrote her a long e-mail as quickly as possible. I used hardly any capital letters, I punctuated haphazardly and I made no considerations for style. I was just trying to tell her what happened at the party. She wrote back in the morning: "This is just extraordinary... I really enjoyed reading this... because it is so raw and alive."

At the time, I'd been pleased my friend enjoyed the e-mail, but I hadn't given her response much thought beyond that. Now I remembered those words: "raw and alive." What could be further from my assessment of the writing I'd produced recently: "melodramatic and contrived"? Something had worked in that e-mail that hadn't been working now that I was actually trying to write a book. And whatever it was, I needed to recreate it.

I went upstairs from my basement bedroom and took a Trader Joe's beer out of the fridge. Back at my desk I drank it too quickly, then opened a new e-mail window. I'd decided the first chapter of my book would be about Barceló's painting of a dome at the UN headquarters in Geneva. The project had been a calamity; it had nearly failed multiple times and caused a political scandal in Spain.

I addressed the e-mail to my friend, noted the numbing buzz from the beer, and started to tell her what happened in Geneva, just like I'd done in the e-mail a year earlier. I wrote like that every day for a week. The writing was littered with sentences that began with "anyway," "so," or "the thing is." The tone was conversational, almost as if it were a transcript of me telling the story of the Geneva dome over dinner.

The following Wednesday morning, shortly before my meeting with Dr. Glavin, I finished telling the story in e-mail form. I copied the text into a Word document. I had twenty pages and no time to read them. I hit "print" and then flipped through the warm pages, horrified. There were no capital letters, the punctuation was haphazard and the language was, it seemed to me, exceedingly colloquial. My professor had asked me to get my act together and this was what I was going to bring him.

In his office, I slid his copy of the pages across his desk. He assayed the thickness of the stack approvingly, and I started reading. For forty minutes he said nothing and I didn't dare to raise my eyes from the pages. I cringed every time I had to read a sentence beginning with "anyway" or "the thing is," but I kept going. When I finished, I put my pages down and looked at him for the first time. He was grinning. "This is a triumph," he said. I was floored. "It has pace. It's visual. The voice is young, but once you clean it up…" He was still smiling, obviously pleased, so I smiled, too. He asked me for another fifteen pages for the following week. So, I went back to my basement bedroom and kept writing e-mails, just telling friends and family the story of Barceló's life.

A year later, I sold my book to one of Spain's most prestigious publishers and in May 2012, two years after I graduated from college, it was published throughout the Spanish-speaking world. I wrote much of the first draft in e-mail form but even when I was writing directly into Word, I always reminded myself to just tell the reader what happened.

~Michael Damiano

It's a Product, Prudy

It took me a long time not to judge myself through someone else's eyes.
~Sally Field

*L*ike most writers, I was over the moon when I sold my first poem. I was in high school, and I decided it was easy! You just wrote something, sent it in, and waited for the check. Right? Alas, wrong, wrong, wrong.

To be fair, I did all right for years. I wrote articles and short stories, submitted them and, most of the time, they sold.

Until I wrote a novel, which I would rewrite from prologue to epilogue four times over five years, and get rejected more than thirty times before I finally sold it to a New York publisher. Those were unquestionably the most exciting yet frustrating years of my writing life; however, two lessons emerged that have stood me in good stead. And, surprisingly, they didn't come from another writer, but from my late husband.

Jack's family had been in the wholesale business in Cincinnati for three generations, and Jack had been in sales for the majority of his working life. He knew how discouraging it was to fail to make a sale, and he was genuinely kind and understanding when I received one of my myriad rejection letters.

As time passed, he also grew a little tired of my angst, so one day he sat me down. "Prudy," he said, "let's say you go into a dress shop. You try on ten, even fifteen dresses, but you walk out without buying a single thing. Did the store fail? Did the clerk fail? Did the dress designer fail?" He paused for dramatic effect. "No," he said at last. "No one failed. There was nothing the matter with the dresses. The simple truth is that this particular store didn't have what you wanted.

"Get smart," he said. "Think of your novel as a product, not as a piece of your soul. If you think of the novel as being separate from you—Prudy, the person—you won't take the rejection so hard. The publisher who sent the rejection isn't saying you're a lousy human being or a wretched writer or that your book is bad. He's merely saying it doesn't meet his needs."

Jack made sense and, heartened, I began work on yet another revision. As I proceeded chapter by chapter through the novel, I recognized that his words contained still another bit of writerly wisdom: If you want to buy a prom dress, you don't go to a store that specializes in casual wear. Translation: the salesperson/writer must know the market, i.e., the publisher or agent who likes his or her product/genre.

The novel sold the next time out. Since then, I've written five more novels, eighteen regional histories, a how-to book about writing your first novel, and a ghostwritten autobiography.

They've all sold.

Thanks, Jack.

~Prudy Taylor-Board

Fire and Spirit

In everyone's life, at some time, our inner fire goes out. It is then burst into
flame by an encounter with another human being. We should all be thankful
for those people who rekindle the inner spirit.
~Albert Schweitzer

When I was sixteen, I wrote horrible poetry—God-awful rhyming nonsense full of clichéd images like thorny roses and dripping blood. Most of it, no, all of it, was about boys I liked who didn't like me back. In my youthful misery, I swore I was the next Sylvia Plath. I thought my poetry was fantastic because I hadn't yet been crippled by the self-doubt of a more mature writer. I believed in myself and my writing to such an extent that my confidence probably bordered on delusion, but hey, I'd grown up in the eighties and gone to school when the self-esteem movement was in full swing. Every other after-school special promised me that if I put my mind to it, I could do or be anything I wanted. And I believed it.

Convinced of my genius, I sent a package of my poetry, all hand-written in blue ballpoint pen on notebook paper straight out of my Trapper Keeper, along with an improperly formatted cover letter, to one of the most famous editors who has ever lived at one of the most prestigious presses in the world. As an adult, I would rather die than do something as shamefully amateurish, as brash, as career-destroying as this. As an adult, I cringe to think that I did this at sixteen.

For several months, I heard nothing. I turned seventeen and still heard no reply, and I decided that the famous editor knew nothing of great writing and was clearly a fool. But one day, I came home and found an enormous package waiting for me on the doorstep. It was so heavy that I had to drag it into the house. Winded and confused, because my birthday had long since passed and I certainly didn't have the money to order anything, I looked at the return address: Famous Editor at Prestigious Press, New York, New York.

He'd sent me books. Lots and lots of books. Mostly poetry, but also novels. And he wrote me a very long, personalized letter.

"These are the books you won't read in school. These are the books that will help you as a writer," he wrote.

Nikki Giovanni, Charles Bukowski, Jorie Graham, Seamus Heaney, Sharon Olds, Adrienne Rich, Tom Robbins. He was right. They didn't teach these writers in school, and I couldn't wait to read them. I figured if they didn't teach them in my eleventh grade AP English, then they had to be great. They were.

The books, though miraculous and nearly better than Christmas, weren't the best part. He'd written that my poems had "fire and spirit," that my writing was filled with passion and exciting imagery. Believe me, this was a lie, but the next part was a truth that has never left me. To be a writer, he explained, one must live life thoroughly. Have adventures, seek out extraordinary people, never fear heartbreak, attend as many parties as possible, accept invitations, run with the wild crowd once in a while, go to the beach, pay attention to everything, read constantly, and never, ever stop writing. Never settle for anything less than being a writer. Do whatever else you like, but never forget that you are also a writer.

Being a writer is hard. Sitting in front of a computer, writing and rewriting the same line, trying to find the perfect verb, is tedious, especially when you're certain your friends are doing something infinitely more exciting over on Facebook, and you are missing it. Others won't take you seriously if you haven't published at least two New York Times bestsellers.

"Oh, you want to be a writer. That's cute," they'll say with a smirk.

Rejection can turn you into a cynic or worse, a pessimist. Your mother will suggest more lucrative careers. You will lose your naïve enthusiasm. I did. But I never forgot that I am a writer, and I never stopped writing or reading.

I've received hundreds of rejections. My writing has been skinned alive in workshops. I've been made fun of—and on the Internet no less. Worse, I've used adverbs after dialogue, I write sheepishly. But I keep going. What makes me stick with it? The after-school specials are partly to blame. And Oprah. Don't tell anyone, but I read *The Secret*, and I'm still furiously trying to manifest something. I do believe, I think, all that about accomplishing what you put your mind to, which is a cliché and we writers need to avoid those, of course.

In my darkest moments, though, when the self-doubt bears down on me, when I hate my work, when I have no original ideas and my friends are all more successful, I remember the letter from the famous editor. I think of his advice and how I've followed it twenty-some years later. I remember that my poems have "fire and spirit," which was a lie of course, but it gave me hope and still does, because what truly possesses fire and spirit is me and the writer I have always been. I remember the box on the doorstep, waiting for me like Christmas. My sixteen-year-old self believed that anything was possible. A famous editor took the time to write me a personalized letter and send me more books than I could lift, so I keep writing and submitting because I would never want to disappoint either of them.

~Victoria Fedden

Treat the Rectangle Carefully

Thousands of geniuses live and die undiscovered—
either by themselves or by others.
~Mark Twain

I stood at the front of my classroom and drew a stick figure on the whiteboard. Next to it I drew a rectangle.

I turned around to my sixth-grade students and announced, "This little stick man is you. This rectangle is what you write for me. When I talk to you about how to fix this," I said, pointing to the rectangle, "I am not talking about what is wrong with this." I moved my finger to point to the stick figure.

Just to be clear, I pointed back to the rectangle again. "This is not the same as," I moved my finger to the stick figure, "this."

Every September, I start my first writing lesson with this conversation. Many writers have trouble separating comments about their work from comments about them, and I think this is especially true for young writers.

But now it was May, and the kids were finishing up their last big writing assignment. They were told to describe a time when something funny happened at a serious event. It had to be first-person narrative, and they were to write about one thing. This is always challenging for sixth-graders because most of the time they want to write a laundry list of events, call it a story, and say they're done.

Naomi's first story for me in September consisted of six sentences: *This summer, I got to sleep in every day. I helped my mom take care of the garden. I learned to make pancakes. We went to Worlds of Fun. It was fun. The End.*

Over the school year, things started to click for Naomi, and her writing skills began to blossom. When I introduced this final assignment, Naomi was excited to tell about a wedding her family attended during Spring Break. I looked over her story chart that Tuesday and saw that she correctly completed the character and setting boxes. She also filled in several notes for "rising action," and correctly labeled her dad running down the aisle as her "climax."

Naomi laid her completed draft on my desk Friday morning. I told her we would go over it during class that afternoon, so she could complete her final draft over the weekend. I read her draft during lunch, and her story was fantastic:

My cousin, Becca, was getting married, and she wanted her dog, Aspen, to be in her wedding.

I found myself smiling as I read because Naomi was using every tool we had covered in our lessons.

"Make sure your brother walks Aspen before the ceremony," Aunt Kathy told Becca. "You know what Aspen does if she gets too excited."

I was laughing out loud as I finished Naomi's story. It was wonderful. All we needed to go over Friday afternoon was some spelling and punctuation errors. It was the best thing I'd ever read of Naomi's.

I sat with her at a round table that afternoon and had her read her story out loud. As she read, I marveled at how much of her own personality was coming through in her writing. Additionally, Naomi found some spelling errors and a run-on sentence without any prompting from me.

The pitch of her voice got higher, and her pace quickened.

"After the minister prayed, Aunt Jennifer stood up to sing 'The Lord's Prayer,' Aspen never liked hearing Aunt Jennifer sing…"

"Right there, Naomi," I interrupted. "The sentence ends right there. You need to put a period after 'Prayer' instead of the comma."

Naomi stopped reading. She stared at her paper for several seconds.

"Right here," I said again. "Here's where you need to put a period."

Naomi erased the comma and replaced it with a period. Instead of continuing reading, however, she just stared at her paper.

"Go on," I said. "Finish your story."

Naomi started reading again, but now her voice sounded tight, like someone was choking her. I thought she might have just swallowed some air until I noticed giant tears running down her cheeks.

"What's wrong?" I asked, suddenly shocked. What in the world had just happened?

Naomi's breathing quickened, tears were streaming down her cheeks, and she began hiccupping and sobbing.

"Naomi, what's wrong?"

She gulped, panted, and finally choked out, "This is the best part of my story, and all you could say was that I needed a period here."

The floor dropped out below me, and my stomach knotted. We had been rushed after lunch, and I never told Naomi that I thought her story was wonderful. I just sat down with her and started telling her what needed fixing.

Suddenly, my "stick figure" was holding her "rectangle," and there were big tears running down her cheeks.

How could I have been so thoughtless?

The best lesson in the world can fall flat if I forget how fragile people really are. Maybe I can show on a whiteboard that we are separate stick figures from our rectangles of work, but sometimes we wrap those rectangles around our heart, and it hurts when someone points out what needs to be fixed. We are not the rectangles we produce each day, but our rectangles are precious to us. Naomi reminded me again to treat the rectangle carefully because some days those rectangles are the only thing that makes us feel good about ourselves.

~Suzan Moyer

The Work Must Speak for Itself

When your work speaks for itself, don't interrupt.
~Henry J. Kaiser

I t is one of my strongest memories of college.

I was taking my very first fiction-writing workshop. Not that I really needed it, or so I believed. I had won writing awards in high school; my teachers had praised my stories and essays to the skies. This workshop, I believed, would simply confirm what I already knew: I was a literary genius, and it was only a matter of time before I was published and thus famous.

Instead, I sat through one of the most brutal critiques I have ever had, squirming and red-faced while my beloved masterwork was taken apart from top to bottom. Characters? Flat. Plot? What plot? Descriptions, bordering on purple. Nothing was left when my classmates were through.

Then, just as I began to think the nightmare was over, came the worst moment: The professor stood up and carefully drew a narrative arc on the blackboard, that classic model of storytelling. Rising tension, climax, resolution. Three simple stages, three acts. "Next time, start from there," he advised.

When he sat back down, I started to speak, to explain what I really meant, to point out all the wonderful things in my story that they had so inexplicably missed. How could they not understand?

How could they not see what I was describing? How did they all simply not get it?

But before I could get out the words, the professor shook his head. "Authors do not respond," he ordered.

I stared at him, dumbfounded. "Why not?" I asked. (I say I asked, but squawked would be more accurate. I was just thankful my voice wasn't shaking the way my hands, hidden under the table, were.)

"Because," he said—and he gave me a smile then, a sympathetic one—"the work has to speak for itself."

It took me years to understand what he meant.

At first, I took his statement literally. If it's not in the story, then it needs to be. You can't stand over every reader's shoulder, explaining, "What I meant was…" Once the story is out in the world, that's it; it's up to the author to make it as clear as possible beforehand, to make sure every necessary detail has been included.

So I packed my stories with those very details. I fattened them up with flashbacks, asides, everything I could think of to make sure that readers understood exactly what I meant. I spelled out everything, and then repeated it just to be sure. And through the rest of that workshop, I took every piece of advice, trying to write my stories to satisfy everyone, a practice I continued once I graduated and moved to a big city with dreams of literary stardom dancing in my head. Friends, relatives, editors, co-workers: I listened to them all, and tried to write for them all.

Not surprisingly, my overwrought fiction did not succeed, and eventually I put writing aside, disheartened and frustrated by the endless rejections I received.

Many years later, however, I was reading a book review online. When I scanned the ensuing comments, I realized one of them was from the author herself, directly replying to the reviewer. And not just a reply; it was an angry, violent response, criticizing the reviewer's critique, accusing him of lack of understanding, lack of comprehension, lack of intelligence. How could this reviewer not see what she, the author, was trying to say? How could he not understand? How could he come up with such a gross misinterpretation?

"But the work has to speak for itself," I said aloud.

And that's when I realized: yes, but not quite as I had originally believed. It is not a directive to explain everything, to please everyone. It is about riding that fine line between craft and confusion, between explanation and narrative. It is about choosing what you think needs to be said and working to make those points clear, while at the same time accepting that the rest may very well be misunderstood, for reasons beyond your control. The reviewer's critique was not flattering, and much of it was specific: a character that felt like a stereotype, an unbelievable plot twist. But it was also quite clear that the reviewer disliked many works in that genre.

It was in part, then, an issue of craft, and in part, an emotional response that was simply beyond the author's control. What I had missed in that workshop, all those years ago, was how to distinguish between the two. Yes, the work has to speak for itself, but the author can only control what the work says, not the responses it provokes.

Armed with this newfound understanding, I began to write again. I joined a new workshop, and then another, and another. I read through my critiques and worked on staying detached, on evaluating the advice I was being given, piece by piece. I accepted some, and rewrote accordingly; I disregarded the rest. I let my classmates tell me what they saw and didn't see, what they understood and found incomprehensible, and I learned to write in a way that communicated more clearly the most important parts, without putting in the kitchen sink.

But, most importantly, I learned that some people will simply not get it, ever, and to let those critiques go.

The work has to speak for itself; it's up to the author to make sure the work says, clearly, what she wants to convey.

And that's all.

~L.S. Johnson

Stickler for Details

It was while making newspaper deliveries, trying to miss the bushes and hit the porch, that I first learned the importance of accuracy in journalism.
~Charles Osgood

arly in my writing career, I penned a monthly column for the *Myrtle Beach Area Business Journal*. Aptly named "Face to Face," the column was a creative way for me to introduce the greater Myrtle Beach area to an individual community member.

I loved discovering interesting details about people's lives and incorporating that information into an eloquent profile. It was often challenging and always rewarding.

I will never forget my August 2005 assignment: interview the local postmaster. It was a rather ordinary interview. We met at a coffee shop and chatted over a couple of cups of brew. I introduced myself and explained the name of the column. He said his last name was Neat. I liked it; it sounded catchy.

Mr. Neat and I talked for more than an hour. He told me that working as a postmaster was a dream of his that stemmed from boyhood. "I thought postmen just drove around in their Jeeps all day," he said with a laugh. He then filled me in on his academic background, family life, and love of the sun and surf.

Later in the interview, we talked a bit about his musical tastes, work ethic, and personality. Neat described himself as "a stickler for details who likes things done right the first time."

I kept that quote in mind as I went home to write up my profile. I was extremely cautious about my grammar and punctuation; I didn't want any errors in my copy. The next morning, I submitted the profile on Postmaster Neat to my editor. I was excited about the story and couldn't wait for it to go to press.

A week later, the publisher came into my work area with a copy of the new issue. "Melissa, we need to talk," he said. He pulled a chair over to mine and opened the journal. He pointed to the heading and said, "His last name is Leat, not Neat."

I stared at the boldface heading. I might as well have written profanity. It wouldn't have been any more humiliating.

"Does he know?" I asked my publisher. "Has he seen it?"

"He's the one who called me about it. He's pretty upset."

"I'm so sorry," I managed to respond.

But I couldn't say anything else. I felt a lump rise in the back of my throat, and tears began to leak from the corners of my eyes. I ran outside and cried. It was one of the most embarrassing mistakes I had ever made, and I couldn't make it go away.

I started to think about how I could have made such an enormous error. He told me his name over the phone when we first set up the interview. It sounded like Neat. I thought that was what he said in person when I shook his hand. I even said, "Neat name," as we talked. It never occurred to me that I was calling him the wrong name. Then I thought about him telling me how important details are and that he likes things done correctly the first time. And I cried some more.

A few minutes later, the route to my error started to become irrelevant. I needed to focus on making things right. So, I fastened my big-girl britches and went inside to talk to my publisher.

"What can I do to fix this?" I asked him. "Can we redo the story in next month's issue? I'll even rewrite the piece if you'd like."

"We won't be able to do that, Melissa," he said. "The best thing to do in this case is apologize and move on."

So I did. I called Mr. Leat and left a message. I apologized for my novice mistake and offered to buy him a cup of coffee. I left my number for him to return my call. Then, a few days later, I handwrote an apology letter and mailed it to him.

Luckily, my publisher forgave me, and I didn't lose my column. But I never heard from Mr. Leat again, so I don't know whether he forgave me or not.

As humiliating as the experience was, part of me is grateful for it. It made me a better fact-checker. Now, when I conduct an interview, I ask for business cards or for the person to write his or her name for me. I don't rely on my sense of hearing alone.

I triple-check everything. I am a stickler for details. And from now on, I am trying to do things right the first time.

~Melissa Face

Going Where You Look

If we are facing in the right direction, all we have to do is keep on walking.
~Buddhist Saying

"Slow down before we reach the intersection." I clutched the steering wheel with sweaty hands as I followed the instructor's direction. The car lurched toward the side of the highway, the front tires perilously close to the edge of the pavement, where a six-inch drop-off threatened to flip us over.

"Careful." The instructor calmly reached across and straightened the steering wheel. The car returned to the center of the lane, and my teenaged classmates, belted in the back seat, let out sighs of relief.

"Sorry." I tapped the brake pedal. The driver's ed car rolled to a halt in front of the white stop line.

"Keep your eyes on the road ahead," the instructor said, while I tried not to feel incompetent. "You go in the direction you look."

I remembered the remark several years later, when my mom and I reached a crossroad in our writing careers. We'd been writing separately, pursuing different paths on the way to publication. Whenever we got together, we talked about our stories, books we enjoyed reading, and the latest trends in the publishing industry, which we gleaned from writing magazines whose subscriptions we shared. We loved writing, though we weren't making progress toward our goal of getting published.

"Romances are popular," Mom said, during one of our chats. "We should write one."

"We? As in the two of us, working together on the same book?"

She nodded. "I think it'll be fun. I'm tired of facing a blank screen every morning. If we took turns, there'd always be something to build from. We could be each other's writing imp. You know, the little pixie who sneaks into the computer late at night and magically makes words appear."

"Think so?" I said. "I'd be tempted to trim the wings off any imp who changed my stories."

Mom thought about that for a minute, then admitted, "Yeah, me, too."

Still, the idea of writing together was appealing, and we kept coming back to it. After a few months of indecision, we decided to give the imp a chance to show off her talents. We outlined a romance novel and got started. I worked as first-shift imp, writing in the morning before leaving for my day job. Mom showed up at the house just before I drove off and took over the computer keyboard.

The rough draft progressed rapidly. Mom had been right—the imp made the work much easier and a lot more fun. We both looked forward to getting to the computer each day to see what twists and turns had taken place while we were gone. We both also wanted to make sure the work we left during our respective imp-stint was as interesting as we could make it.

Rewriting and editing presented challenges. The imp was great at creating, but not so good at revising. After a few ugly arguments, we established one unbreakable rule: When in doubt, delete. If we simply could not come to a compromise, we deleted the offending word, line, paragraph, or scene, and started anew—with one change: We worked together on the new part, instead of separately. We red-penciled revisions over lemonade and cookies while sitting at the picnic table on the sunny back porch, and heated disagreements turned into what my dad called "giggle sessions." We couldn't help it—we were having fun.

We finished the first book and began sending queries. We got some good feedback from agents, and a couple of them asked to read a few chapters. Despite the initial encouraging remarks, as the months went by, rejections piled up: Too much mystery. Where's the romance? Contrived plot. Sorry, not for us.

From experience, we knew the best way to keep from dwelling on the disappointment: Start the second book while we shopped the first. Once finished, we bravely sent off our second effort — and fared no better. We began a third, grinding out a set number of words each day and turning our imp-stints into grim marathons. When romance number three reached rewrite status, the giggle sessions became relentless quests to root out every error and produce a saleable manuscript.

In the summer of our battle with manuscript three, a convention for romance writers came to town. Despite the steep fee, we needed the inspiration, so we made reservations. We spent three days attending lectures, signing up for agent conferences, and networking with other authors.

Yet instead of inspirational, we found the event dispiriting. With the exception of an elite few, most attendees were just like us: hopeful and struggling. And we learned about the terms of the writing contracts we'd be expected to sign — should our work ever be accepted — which included relinquishing almost all rights. Were we working so hard only to end up for-hire hacks?

"We're never going to break in," I said, as we drove home on the last day. "We have better odds of winning the lottery or getting struck by lightning than we do of getting a romance published."

"I agree." Mom's voice was low. "Maybe we should give up."

"Do you want to?" I looked at her, and the car drifted to the right. With the practice of years behind the wheel, I straightened it automatically, and my high-school driving instructor's words came back to me. Before Mom could answer, I said, "Maybe we ought to look where we're going."

"What do you mean?" Mom asked.

"It's like driving." I gestured at the highway. "We've taken our eyes off the reason we started writing together, and we've strayed off course. We want to be published, sure, but the main reason was to have fun doing what we both enjoy."

"You're right." Mom let out a breath. "I haven't been having fun for quite a while."

"Me neither."

"So what now?"

"I still want to be published," I said. "I just don't think we're cut out for romances."

"Actually, we stink at them," Mom said, and we laughed together for the first time in ages. She added, "I think I know why, too. We only started writing romances because they're popular, and we thought it was an easy road to publication. There's no real heart in our stories, not like some of those authors at the convention. They love romance. We don't."

"True. I'd rather have the heroine pursued by a killer than a boyfriend."

"I agree. We should have paid more attention to the rejections. Apparently, our preference was obvious to everyone but us."

"Now that we've figured it out, we could try writing a mystery. They sell well."

"Isn't that the same road we were just on?" Mom asked. "Rather than picking a genre, let's write a book we'd like to read."

"Sounds like a plan." I smiled at her. "I'm looking forward to working with the imp again."

I flipped on the directional and slowed to turn onto the exit leading us home, and we launched into a conversation outlining the plot of a new book.

The SkyHorse, our young adult novel, was published by Musa Publishing last year, using our joint pen name, HL Carpenter.

~Lorri Carpenter

And
I Get Paid for This

The secret of success in life is
for a man to be ready for his opportunity when it comes.
~Benjamin Disraeli

There have been journalism assignments where I chuckled to myself and thought, I'm getting paid to do this. This thought crossed my mind while sitting on a bleacher, watching a high-school kid named LeBron James play basketball. The same thought crossed my mind while joking with comedian Ron White. And it brought a smile to my face as I interviewed drivers in the NASCAR circuit.

Writing is a joy. Writing as a livelihood was beyond my wildest dreams.

Getting published was beyond my wildest dreams, and I didn't dare fantasize it could become a career. Girls grew up to be nurses or teachers.

It was a teacher who sparked my dream. In eighth grade, Mrs. Louise Boyer, my language arts teacher, read the rough draft of a book I had written just for me, just for fun. When she returned my handwritten novel, she asked, "Have you ever thought of getting published?"

Well, no.

"You should," she said simply.

She made it sound so easy. She sparked a crazy idea in me and encouraged me to become a writer.

•••

If you want to write, write in whatever circumstance you find yourself. If you're a high-school student, find the school newspaper. If you are a mom with small children, find the local community newspaper. If you are involved in an organization, compose the group newsletter. If you are grieving, write a journal because it could become the basis of a self-help book. But open your eyes and look at your surroundings. There are interesting people all around, and you can tell their story through your written voice.

Doors will open to the best career ever.

As a young mother with two children, I wrote press releases as a volunteer with the local parent-teacher organization at the elementary school. After a year with the organization, the community newspaper needed a feature writer. They knew me from my press releases, and they offered me a job.

Those were good years, conducting interviews in strip mines and grain elevators, writing articles about celebrities who were coming to town and the "celebrities" who lived among us.

With each assignment, I discovered new contacts, new sources. A writer with integrity earns the trust of managers and sources. One assignment leads to another. A writing career is built one article, one source at a time. And if you get writer's block, play with words and themes. Once you get the lead, the rest of the story follows.

My career was journalism. I got paid to tell the stories of others. No two days were the same. One day the agenda was covering a mayor's breakfast; another was an interview with John Madden; another day could bring an interview with a one-hundred-year-old resident.

It was my dream job.

Over my twenty-four years in print media, journalism has changed. It is no longer interviewing a subject, getting quotes from at least two sources and writing the report. Journalism today incorporates not only newsprint, but online publishing, photography, video, blogs and social media.

This only means more opportunities for a writer.

As I managed a newsroom, college interns would bemoan the job market.

"It's not where you start," I'd say. "It's where you finish."

It's true. I started writing press releases about star students in the local grade school. It led to writing about star athletes and everyday heroes who live among us. Everyone has a story to tell, regardless of income and vocation.

Take the opportunities presented. Write for the school newspaper. Publish a blog on your favorite hobby or interests. Cover high-school sports.

Writers write. Delight in the fact you are getting paid to communicate through the published word. And when the word gets out that you communicate well, be ready for the next door to open. It worked for me.

~Tammy Roark-Proctor

Chapter 5

inspiration
for

Wrestling with
Writer's Block

Writer's block is a disease for which there is no cure, only respite.

~Terri Guillemets

Turning Blocks into Stepping Stones

One of the secrets of life is to make stepping stones out of stumbling blocks.
~Jack Penn

When I first joined my writing group, I was no stranger to blocks. They were installed on every cabinet, toilet, door, and crib, preventing my newly motoring toddler from a myriad of unthinkable accidents. Building blocks littered the floors, and although I occasionally tripped over one, I liked the minefield reminder of how blessed I was to finally have a child. Blocks were a good thing.

My writing group was good, too. It unleashed a creative side that constantly revitalized me. It was as if my brain had been tapped. Stories and words flowed as abundantly as maple sap in the sugaring season.

"I'm off to tap!" I'd announce and disappear into the computer room where time flew by. I'd imagine myself as Ginger Rogers, my fingers tap dancing a percussive tune across the keyboard. Words teemed, paper was plentiful, and my printer hummed constantly, spewing out the copies of my supposed next bestseller. Committed to my goal, I purchased the Costco-size box of manila folders to mail out manuscripts. I felt enthused and invigorated and so much like a writer that I even dared to claim the title when I was asked what I did. Then, without warning, the rhythmic staccato of the keyboard slowed.

My thoughts and words dried up. I got up from the computer to take a break and literally stumbled over one of my daughter's blocks. The universe has a funny way of speaking to me. I self-diagnosed my ailment: writer's block.

Reflecting on that time, it wasn't one specific instance, but a steadily growing pile of rejection letters, doubt, and critical voice that turned my happy tapping into the funeral dirge "Taps."

I continued attending our meetings every three weeks, where inevitably one of the writers would announce that her story was being picked up by a magazine, book or newspaper. We'd applaud as she'd ceremoniously slip a copy of her piece into the group's ever-expanding binder of published work. Entering that book seemed as elusive to me as entering The Land of Oz. I wanted in, but I was out. I didn't feel jealous—well, maybe a little—but mostly I felt inadequate and fraudulent.

Our group had an expression: "Life gets in the way." We all knew it was code for, "I've made everything else a priority in my life besides writing." And, boy, did I have convenient and justifiable reasons for life to get in my way.

My husband and I purchased our first home, moving us about thirty miles away. I dove into my new life—painting, planting, decorating, and finding new friends. Writers' group meetings that formerly took twenty minutes to get to now required an hour's worth of travel time. I've got nothing to share, I'd tell myself. Five hours (counting travel and meeting time) is a long time to be away from my family on a Saturday. Occasionally, I sat at the computer, but invariably spent more time hitting the Delete button than the Save. I edited and criticized as I wrote and routinely told myself how trite, dumb and blah my work sounded.

"I got another rejection," I announced glumly at a meeting I finally attended.

"Where else are you sending it?" asked Sallie.

"There's a children's book writers' conference you should check out," chimed Jean. "You can meet editors face to face. You have a presence."

"Maybe it's your cover letter," offered Dierdre. "Let's go over it."

"What about writing an article?" asked Linda. "Most book authors say they broke into the business that way."

With every well-advised question, my defenses swelled, and my block loomed larger. I wanted to do it my way. My way was that an editor would read my work, love it, and offer me a book contract. I wanted things to work exactly as I'd planned. The only thing was—they weren't.

Fay Weldon, the novelist, says, "If it's approval you want, don't be a writer." That's when it hit me. The purpose of my writing group wasn't the whine-and-pity party I was hoping they'd throw. They were there to push and prod and validate my will to write. Before me were seven women goading me to flip a block into a stepping stone, if only I was willing to turn it over.

As I saw it, there were only two options left: walk away from writing... or write.

It wasn't easy or comfortable, but I started. First, I wrote in my journal, pouring out every doubt and desire I had. This stuff wasn't publishable—it wasn't even nice—but it certainly was cleansing and therapeutic.

Next, I devoted the first fifteen minutes after waking to writing. I absolutely refused to peek at or answer e-mail during that fifteen-minute magic period because it always zapped my energy and drained my time.

I attended my first conference and felt so charged and positive that I knew I was in the right place. And, most importantly, I recommitted to group meetings, knowing that even if I didn't have something to share, I provided an important source of feedback for those who did.

Always mindful of our goal to be published, B.J. initiated her star program, offering stars to anyone who sent out a manuscript. I thought it was corny. After all, I wasn't five. But my way wasn't working. The truth was that the stars jumpstarted me. And I have to admit, I liked seeing them under my name. They were tangible proof that I was writing and submitting.

Deadlines also work for me, and knowing the group was arriving at my house for a meeting, I crammed the night before. Admittedly, my first draft was rough, but with a table full of women laughing, I felt encouraged to smooth out "How Hard Could It Be?"—an essay about all the stupid things I'd done over the years to save money. A month later, a prominent Southern California newspaper published it. I had entered "The Book." I felt as if I'd arrived in Oz.

Funny, I'd been lost for so long—off-course and off-track—but the group brought me back, and I couldn't stop humming "Follow the Yellow Brick Road."

~Tsgoyna Tanzman

Variation on a Theme

We don't see things as they are; we see them as we are.
~Anaïs Nin

"Writer's block," that common phrase, is not an apt description
For what, in fact, ensnares me when I lose my inspiration.
A block suggests external things are keeping me from writing,
When, actually, internal things are really what I'm fighting.

Concrete blocks and road blockades are images I see
Whenever someone mentions the phrase "writer's block" to me.
I need a sharper image for what ails my concentration
When brain fog fails to stimulate my keen imagination.

When creativity falters, and ideas are barely crawling,
When typing is pure torture, and my output is appalling,
I've never thought that "writer's block" sums up the situation
As well as, say, another phrase—like "writer's constipation."

~Wendy Hobday Haugh

When Words Really Matter

The difference between the almost right word and the right word is really a large matter—it's the difference between the lightning bug and the lightning.
~Mark Twain

I'm not ashamed to say I write for money. Forget the muse. As a full-time freelancer, I write for a living, and have done so for more than a decade. I've penned articles on topics ranging from animal dissection alternatives to angioplasty, toddler dental traumas to bridesmaid drama. It matters not whether I'm ghosting a sales-coaching book or editing a medical course for emergency-room docs. Make me an offer, promise a decent amount of money, and I'm your girl.

No, it's not as simple as brewing coffee or digging ditches, but as a service journalist, most of my work isn't brain-taxing stuff. Sure, I cover subjects that are new to me occasionally, and I stretch myself to come up with new approaches to evergreen subjects (unlike the ditch-digging analogy above). On the plus side, I rarely experience writer's block. Sure, some days I don't particularly feel like writing, but that's not writer's block. That's writer's apathy.

So why was I so blocked when it came to writing a simple, two-page pitch?

It didn't matter that I've written more than 1,000 sales letters of one form or another—queries, letters of introduction, cover letters to accompany essays—during the past eleven years. This was a different kind of pitch.

In the adoption world, we call them "dear birth mother letters." It's the document you create to introduce yourself to a woman who's expecting a baby and considering adoption. (Technically, that nomenclature isn't accurate—you only become a "birth mother" after you place a child for adoption.)

Think about that. You're given a measly few paragraphs to catch this woman's attention, to explain why you want to be a parent, to showcase your strengths as a person, to demonstrate why you (and your husband) are deserving of her baby. How can you possibly encapsulate that in a few hundred words? And what if you don't pick precisely the right words?

Yes, I write for a living. But now I was writing for my life—the life I hoped to have as a parent.

I was, in all senses of the word, blocked. I thought I knew what I wanted to say. Several adoptive parents sent me templates. I had samples to model. But I was still stuck.

I would sit down at my computer, stare at the screen, and think, "This is the most important letter I will ever write." Normally, I'm a fan of "pretty good" when it comes to my work. Pretty good is almost always good enough. That wasn't the case here.

I had some false starts, struggling with the right mix of information and style. I abandoned the writing process completely for a couple of weeks, instead digging through photo albums and looking for pictures where Erik and I looked young yet mature, carefree yet responsible, smart yet personable. I chose pictures that would reflect our personalities and our as-yet-unproven-but-hopefully-stellar parenting abilities. And, yes, I included pictures of each of us with children (smiling, happy children) to create a subliminal message of "Hey, they look like great parents."

And, finally, I remembered the number-one rule of writing—consider your reader. I stopped worrying about what I should include or what I thought I wanted to say, and focused on what I thought my child's birth mother would want to know. Sure, I wrote a little bit about our history together, our hobbies, our families. But the heart of the letter was about her baby—and what her baby's life would be like if she chose us to become parents. I wrote, edited, and rewrote. I sent it to my adoption attorney, who suggested I make some changes. (You know the drill—when an editor says, "You've got a great start, but...") I made the changes, and my lawyer said she liked the new version. My husband liked it. My mom liked it. My best friend liked it.

Most importantly, a young woman named Jodi liked it. She'd learned about us through our attorney, and asked for my (painstakingly crafted) letter. She thought we sounded down-to-earth, laid-back, and fun—and she called us after reading it. We met her two weeks later, and she chose us to adopt her baby. Just six weeks after that, Ryan was born and became our son.

Now I know that it wasn't that I was immune to writer's block. It was that none of my assignments up until then had mattered to me that much. Even the big features for glossies I'd tried to crack for years eventually came down to nothing more than a byline, a clip, and a check.

It wasn't until I had the chance at my dream assignment—the one I truly wanted—that the words got stuck. Eventually, though, they came to me. They may not have been the perfect words, but they were the right ones. My words created a connection between writer and reader—between Jodi and me—and so much more.

~Kelly James-Enger

A Time (Not) to Write

The pause is as important as the note.
~Truman Fisher

When I was working on a novel, I found it easy to get up at four in the morning and write for two hours before work. Two years, two novels, and at least two hundred rejections later, I was still rolling out of bed with endless energy to write. Then my work situation changed. I stopped teaching on Mondays and Fridays, so I told myself these were my days to write. Instead of two hours, I had eight hours. I became even more prolific, and I started publishing. My short stories appeared in dozens of journals, I won a few contests, and I was even nominated for a few awards. I named my muse Trusty, and we made a good team.

Then, inexplicably, I hit the Berlin Wall of writing blocks, as if I had reached an impasse and run out of gas at the same time. Though I felt immobile, the piles and piles of ideas on my desk told me something else was going on. I wasn't so much dealing with writer's block as writer's burnout. So I organized. I stacked my ideas into neat little Post-it note towers—the first time my desk had known "neat" in years—and stared at my computer screen, waiting for Trusty. Nothing.

"You have to chain yourself to your desk and write every day anyway," a writing compadre told me. "Even when your muse doesn't feel like writing."

"Easy for you to say," I said. "You always feel like writing. And it's always good."

"Not true," she said. "I throw a lot away."

"The problem is, right now I'm not writing anything."

"Write 'Mary had a little lamb' a thousand times."

"I probably won't do that. Got anything else?"

"Write from prompts," she said. "There are thousands on the Internet."

"I've tried them. I never…"

"Do timed writing exercises. Use photographs as prompts. Record your dreams. Lyrics! Write anything that comes into your head."

"I guess I could write 'I need a nap' a thousand times."

"Great!" she said without irony. "And when you're done, fling your pages into the furnace to get the gold," she cheered. "Ram your idea icebergs for the shards!"

"What kind of coffee do you drink?" I asked, exhausted.

Despite the silly metaphors, I told her I'd give her advice a test run. After all, this is the wisdom almost all books on the craft of writing impart: discipline, routine, commitment. Write twenty pages to get twenty lines. Burn your first novel. Dig through the ashes to find that one brilliant yet fading ember.

I had gone through periods of writing drought before, but for the last ten years Trusty had always returned, always unannounced—in weighty times of sadness, in frenetic times of boundless energy, on a rainy November day in Munich, on a noisy beach in Brazil. She'd never gone on holiday for more than a few days.

Even if writing seemed to be an impenetrable brick wall, I was always sure one morning I'd wake up, go to my computer and just start writing something I loved. But after writing two hundred pages of metaphorical garbage, none of which came even close to being gold, embers or shards of icebergs (whatever that meant), the day came when I had to admit my muse, Trusty, was either dead or at least on extended sabbatical in Costa Rica. Maybe she'd joined a convent.

That day, I stretched, got up from my computer and went for a walk. I said to myself, "If Trusty's going to be that way, let her find me this time." There's a time to write, and there's a time to play hard-to-get with your muse, a time to walk away from your words and just enjoy the silence. I walked in the forest behind my house, through the old town in Munich, up and down the Thames in London. I people-watched. I started taking photographs. Sometimes I even turned the camera around and took goofy pictures of myself.

Even when I was home at my computer, I refused to write prose. I surfed and chatted, wandering from site to site. I convinced myself that maintaining my Facebook, Twitter, Goodreads, StumbleUpon and blog presences was important, too. I dallied. I played Scrabble, Lexulous, and Words with Friends. As long as they weren't my words, I was fine.

I read all the books in my office that had been stacking up over the previous year. I read David Foster Wallace's *Infinite Jest*—or at least I tried. Supportive friends sent me books. "You'll love this," a friend said. "He writes like you." Not like me lately, I thought, unless this is a book of shopping lists.

When I confessed my problems to my writers' group, they sent me their own stories of writing worries and weariness, from burnout to frozen shoulders. The leitmotif was obvious: There is a time not to write.

Comforted, I played hard-to-get for a few more months. During this time, though, I wrote a few book reviews for friends (my muse had never been much help with this sort of writing anyway). I concentrated on editing for other people. Ironically and perhaps a tad dishonestly, I gave a few interviews on my approach to writing, hoping to actually find a new way in. And one day it happened—as always, unexpected.

When she finally returned, I took a long look at her and shook my head. She didn't look like my muse, Trusty, at all. It was as if the muse agency had sent one that sort of looked like Trusty but had a slightly droller sense of humor. She wore reading glasses and complained of jetlag. She was snarkier and older.

But she had mud on her shoes—from the forest. She knew every inch of the Thames Path in London. She boasted that she'd read *Infinite Jest*—or at least she'd tried. She grumbled but never apologized for her absence; she simply sat down and started knocking down my neat towers of ideas, casting them into the furnace and handing me tiny—quite tiny at first—shards of gold.

~Christopher Allen

Fires in the Night

Your talent is God's gift to you.
What you do with it is your gift back to God.
~Leo Buscaglia

At the end of a cold and rainy day, I retreated to the sofa with a steaming cup of chocolate and my grandmother's scrap quilt. As the night shadows gathered at the windows, a fire crackled in the fireplace, casting an orange glow about the room. Its warmth reached out to me, but the chill in my heart remained.

For three months, I had not sat down at my desk to write. Not one single word. After years of freelancing, I knew what it meant to encounter writer's block. I knew all about rejection letters (I had enough to wallpaper my office), but this time it was something more: I was thinking about giving it up for good.

While I had been blessed to see my work in a number of publications, I was growing weary with the struggle. Maybe I had nothing more to offer.

And so, for three months, my pen lay still.

It wasn't easy. Some nights I tossed and turned till dawn, wrestling with words and phrases that formed in my head, refusing to get up and write them down. But like a quarrelsome child, the words demanded to be heard; they would not leave me alone.

As I watched the fire's flames lick the stack of logs one night, I was struck by a bizarre thought: What would happen if I lit a match to my desk? The computer. Files. Books. Everything. Would that silence the words? Would anybody notice?

The daunting voices in my head answered quickly. "Not one person would notice, nor care," they assured me.

Deliberately, I rose from the couch and phoned Cindy, a friend in New Jersey. I knew if anybody could cheer me up, she and her undying belief in my abilities could.

Immediately, she sensed my mood. "You sound depressed, friend." (She has a pleasant habit of calling me that.)

"Yes, I am depressed," I told her. "I am so depressed that I am considering starting a bonfire with my desk."

She laughed at first, but then her tone turned serious. "Dayle," she said, concerned, "how can you even think about such a thing? You don't want to destroy the gift God has given you."

We talked a long while, and by the time our conversation ended, I felt better, but still unsure as I plopped back down on the sofa.

The flames in the fireplace burned low now. The room had grown cold and dark, chilling me to the bone. I walked over to stoke the fire, and, when I did, flames shot up, filling the room with hot red colors. I had stoked the fire in this manner hundreds of times before, but this night the flames held a clear message for me: Fire left alone will soon burn out, but stir it up, and it becomes a powerful source of light and warmth.

As the fire blazed, I took great comfort in the message it brought. I knew Cindy was right. God had given me a gift, but if I failed to use it, soon it would be nothing more than a pile of ashes. Surely, the gift was still in me, just waiting to be rekindled. I remembered the verse of Scripture that says, "Stir up the gift of God which is in you" (2 Timothy 1:6 NKJV).

Armed with a new sense of purpose, I marched into my office, switched on the lamp, powered up my computer, and wrote the story you are reading. It feels good to be back.

~Dayle Allen Shockley

Editor's note: We are happy to be of service!

Hope Comes in the Mail

The worth of a book is to be measured by what you can carry away from it.
~James Bryce

I used to joke that I had made literally hundreds of dollars in my career as a writer. By the time I turned thirty, I'd stopped laughing.

Life was catching up with me, and what did I have to show for it? A drafty apartment, a thick stack of bills, and a filing cabinet overflowing with unpublished stories and rejection letters.

I started thinking maybe it was time to grow up.

In my heart, though, what I meant was give up.

I grew depressed. I moped around the house. And slowly I lost the ability to write even the un-sellable work. The dream I'd had since I was old enough to hold a pencil was dying, and I didn't know what to do about it.

The icing on the cake came when I lost my job just before Christmas.

On Christmas Eve morning, I slumped across the parking lot to check my mail, expecting more bills I couldn't pay and, of course, a couple of rejection letters.

There was no return address on the package. I remember standing at the mailbox as an icy wind whistled around me and tucking the rest of the mail under my arm to open the box.

Inside was a worn, dog-eared copy of *Chicken Soup for the Writer's Soul.*

I'd like to say that the clouds parted and a single sunbeam fell across the cover... but it didn't. I felt like crying.

Even more, I felt like tossing the book into the trash. The last thing I wanted to do was read about a bunch of people who were doing what I couldn't.

Instead, I tossed it on my desk and forced myself to read a couple of pages a day during breaks from the want ads.

By page five, I realized there were others out there who had felt what I was feeling. By page twenty, I started thinking: Maybe if they could do it...

By the middle of the book, I was working again and, more importantly, I was writing again!

In the pages of *Chicken Soup for the Writer's Soul*, I found the hope that I'd lost, the encouragement I'd needed, and the pure joy of writing I'd forgotten amid stacks of letters that all started: "Thank you for your submission. Unfortunately..."

When I turned the last page, I gathered all my rejection letters and burned them.

That was almost ten years ago.

Two mystery novels later, my agent is hounding me for a sequel for the shelves this fall.

My goal of coming home and writing full-time has finally come true.

I still don't know who sent me that battered copy of *Chicken Soup for the Writer's Soul*, but I hope they've seen how their kindness has helped me recapture my dream.

Whoever you are, my friend, if you're reading this... God bless you!

~Perry P. Perkins

Lend Me Your Ears

Action always generates inspiration.
~Frank Tibolt

W riter's block. I'd heard it described many times by fellow writers, yet never experienced it first-hand... until that muggy summer day.

I ventured outdoors, searching for any kind of inspiration Mother Nature could send my way. Ducks lazily glided across the water along the canal. Church bells faithfully chimed the hour.

Nothing... I felt as empty as the dried-up watering can I'd spotted earlier.

Sighing, I headed back through town, wondering how I'd ever fulfill an upcoming writing assignment.

That's when I heard it... happy laughter coming from an open shop window. A gray-haired woman positioned behind a counter incessantly chattered like a magpie to one of her customers. Like one of the colorful magnets on my apartment refrigerator, her voice drew me inside. Pretending to rummage through secondhand items on aisle after aisle, I shamelessly eavesdropped, feeling my senses come alive as I listened to her humorous, adventuresome tale.

Scarcely realizing I'd acquired several knickknacks along the way, I approached the counter just as the cashier concluded her story. She waved farewell to her friend before turning her attention my way.

As she rang up the items I'd selected, I mustered up enough courage to speak.

"I couldn't help hearing your amusing tale," I shyly began. "I just wanted you to know that it really made me smile." Others in line agreed enthusiastically.

Was it the sunbeams shooting through the window that illuminated the woman's face, or just the sheer pleasure of captivating an audience for a few moments in time? I'd never really know the answer. But, suddenly, inspiration filled my very soul.

With a spring in my step, I hurried home, eager for the first time in days to jot down my thoughts.

And that, my friend, is when it hit me: It wasn't writer's block I'd experienced at all. It was, in fact, "listener's block."

I vowed to never come down with such a malady again.

~Mary Z. Whitney

44

How I Got My Creativity Back

When patterns are broken, new worlds emerge.
~Tuli Kupferberg

Like every writer, I go through occasional periods of writer's block—days when I feel stuck, when I sit at my keyboard and no words come. Usually, I force myself through it, and the next day, the words come easier. But in my first semester of graduate school, I experienced writer's block like never before, a new monster that lingered for weeks and months. Simply put, I sank into a creative rut. Nothing I wrote seemed interesting. None of my ideas seemed worth pursuing. I was exhausted from teaching and from my own studies—there were always assignments to grade, books to read, academic papers to write. I did not feel inspired by the world around me; rather, I felt overwhelmed. I wanted to shut off my brain and turn off my computer for good.

But that didn't make me feel better. If anything, when I pushed away my creative-writing projects, I only felt worse. Writing is how I process and deal with my life, how I make sense of the world. When I don't write, I don't feel like my best self. I don't feel like myself, period.

So I came up with a plan. Each day, I would try one new activity to attempt to get my creativity back. Day by day, I hoped that I would rediscover and reconnect with the curious, inspired writer within me.

The first day, instead of using my lunch break to grade papers in my dark cave of an office, I brought my sandwich and apple outside and spent an hour people-watching. I picked a stranger to be my "character." Then I closed my eyes and tried to really get inside this character's head. I asked myself, "What is he thinking, feeling, worrying, wondering? Where is he going? What memories does he have?" I took out a pad of paper and spent twenty minutes "free writing"—writing without thinking too much or editing myself. I couldn't remember the last time I'd written a story by hand instead of on my computer. My pages looked sloppy, my handwriting messy, with words crossed out and cramped words squeezed into the margins—but to me, each page was beautiful. I wanted to keep writing even longer, but I had to go inside to teach my class.

The next day, I changed my routine by walking home from school instead of taking the bus. Usually, the two-mile commute to and from school was just another thing to hurry through. I would spend the whole bus ride home glancing at my watch, wishing the bus would go faster so I could get home and start chipping away at my piles of grading and reading. (Instead, drained and depleted, I usually ended up vegging out in front of the television for a few hours.) But this day I decided to re-envision my trip home as "me time"—an hour or so for me to wind down from a hectic day at school and take in the world around me.

And guess what? When I slowed down my daily trip, the commute home didn't feel like a chore—it felt special. I noticed little things like hummingbirds, squirrels, and the unique purple of the sky as the light faded to evening. I reached home feeling rejuvenated instead of exhausted. I made a healthful veggie pasta for dinner, cleared aside my papers and books, and sat down to write—not for school, not for work, but for fun. For myself. The next day, I walked home again, only this time I also took a notebook with me so I could jot down notes right when an idea hit me.

The rest of the week I spent trying new things. Nothing fills my "idea well" more quickly than traveling—experiencing new places, embarking on new adventures, meeting new people. But I couldn't just pick up and leave town. Instead, I decided to "travel" by trying new things right at home.

I ventured into a Peruvian restaurant I had passed many times but never had the nerve to try, ordered the first thing off the menu that caught my eye, and wrote a poem about the flavor and texture of the food.

I watched a YouTube video on how to knit and spent a few nights wrestling soft blue yarn around knitting needles, and a story idea flashed within me about a man seeing pictures in a ball of yarn.

I dabbled in painting, an art form I had loved as a child, and ended up using my fingers to smear gobs of paint across the page. It had been a long time since I had allowed myself to be creative without the added burden of wondering if my creation was good enough.

As I washed the paint from my fingers, I felt wonderfully free. I knew I had tunneled my way out of my uninspired hole. I've kept these activities as part of my life to keep my daily routine richer, more spontaneous, and less draining.

I still get writer's block occasionally. When I do, it is usually related to the specific project I am working on. One thing that helps me is to focus on what I know instead of worrying about what I don't know. I often struggle with "the muddle in the middle" of a story. Perhaps there is a later scene I want to write, but the middle is tripping me up. My solution is to skip forward and write the ending. Then I can go back and write the middle. I've found that ideas tend to come once the ending is in place. Similarly, sometimes I get blocked when I'm at a "fork in the road" in my story: There are multiple routes my story could take, and I'm not sure which one is the "right" one. When that happens, I try picking one route—one way the story could go, one thing that could happen next—and write that. If it doesn't feel right, I can always go back and change it. But often picking one way for the story to go is enough to get me through the block and writing again.

I feel fortunate to have found something I am passionate about, something that allows me to escape into the magical realm of make-believe on a daily basis. Ever since I regained my creativity, I appreciate it much more. Creativity solves problems and inspires curiosity. Creativity unleashes big, beautiful dreams. Nurturing my creativity has not only made me a better writer, it has made me a better person—more optimistic, compassionate, and open to life's unending possibilities.

~Dallas Woodburn

inspiration for

The Healing Power of Words

Words are the physicians of a mind diseased.

~Aeschylus

45

Telling Stories That Matter

There are no ordinary people. You have never talked to a mere mortal.
~C. S. Lewis

he call came as so many in my writing life do — unsolicited. The voice at the other end of the phone was soft, and the words were polite. The caller was an administrator at a local senior living facility. Her proposal: Might I want to meet with a group of six women, all in their seventies or eighties, who had ended up in that place?

My initial thought: This isn't much of a story.

Then came the content and context: All of these women were survivors of the Nazi Holocaust. All of them had scarred lives, horrible memories, ghastly stories of loss and pain. And in their twilight years, they had found one another.

I was instantly looking at my calendar to find a time when I could get to the facility and learn more.

Call it a writer's intuition — a conditioning that comes after years of covering stories that may sound fascinating and turn out not to be, and the flip side of the coin: stories that may sound daunting that turn out to be remarkably powerful.

I was betting on the second scenario.

Even before I kept my date at the senior care facility, I alerted a hard-bitten newspaper editor about the potential story. She was mildly interested.

Again, writers tend to look at all potential stories with more optimism than editors do. A sweeping generality, perhaps, but curious writers tend to see the glass half-full—and editors, with a "show me" attitude, see it half-empty until proven otherwise.

My preliminary visit with several of the women revealed a lot. They would not be easy subjects—they were guarded and a bit suspicious of me. But there also was a sense of urgency easier felt than explained. They wanted to tell their stories. They wanted to tell them soon, as the relentless march of time numbered their days.

Over tea and cookies, things got more comfortable. Another lesson of journalism: I'd learned long ago to somehow manage face-to-face/eye-to-eye contact when the subject is tough.

Let me cut to the chase:

The editor I'd contacted wanted the story. And she wanted it to take the form of a modified photo-essay. Those faces would speak volumes, and we both knew it.

The photographer was carefully chosen: a woman with innate warmth, a pro at getting the visual details that make you stop in your tracks.

On an ordinary weekday afternoon, she and I arrived at the senior center. Six women sat shoulder to shoulder, and even their body language revealed deep connection.

They were bonded. They were sisters, not biologically but surely soul-to-soul. And they had each other in a sometime tough world.

For the next three hours, their stories spilled out. Sometimes, it was hard to listen.

There were tales of brutality and humiliation, partings with parents, unspeakable fear and ultimate renunciations.

As each woman spoke, the others seemed to form a protective honor guard around her without ever changing their seats or moving at all. Impossible to explain—awesome to witness.

The gifted photographer shot her digital photos. And after a while, the survivors seemed to forget there was even a camera in the room.

I'd deliberately left my tape recorder at home, and went back to the original tool of journalism: a reporter's notebook. Between jottings, I could look at them—and hopefully send messages of support.

Sometimes, it was hard not to gasp at their stories. Several times, I just had to reach out and touch a hand, pat a shoulder, offer a tissue.

The last picture the newspaper photographer shot was of the six women, arms linked, walking resolutely back to their apartments, somehow looking years younger than they had just hours before.

They had told their stories. They had spilled out the pain and terror of the past. It felt cleansing.

I went home and wrote like a woman possessed. I had to get those stories down. I had to let those voices be heard.

The story that ran the next week led to an avalanche of mail. It had touched many.

And the ladies became instant celebrities in their little universe.

And the lesson for me?

Trust instinct. It's not always right. It sometimes leads to dead ends and wasted time.

But after three decades of writing, I still stumble on stories that excite me as much as the first few I ever tackled.

And the best of them are seldom about the rich and famous.

They are, instead, about ordinary/extraordinary lives.

And as long as I can find them, I'll go on telling them—and recognizing what a rare privilege it is to be a writer.

~Sally Friedman

The Small Miracle

Numbing the pain for a while will make it worse when you finally feel it.
~J.K. Rowling,
Harry Potter and the Goblet of Fire

Choosing to write was actually not even my idea. I had no interest in it, no thoughts about it, and no need to start.

Several years ago, I found myself severely overweight, facing multiple spinal surgeries, smoking a half-pack a day, and turning my frustration on anyone who crossed my path. I was a mean and ugly person. It was about that time that someone, taking her life in her hands, suggested I seek therapy.

"I'm not crazy! What the heck do I need a therapist for?"

Seeing no way out, putting my marriage, friendships, and family at risk of hating me, I bit the bullet and found someone just down the street. Oh, she was in for it, I smirked to myself.

That first meeting was spent staring each other down. It was the proverbial gunfight at high noon. I looked at her; she looked at me.

"Well, let's talk about why you're here," she said in that quiet and calm therapist voice.

"I don't know!"

It must have surprised her because she shifted uncomfortably in her chair.

"What's the deal with this couch anyway?" I said, trying to deflect her by changing the subject. "Is this supposed to comfort clients?"

It was upholstered with a dizzying floral material. I could almost smell the flowers.

"If you're not able to tell me what's going on, I want you to write it down and bring this back next week." She handed me a notebook. I grabbed it and left the office annoyed. Great, I thought to myself, now I have homework. Not only am I crazy, but now I am being treated like a child.

I stared at that notebook for days and wrote nothing. My behavior didn't change, and my anger only grew. So when my next session came, I didn't have anything to talk about. I didn't know her. I didn't trust her.

"You're gonna have to try writing in that book or you're wasting my time and especially yours." She paused. "Look, why don't you start with 'I feel…' and see where you go from there."

Again, I stared down at a blank page for the next several days. Then one evening, out of pure spite, I wrote "I feel" and it started a flood. Page after page of my deepest thoughts and feelings scribbled on the paper as if some puppet master was guiding my hand. Ink stopped and started in places that I never went back to fill in. This was my mind, my vulnerability on paper. Tears fell to the page, and the ink ran down, blurring other words. I didn't care. It felt so freaking good. I journaled until my hand seized with pain. Then, suddenly frightened of my actions, I quickly closed the book and threw it across the room in anger. I didn't know what was in there. I was afraid of what was in there. Scared of my own words, terrified of own thoughts, I wept most of that night.

Not opening the book again, I took it to my next session. Pinching it slightly between my thumb and forefinger, I handed it to my counselor like it was diseased.

"Read it," she said sternly and threw it into my lap. I took a breath and opened up to the first page. Big letters, small letters, scribbles, ink that bled so deep into the page that it tore onto the next. What the heck? My eyes blurred, and the only word I could make out over and over again was PAIN. This was my physical and mental pain written down, starring at me, taunting me. It was that one day, in that one moment, when I realized why I had become so ugly. I was projecting all my pain onto other people. It was an epiphany for me.

I continued writing in my notebook for over a year until I became myself again. I started eating healthy and managed to lose over one hundred pounds. I quit smoking. Today, I still struggle with my physical pain, but I learned I can channel it in other ways—by reading my favorite books, watching my favorite movies, and writing. Then one night, during the worst snowstorm I had seen in Pittsburgh, I closed my eyes, lay on my bed, and just listened. It was as if I was meant to do it. My fingers took their places on my lonesome keyboard, and I wrote my first story, "The Storm." Now, three years later and my hopes of healthier years to come, I look back and remember that awful time, which seems so long ago. Becoming a writer wasn't what I had planned, but it was the small miracle that saved me from myself.

~Carisa J. Burrows

Healing Myself by Helping Others

Dare to reach out your hand into the darkness,
to pull another hand into the light.
~Norman B. Rice

During my sophomore year in high school, I nearly killed myself. It wasn't intentional suicide, and it wasn't suicide in the traditional sense: I didn't turn to drugs, knives, or reckless behavior. Instead, something just as evil beckoned me toward death—an eating disorder.

More than a year after my diagnosis and the start of my recovery, I sat in TAG (my high school's Talented and Gifted literature class) with the other juniors and seniors. We were just back from Christmas break and were still dragging from days spent staying up late and lying in bed until noon. We weren't exactly prepared for a big project. However, our teacher, Mrs. Miller, was. As soon as the final bell rang, she hit us with it: she handed out thick packets with the details of our big third-quarter project, and several of my classmates groaned.

"Okay, guys," Mrs. Miller said, clapping her hands. "It's third quarter. That means ISPs—you'll be doing your Independent Study Projects."

Another round of groans went up around me.

"Really, Mrs. Miller? Can't you cut us some slack? We're so busy right now," Carson, one of the seniors, moaned. "Caroline and I have Cotillion stuff like every night. Not to mention scholarships."

"And those scholarships are evil," Caroline agreed.

Mrs. Miller ignored them and continued. "Every year, we have a theme. Last year, if any of you remember, TAG students presented ISPs about what they were passionate about. That was the theme. This year, we've been talking a lot about happiness. In *Anna Karenina*, for example..."

"Hate that chick," Carson mumbled, none too quietly. Beside me, Colleen laughed.

"...we talked about the true meaning of happiness in our Socratic Seminars. So this year I want all of you to research something that has or may be a roadblock to your happiness; look into what could potentially keep you from being happy."

Carson's head made a *thunk* as it hit the table. Cody looked at Mrs. Miller skeptically.

"Um," Stephanie said, raising her hand, "what if we're always happy?"

"What if we're not like Anna Karenina?"

"What if we don't know what will make us unhappy? We're not psychic. At least... not all of us."

I watched Mrs. Miller carefully, my arms folded. She didn't flinch. Instead, she smiled. She looked at me. We'd already talked about my project. When she had mentioned it briefly before Christmas break, I'd gone to her with an idea. I'd known that, in order to be happy in the future, I had to work through what had happened to me in the past few years. The Independent Study Project presented the perfect opportunity to do that. So, while the rest of my classmates complained, I was already partway through the hardest project of my life: I was writing a memoir about my diagnosis and the beginning of my recovery from anorexia nervosa. I was revisiting my encounter with depression and the shadow of death, taking poems that I had written during that time and using them as a basis for each chapter. Some may have said that pulling things out of thin air for pure fiction was the hardest kind of writing, but I disagreed. Diving into my past was the most difficult thing I'd ever done.

But I made it. In the spring of my junior year, I completed the first draft of my memoir. Mrs. Miller sat down and talked to me about the next step.

"What if," she said, during our private meeting, "you tried to get it published?"

I stared at her for a moment. It had been a dream of mine since I was little, curled up on my bed with stories like *Little Women* and *Treasure Island*, to be a published author. Getting my memoir published would be... amazing. It would give me a chance to spread awareness about eating disorders and give "outsiders" an inside look into what went on in the mind of someone suffering from malnutrition. It would give me a chance to inspire unhealthy people to fight against their eating disorder. It would even, perhaps, give me a chance to save a life.

"E-books are becoming popular. You could try doing it on Amazon.com for Kindles."

I thought for a second, and then lifted the lid of my laptop. "Okay. Let's do it."

Together, Mrs. Miller and I looked up the terms and conditions for selling an e-book on Amazon. Together, we edited my story multiple times, passing the rough draft back and forth for several weeks. Finally, in July, *The Camera and the Calculator* was available for Kindles. It was one of the proudest moments of my life.

As intended, writing and publishing *The Camera and the Calculator* helped me address a major roadblock to my happiness. It gave me the opportunity to revisit and move on from the terror of my years with an eating disorder. Accepting what had happened also allowed me to be more open about my past. I gave an interview with a reporter from the local newspaper about my sickness, and presented my story to several groups in the community.

My experience, both with anorexia nervosa and writing my memoir, made me stronger. If you have dreams of being an author, I encourage you to pursue writing (especially about a difficult time in your life). If you have been intimidated by editors and big publishing houses, e-books are a great place to start sharing your writing. And no matter what difficulties you may face, you can accomplish anything you set your mind to. I turned the darkest time in my life into a positive experience, and I learned to love myself again in the process.

~Jessica M. Ball

My Muse

Let us be grateful to people who make us happy;
they are the charming gardeners who make our souls blossom.
~Marcel Proust

"O ne day, you will write our love story, which will make thousands cry," my husband wrote in a love letter he sent to me in 1972. He called me his "English Rose," and "one of the talented few who could touch hearts with your written words." He was, and still remains, my greatest source of inspiration.

As a child, I loved to read and would often squirrel myself away in quiet places to escape my abusive circumstances. My father, a family doctor in the small town where I grew up, abused me sexually and verbally; my mother abused me physically. With no one to rescue me, I sought solace in books and writing, as well as my classes at school, where I maintained straight A's most of the time.

As a teenager, I disappeared into the comforting lap of literature, especially poetry. I memorized my favorite poets: Keats, Shelley, Wordsworth, Emerson. Cooped up in my bedroom, I would recite the poets' lines, savoring the cadence, rhythm and beauty of their carefully crafted words. They became my secret friends, people my parents could not banish from the house. I formed a kinship with them, as their poetic voices inspired my own poetry.

At sixteen, I announced to my parents that I wanted to become a writer. My father mocked me, saying: "Writers are failures. You will grow up to be a failure." My mother agreed with him, as she always did. From that point forward, the words "writer" and "failure" resonated in my mind. Already crushed by my father's continual abuse, I decided to become an English teacher instead, as they expected.

Having graduated valedictorian in high school, I entered college to major in English and history, which required writing numerous papers. The library became my second home and a welcome retreat where I could research material for my projects. A friend asked me: "How can you stand writing all those papers?"

"I love it," I responded, eager to begin each new assignment.

In graduate school, I chose my first love, English, as my course of study. I soared through an entire course on Hamlet solely on my writing skills, earning all A's and my professor's admiration. With A's in most of my graduate courses, I knew I had found my niche. In addition, I was encouraged by my professors to become a writer, a fact I never shared with my parents, knowing what their response would be. My favorite professor, having graded my two seminar papers, wrote: "You write so beautifully and with such inspiration, it's always a pleasure to read your papers." She urged me to publish the papers, but fear stopped me. She did not know the seeds of failure had been planted inside me by my parents.

Having obtained my master's degree in English, I moved to Florida to teach middle school English and history. Though I loved the students, teaching was not my true calling. Disappointed, I quit teaching and found a job as a copywriter at an AM/FM radio station nearby. With a salary equal to the teaching position I had left, the job required a fifty-hour week of writing commercials ("spots," as they're called in advertising) for local businesses. Efficient and imaginative, I soon became a favorite with the merchants. Rarely did they make changes to the copy I submitted for their approval. I was again in my element.

My life was to take a more meaningful direction, though, when I met my future husband, Ty, an announcer and Chief Engineer at the radio station.

"Your writing is as beautiful as you are," he wrote in one of his many love letters to me before our marriage. "Your words flow effortlessly on the page and from your heart," he wrote in another. Unlike my parents, he believed in me. Unlike my parents, he praised the talent I prized the most. How could I not love him, my gentle muse? I married him less than a month later and left my parents behind, trusting I had found my soul mate.

Through forty years of marriage, my husband patiently transformed me from battered child into a confident woman, willing to take risks with my writing. Although I encountered some rejections, I shouldered on, believing in my talent, as he believed in me. Though our marital path was strewn with roadblocks along the way, he made me stay true to my course, always willing to steady his wayward traveler. He even typed, without complaint, my many manuscripts for submission. My dream was his because he knew writing was what made me happy.

Finally, my magic wish was granted. I did become a published writer. Poetry, essays, children's stories, gardening articles, and then, a book fell into my writer's cache. No one was prouder than my husband, witness to the tears and smiles along the way.

"Look, look," he said once to an employee in a bookstore where we were browsing, as he pointed out an essay in the book. "This is what my wife wrote. Read it!" I was his phoenix risen from the ashes; he was my muse.

In January 2012, humbly and in honor of him, I took on the most daunting task of all: writing his obituary. For three years, we had battled his brain cancer together, and now the end was near. Fighting my emotions and fears, I wrote that he was "my husband, my friend, my one true love and guardian angel who had rescued me from a childhood of horrific abuse." What I didn't say was that his optimism and support had also turned me into the writer I'd always dreamed of becoming. He took me under his wing and taught me to fly away from the bitter past into a future we built together.

Taking his hand in mine as he lay in the hospice bed, I asked if he would like to hear the obituary I had written for him. He nodded yes. When I was done, he turned to me, blind from the cancer, tears trailing down his cheeks, and said: "That was beautiful. Thank you for reading it to me before I died."

My muse died on our fortieth wedding anniversary, March 31, 2012, but he is with me in spirit. With his words from 1972 in my heart, I turned to my writing as relief for my mourning. Devoted husband that he was, he wanted me to persist; he wanted me to write. Now I write the words he still inspires. I write for all who grieve. I write for all who aspire to be writers and who are inspired by angels like mine. I write for all of us who scatter our words like stars into that great dark abyss, uncertain of the outcome. I write for him, for me, for everyone who perseveres beyond the barriers… always and forever.

~Josie Willis

Stories Along the Way

We must embrace pain and burn it as fuel for our journey.
~Kenji Miyazawa

The morning was cool for August... but, then, it was always cooler at my grandparents' farm up in North Canton. I wandered out into the side yard with its giant weeping willow and played-out fruit trees. I was a month shy of ten, and my father had been rushed to the hospital late the night before following a heart attack. All of us kids, except my oldest brother, who was in college, had been sent up to our grandparents' place. I'd been sick shortly after we'd arrived and was still feeling washed-out and wobbly legged.

I stood by the porch steps, staring at my grandmother's pink and blue morning glories. There was a rusty drainpipe lying alongside the unpaved driveway, spilling its water out onto the sand and pebbles. I picked up a yellowed willow leaf and set it down in that stream. Entranced by the burbling sound of the water, I followed my leaf friend as he bobbed along, making up a story for myself about where he was heading and what adventures he was having. Then I decided he might be lonely, so I found a "lady" leaf to keep him company. And when I'd made up all the stories about them that I could possibly come up with, I let them live happily ever after.

Thirty-one years later, that memory-picture is still vivid to me... so vivid that I've often felt as if I could step back in time and right into it. It was the first time that I clearly remember making up a story to help me through something that was very frightening to me. Creating that story comforted me in the wake of my dad's heart attack. Oh, I had scribbled stories before (little stories about my cats, lavishly illustrated in red, black, and green ink, or endless sagas about the characters in my favorite books). But nothing had ever given me the sense, as this did, of what makes writing magical for me: namely, the ability to step outside of yourself into other worlds, other lives—even if they're the lives of two yellowed willow leaves—and, paradoxically, heal your own pain and loneliness. "The stories people tell have a way of taking care of them," says Badger in Barry Lopez's book, *Crow and Weasel*. "Sometimes a person needs a story more than food to stay alive."

I needed that story.

Twenty-four years later, the powers that be gave me the opportunity to learn that truth anew. Granted, it was not an opportunity that I had sought—indeed, it was one that I would have given anything to give back. On July 11, 1995, my husband, Tim Spooner, was killed in a freakish car accident, tearing apart the world that we had created for ourselves and our three-and-a-half-year-old daughter, Marissa.

I struggled out of my own personal wreckage and slowly, painfully began writing again. Less than a year later, I began writing a time-travel novel, *Souleiado*. My recently widowed artist heroine, Miriam Souleiado, has been chosen by some particularly restless spirits to solve a mystery that ruined their lives. Traveling back to the late 19th century, she finds out the truth for them as well as a few home truths for herself.

In my previous writing, I had always stopped short, unwilling to push myself that extra distance and focus on what most needed focusing on. I'd been able to dazzle most folks with my wordplay and make them think I was being completely open and forthright with them. "How well she describes feelings," a published poet had written to a friend's father after he'd shown her some poems I'd written back in junior high. And that was the truth of it: I had described feelings, but I had not put myself right in the midst of them.

In short, I had been hiding behind my own words. And doing it very well, I might add.

Not now, though. Miriam gave me the mouthpiece I needed. Through her, I could finally give voice to all the grief, pain, and loneliness that were surging through me, and I did not hold back. And during the three years I spent in Miriam's company, both in our own time and in the past, her healing became my healing.

Funny, but when I stop and think about it, both those stories, crafted so many years apart, were about healing myself. Miriam's story was infinitely more complicated than that of the little willow leaf making his way down the stream of water. But both Miriam and the leaf were on journeys—and telling their stories helped me on mine.

~T. J. Banks

50

Word by Word

She was no longer wrestling with the grief,
but could sit down with it as a lasting companion
and make it a sharer in her thoughts.
~George Eliot

"Hey, what's this?" my husband called from across the living room. I glanced over at him. With his head buried deep inside the drawer of the computer cabinet, I could barely see him. I sighed. He was trying to clean up, bless his heart, but the mountain of paper inside that desk was overwhelming.

We were in our far-too-tiny living room in our far-too-tiny house in a semi-safe neighborhood in northwest Indiana. We'd moved there nearly two years before, willing to make a few sacrifices to be closer to our respective families.

But that's when things started falling apart, I thought, as I made my way over to my husband, dodging the toys our children had left scattered on the floor. That's when I lost my job. That's when Kathy died.

And I stopped writing.

But now my husband, Jeff, was holding out a thick sheaf of papers. I reluctantly took it from his hands.

Reading the title, I sank back on the sofa. Meanwhile, our two children entered the room, giggling and playing. Katie was seven; Sean was three. No matter what happened, it seemed, those kids were always happy. Sometimes, I'll admit, it was the only thing that kept me going. I reached out and wrapped Katie in a hug as I held the papers in my lap.

"Death on Deadline," I said out loud. I put the papers back on the floor and leaned forward, putting my head in my hands, willing myself to start cleaning up the place. Lately, it seemed, I hadn't had the energy to do anything.

But my husband was persistent. Now that he'd extricated himself from his papery prison, he was curious.

"This is your book, right?"

I didn't answer. He was right, of course; he likely already knew that. Two years ago, I'd had this great idea. After being a reporter for fifteen years, I decided to write a murder mystery based in a newsroom. My husband encouraged me.

The story would be lighthearted and funny, written with a decided Ozarks twang. We'd lived there for almost a decade, and I'd loved it. So I assembled a cast of quirky, creative types in my head and created a heroine—a young, single reporter a little too nosy for her own good.

I created my own deadlines, striving to write 1,000 words a night. I made an outline, determining what would happen in each chapter, and fleshed out the details.

I tackled my project word by word, chapter by chapter. I developed a main plot, threw in a few red herrings, added a dash of romance.

It was fun—I loved writing. I'd been writing all my life. Even when I was little, I'd make up stories for my family, read them out loud, offer them as gifts.

It seemed natural, then, to become a reporter after college. I didn't make much money, but I got to write every day, interviewing subjects about their lives, their loves, their passions, and crafting their words into stories for everyone to enjoy. Everyone had a story, I knew—they just needed the right person to bring it to life.

I'd met my husband at a newspaper; he was the sports editor. Despite the fact I didn't know a football from a French fry, we clicked and were married two years after we met. Six years later, we were blessed with a daughter, and four years after that, a son.

We both worked at newspapers. We assumed we always would—until people stopped reading them, and reporters became an endangered species. But we'd managed to survive.

Then we'd moved here, to this little house, and it seemed like we'd become cursed. My section at the paper was eliminated. My four cats, which had thrived in the Ozarks, became ill and died, one after the other.

Then my husband's mother died suddenly from a stroke, leaving our kids without their devoted grandmother.

And less than a year later, my funny, sweet-natured sister Kathy complained of a terrible headache and went to sleep on her couch. In the morning, when she tried to get up, she collapsed. Three days later, she died, the victim of a stroke as well. She was forty-eight.

When her heart stopped, mine broke—utterly and completely. I truly felt like the world had ended. It actually surprised me when I would go outside and see people laughing, talking, driving to work. Didn't they realize Kathy was gone?

I limped through each day. I stopped writing. Despite my husband's constant encouragement, it was like the creative part of me had disappeared. I wondered occasionally if it would ever come back.

But now my husband was sifting through the papers I'd discarded.

"This is your book," he confirmed. My daughter wiggled from my grasp to look over his shoulder.

"A book?" she asked. "Mommy writes books?"

My husband nodded and gave me a look. "She does... she did," he said. Then he looked at me. "You wrote all this—you need to finish it."

He was right. I did. I just couldn't. But my husband was relentless. He knew what I was going through; he'd been through it himself.

He pulled me up from the couch, led me to the computer.

"Write," he said firmly.

I waved a hand listlessly. "Tomorrow," I countered.

I glanced at the keyboard, at the computer screen. When I'd

mentored young reporters, I'd always told them that when they got stuck, they needed to write something, anything, even if it was bad.

But now, that blank screen seemed incredibly intimidating. And every task was easier "tomorrow."

"Today," my husband insisted.

My daughter was next to him, echoing him. "Write me a story!" she said.

I looked up at him, and then looked into my daughter's wide blue eyes. Suddenly, thankfulness that they were there washed over me like a wave. I realized that I needed to write—something, anything—right then. It was up to me.

I was a writer. Writers write. And while I could make all the excuses I wanted, at the end of the day, I would either have words—solid, real, reassuring words—on a page, or I wouldn't.

I didn't know how much time I had left to write, after all. A year, a decade? We all make plans, all assume we'll live forever, put off our dreams until we have time.

I felt a surge of energy I hadn't felt in months. I would write. I would finish my book, I would publish it, and I would write another.

But right now, I'd write a story.

I wiped my eyes. "What should we write about?" I asked my girl.

"Trolls!" she said promptly.

I laughed. I hadn't heard the sound in so long, it sounded strange. But good. I set my fingers on the keyboard.

"Once upon a time, there was a little troll…"

The troll led me on the path back to my book, which I published two years ago.

It was a long path, and it wasn't easy. The first step was sitting down again and writing—taking it word by word.

~Diane Majeske

51

The End
Was Only the Beginning

*The world is round and the place which may seem like the end
may also be the beginning.*
~Ivy Baker Priest

I t was August, and life was finally good. I was curled up on my couch under the air conditioner that Saturday afternoon when the phone rang.

"Dad's in the hospital." It was my ex, James. We were still friends, and his parents still considered me a member of their family. "You should come." His voice broke. He wasn't the type of person to show his pain. "Please. It's bad. It's real bad." There were muffled sobs between his words.

James's dad, Ben, had been in the hospital before and had gotten better. This should have only been a routine surgery.

"Okay. I'll see what I can do." I hung up and was soon on the road back to our hometown.

James and his mom Dorothy were already at the hospital when I arrived. James's pale face was ghostly white. Dorothy's face was rigid. Ben, however, was smiling. He waved to me as I entered.

"I brought this to help entertain you while you recover," I said. I handed Ben a binder that contained a few stories and some poetry I had written over the years. Reading was one of Ben's favorite hobbies, but I had never shared any of my writing before. He would appreciate the gesture even if my writing was terrible.

Nurses arrived to change Ben's dressings. I caught a glimpse of a massively swollen foot and a flash of green as we were escorted outside. We waited in the hall.

"How is he?" I asked James.

He took my hand in his. Tears sprang to his eyes.

"It's not good. He's refusing the surgery. Without it, there's almost no chance. And if he has it, he might die from the surgery because of his weak heart." The reality of Ben's situation hit me like a bus. He was really dying. I hugged James, trying to comfort him, but my eyes were equally full of tears. I wished there was something I could do to help.

I had to be at work on Monday, so I returned home and James called a few days later. They were trying an experimental oxygenation treatment. It would be several days before they knew if it was working.

Another week passed before James called again. He didn't bother trying to disguise the pain in his voice this time. "The doctors said there's nothing more they can do. We're bringing him home to die. Please come. We need you... I need you."

When I visited Ben that night at the hospital, he was incoherent and didn't recognize me. "Earlier, I told him we were getting back together," James said. "A huge smile appeared on his face. I know it wasn't true, but it made him so happy to hear it. He always liked you... And if you wanted, we could make it true."

I was too distraught to give James a proper answer. Everything was changing so fast.

An ambulance brought Ben home the next day. He was still incoherent. He didn't recognize anyone. He was not in pain but he was hallucinating and terrified of dying. That night, James went to bed while Dorothy sat with Ben. She tried everything to comfort him, but nothing worked. Finally, she decided to read to him. She grabbed the first thing she could find. It happened to be my binder of short stories and poetry. As she read to him, he became calm and quiet, more alert. He recognized her. She read every story and poem in the binder, and when she finished, he asked quite clearly, "Can we go to the library tomorrow and get another book by that author?"

"Yes," she replied, even though I was not a published author yet, even though she knew he would never leave that bed.

Then, he fell into a peaceful sleep and passed away a few hours later.

Ben's words inspired me. My writing helped him find peace in his final hours. With his last words, he reminded me that even a seemingly insignificant piece of writing might mean the world to the right person. His words were a spark of hope in a time of my life that was dark and filled with grief.

The end of his story was only the beginning of mine.

~Robin A. Burrows

I'm in My Element

It's not that I'm so smart, it's just that I stay with problems longer.
~Albert Einstein

When my wife was pregnant with our first child, she decided that she would stay home and write instead of going back to work. "I want to write. I've always wanted to write."

"If you think that's what you want to do, I'll support you all the way."

Seven months later, I sat with our growing daughter, Vanessa, snuggled in my arms, looked at Georgia and asked, "Did you write anything today?"

"No! Do you have to ask that every other day? Stop nagging me!"

I struggled to remain calm. "But you said that's what you wanted to do."

"I do! It just doesn't happen, you know. I need to be in the right frame of mind. A person just doesn't sit down and start to write. I need to get an idea and then plan the outline. What do you know?" She stormed from the room.

Vanessa cried in my arms. I rocked her and wondered what I'd said to upset my wife. "I was only trying to help," I said to my daughter. She stared back at me, blinked and blew a spit bubble. I took that as agreement. "I guess writers are touchy." Another spit bubble proved me right.

A few months later, Georgia joined a local writing group. They met once a week. The members took turns hosting the group in their homes. I was proud of Georgia for finally getting into her writing.

On the nights she hosted the group at our home, I served coffee, tea and snacks to the ladies. While not serving, I sat and listened to the members critique each other's work. Many of them wrote children's stories.

By that time, I'd read so many children's stories, it seemed easy enough to write one. The man who hated English class in school and writing began to write. I started with children's stories and failed. I switched to humor and had a little success. A local monthly free paper started using one of my humor stories in each edition. Sadly, that came to an end when I wrote a piece that made fun of fireplaces. A major advertiser in the paper supplied firewood in the area.

Georgia's group fell apart. She lost interest in writing.

Me? I had the writing bug. I couldn't stop. I plunged forward. The rejection letters poured in. The mailbox was my worst enemy. No one used e-mail in the early 1990s.

In 1996, I moved to another city for a new job, discovered the Internet and an online group called BBS Writers.

My writing life changed. Members of the group included both established and hopeful writers. Two women helped me. One lady, Deb, became my best friend. She told me, "Michael, I know you like to write humor, but in every piece you write, your ending always has a touching side. You should write romance."

Romance? Not for me.

The other lady taught creative writing in a community college. She said, "Mike, you have great ideas, but I'm afraid to tell you, your grammar sucks. Before you write anything else, buy yourself a few grammar books, study them and learn."

Her words stung. Critiques are hard to accept.

I sulked for a week. My friends told me they liked my stories. Who was this person on the other end of a dial-up Internet connection to say my friends were wrong?

I got the grammar books. They landed in the bathroom, where

most of my reading was done. I removed all other reading material. It was me, the grammar books, and a hard, cold seat.

I read them over and over.

In 1998, I wrote a story about the antics I did in the window at the office I worked, sent it to a local paper, and made my first sale. I followed it up with three sales to the *Ottawa Citizen*.

Two more moves came and went. For five years, my writing was put on hold as I adjusted to new places and jobs.

In October 2003, I stood at the front of a chapel in a funeral home in New Jersey. The urn with Georgia's ashes shined brightly under the lights of the chapel as I spoke about our life together and failed to hold back my tears.

That evening, I sat in the silence of my house. My son mourned alone in his room. I turned on my computer and searched for widow and widower support groups. I found my new home. I wasn't alone. Others suffered the loss of loved ones.

I poured my heart out to them. They reciprocated. It was healing to write down my thoughts and feelings. The more I wrote, the better I felt. It was back. Writing soothed me.

I stopped writing about my grief and began to view the world in a different way. In everything there is a message to be told. I looked for those hidden gems that most people fail to see. I started a newsletter to showcase my work and promised my readers at least one story a week.

I never fail to do this. It's my motivation. All week long, I think about what I will write next.

My friends steered me in the right direction: I needed to write from my heart. The first story I sold has since sold twelve more times and made me close to one thousand dollars. It has appeared in several major newsletters. Their subscribers joined my newsletter—more than four thousand at the time of this writing. I've sold three stories to Chicken Soup for the Soul. Several more have sold to other publications. An actor/producer/director contacted me. He wants to make a few short films based on my essays.

I read the work of others. When I come across a good one, I

make a point to compliment them. They reply, "Thank you, Mike. Coming from a writer with your skill, this means a lot to me."

Me? Skill? Maybe I'm modest, but I thought they were better than me.

I work in telecommunications as a project manager. My writing is a release. One day, I hope it will be my living. At night, I look at the television and get bored. I itch to write. The television goes blank with the touch of a button. Blues music plays on the stereo. My fingers move to the music. They dance over the keyboard. A story unfolds.

It took me more than twenty years to make it this far with my writing; I'm not stopping now. One day, it will be all I dreamed it to be.

When I write, I'm in my element.

~Michael T. Smith

Why I Write

The best thing about having a sister was that I always had a friend.
~Cali Rae Turner

Growing up, I dreamed of being a nurse or a doctor. When I got to college, I tried out different majors and ended up deciding that an engineering degree was for me. Writing? To me, that was simply a necessary evil when it came to college assignments and the occasional report at work. I certainly never saw myself writing for pleasure—that is, until life gave me an opportunity to take a closer look at what matters most, and I discovered the writer within me.

My older sister, Barbara, was a dreamer. She wasn't afraid to take risks and try new things. From cross-country moves with nothing but a roadmap and a prayer, to enrolling in college courses just because they sounded interesting, Barbara loved a challenge. She lived her life chasing possibilities and always thought she had all the time in the world to do the things she wanted to do. Sadly, life didn't turn out the way she planned it.

While still in her early forties, she was diagnosed with multiple sclerosis (MS). Over the course of ten short years, the devastating disease robbed her of the ability to walk. Eventually, she became bed-ridden and homebound. Her world shrank, but not her spirit. She refused to believe she would never walk again. She refused to give up hope.

Barbara and I had always been close. We were each other's

biggest fans and confidantes. For years, we faithfully called each other at least once a week. As the MS took its toll on her body, however, we began the habit of talking every night on the phone. I would share with her the antics of my family... like the time my older son decided to see how well twenty-seven newborn chicks could swim in a bucket (yes, by the way, you can blow-dry baby chicks) or when my daughter announced (at age four, mind you) that when she grew up she wanted to be a massage therapist and open up a shop called "Ruby's Rubbers and Scratchers—We Scratch the Itch So Your Wife Doesn't Have To!" My stories became Barbara's window to the world outside her bedroom.

Sometimes, however, our conversations turned to writing and story ideas. My sister was a writer. She had a degree in communications, and prior to her illness had worked successfully in various positions utilizing her writing skills. Over the course of her career, she had been employed by advertising firms, major telecommunications companies, and even a university or two—often being responsible for company newsletters and facilitating conferences. That might be enough for some, but not for Barbara. She hoped for something bigger. She dreamed of someday being a published author. Even as her life drew to a close, she tried to hold on to that dream.

My sister and I shared a lot in common. We both loved listening to classical music and believed that a dish of chocolate ice cream was the perfect stress reliever. Together we went on many an adventure to satisfy our wanderlust, but writing was definitely her dream, not mine, that is until I decided to start a blog when Barbara died.

Barbara's passing gave me a reason to look at my life and re-evaluate what was important to me, to think about what I wanted to accomplish during my time here on earth, especially since her dreams were cut short. Blogging gave me the chance to put into words all of the thoughts swimming around inside my head. I also really missed the nightly talks with my sister, and blogging became a way of replacing our conversations. I began to realize, much to my surprise, that I actually liked writing. As a stay-at-home, home-schooling mother of three, I didn't have a lot of creative outlets. My blog gave me the desperately needed opportunity to express myself. I still never dreamed I would ever actually think of myself as a writer… that was my sister, not me… right?

Several months and hundreds of blog posts later, I have begun to think differently. Slowly, I am realizing that writing has become a part of who I am, and I can't imagine not doing it. On my blog, I am able to "let down my hair" and vent a bit. I see having the chance to put my thoughts into words as a blessing. It allows me to do a bit of soul-searching and maybe, just maybe, seek (and occasionally find) a little slice of peace in my otherwise topsy-turvy world. Writing is also one of the ways I keep the memory of my sister alive within my heart. And who knows, I just might make the dream come true and someday become a published author. But no matter what happens, I have become something more… I am a writer. And I will be forever grateful to my sister for that.

~Pamela Louise Walker

Chapter 7

inspiration for Writers

Mentors Who Mattered

The dream begins with a teacher who believes in you,
who tugs and pushes and leads you to the next plateau,
sometimes poking you with a sharp stick called "truth."

~Dan Rather

54

The Rewards of Paying It Forward

When the student is ready — the teacher will appear.
~Lao T'zu

They say you can only learn from experience. But I'm a reporter, so here's the scoop. The experience doesn't have to be your own!

A long long time ago, when I had long brown hair and fewer wrinkles — so long ago, actually, I had *no* wrinkles — I got my first job in television. You have to remember, this was 1975.

I had bamboozled my way into the local newsroom — there were not many women on TV at that time, and I had gently reminded the management of that. I had no experience on television, but, with a sigh, the news director admitted he might be able to make a twenty-five-year-old me into a TV reporter.

And if he couldn't? No big deal. I had no contract, and my salary was $8,000 a year.

If there was anyone who desperately needed a mentor, it was me. The depth of my inexperience was unfathomable. I had no idea how to report or write or shoot a story for television news. And, just as scary, no one seemed eager to show me. As a result, I will now confess, every night for two weeks or so I went home sobbing. Terrified. Overwhelmed. With no idea what I was supposed to do, let alone how to be successful at it.

It looked pretty bleak for my TV career.

Then one day I was assigned a story on—health care, I think, and I knew that would certainly be the end of it. Not only did I not know about TV, I also knew nothing about the new health care laws. There was no way this was going to work. I was doomed. But I got assigned to work with a veteran photographer named Walt. He'd been around since—well, he was a pro.

Stand here, he told me. Say this. Call this guy. Ask this question. Here's how to hold the microphone. Here's how to use your hands. Here's how to modulate your voice. Here's how to look into the camera. For maybe three weeks he shepherded me at every moment. And soon after, I realized—hey, I love this. And I can do it.

And I've been a TV reporter ever since.

Now, two things. The first, I'm *not* suggesting you do. I was so grateful to Walt that I fixed him up with my sister, and they got married. I told you—this is not a typical thank you for someone who acted as a mentor.

But the second thing? I promised myself I would pass it along. Pay it forward. That when a new kid arrived at my TV station, and I could help, I would. The mentor relationship, remember, is not always easy.

There's a wonderful quote from the *Tao Te Ching*. Lao T'zu asks: "What is a good man but a bad man's teacher?" I thought about that—now a veteran reporter myself and at a network affiliate in Boston—as I shepherded one new kid after another. Some were dismissive. Some decided they didn't need my help. But I learned it's the *doing* it that's the reward, not the gratitude or the results. It's that you're giving your experience to someone whose life you might change.

Here's the amazing secret. The life that changes might be your own. Here's how I know.

Years ago, I had an intern twenty years younger than I was… and that was fifteen years ago, so she was about the same age I was when I started. Sally arrived at the television station with Hello Kitty barrettes in her hair, scuffy Mary Jane shoes, and ripped jeans.

But she had a dream. All she wanted, she told me, was to be my producer in the investigative unit.

All she wanted was to be my producer? I was so touched! At that moment, I decided—okay, sister. The time has come. I didn't reveal my plans to her, but at that moment decided she would be my pay-it-forward girl. I thought—honey, I'm going to teach you everything I know.

A year or so later, Sally had stopped saying "like" every other word, wore little black dresses and pearls, and she and her mother were talking to each other again. Most important, she had become a terrific producer, and sadly, was leaving my TV station to take a fancy new job at a California station. Hurray.

And I thought that was the end of a happy story. Nope. Wait. That's not all.

Years after that, Sally came back to Channel 7 as my producer. (Remember, she'd told me, on day one, that was her dream. Now it had come true. Okay, I admit, it was a dear little dream, but it was hers.)

End of happy story? Nope. Wait. That's not all.

Sally was writing a book in her spare time. While in California, she'd learned the scoop about writing and publishing—and was incredibly educated and connected in that world. Her first novel was a chick lit romance, and she asked me if I could read it and edit it for her.

Well, I love books, right? And I write and edit news stories every day. How different could it be? So I said—Sure. Happy to. But as I was reading her book, I thought—hmm. Ever since I read my first *Nancy Drew*, I've always wanted to write a book. Reading hers, I thought—I bet I could do this. Problem was, I had no idea how.

But Lao T'zu has another saying: "When the student is ready—the teacher will appear."

And—because that's how the universe often works—suddenly the roles were reversed. With an idea for a mystery novel blossoming in my head, I asked Sally if she could mentor *me* in the book world! And she did. (I wonder if she thought—okay, sister, I'm going to teach you everything I know.)

By the end of the next year, I had written my first mystery novel, and it won the Agatha Award for Best First Mystery.

End of happy story? Nope. Wait. That's not all.

My fifth book is now a bestseller, and in a third printing. And the reality is—it all started back in 1975 when newbie me was lost and confused, and a generous mentor came to my rescue. Embracing my turn as mentor—I rescued newbie Sally. And then—because that's how the universe often works!—she rescued me.

Throw someone a lifeline—and it may be your own life that gets saved.

~Hank Phillippi Ryan

55

A Scholar
and a Gentleman

The great thing about getting older
is that you don't lose all the other ages you've been.
~Madeleine L'Engle

Vindication for the decision to become a writer doesn't always come from creative-writing teachers or even editors. One of my most powerful mentors came in the form of a scholar and a gentleman named Uncle Johnny. It happened the Christmas I was eight.

The big day would fall on Friday that year. I was relieved. That meant Uncle Johnny wouldn't be at our house for either Christmas Eve supper or dinner the following day. Wednesday was his day to visit.

I resented Uncle Johnny. His presence at our supper table every Wednesday evening never failed to spoil my enjoyment of the meal. My mother said Uncle Johnny was a graduate of one of Canada's leading universities and had been one of the most renowned literary scholars of his day, but I found that hard to believe.

Uncle Johnny was eighty-six. He had watery, red-rimmed eyes, sagging jowls, and trembling hands that slopped and spilled food and drink. Sometimes, drool seeped from the corners of his mouth. He smelled of mothballs. And he wasn't even my uncle. He was just my grandfather's second cousin, who'd ended up alone in old age. He always arrived wearing an old-fashioned, shiny-with-age, three-piece suit, a snow-white shirt, a threadbare tie bearing some sort of insignia, and down-at-the-heels black shoes glossed to a military shine. A polished fob crossing his vest terminated in the breast pocket that held his gold watch.

Uncle Johnny lived in a once-genteel, now-shabby boarding-house beside the town's newspaper office. His proximity to this print shop facilitated the neatly bound typeset copies of his poems and essays that he never failed to bring to my mother.

He'd present one of these pale blue binders to her each Wednesday as we sat down to supper. "A gentleman never comes calling with his hands at his sides," he'd say as he handed her his gift.

My mother's meal would grow cold on her plate as she read. Uncle Johnny, with shaking hands, dribbled food down the napkin he'd tucked under his chin as he sent not-so-furtive glances in her direction, awaiting her reaction.

Repulsed, I tried to keep my eyes focused on the meal in front of me and ignore Uncle Johnny's effort to get food and drink to his mouth. My mother would finish reading, clutch the binder to her chest, and smile.

"Lovely, Uncle Johnny, absolutely lovely," she'd say. "I'll treasure it."

He'd cast her an adoring, watery smile as he patted his mouth with a corner of his napkin.

"Thank you, my dear," he'd reply softly, casting a gentle nod of appreciative acknowledgement in her direction. "You're too kind."

On Wednesday of Christmas week that year, aglow with hopes and plans for the Yuletide, I was willing to view even Uncle Johnny's weekly dinner visit in a kinder light. He wouldn't be around to spoil any of the Christmas feasts.

That morning, my mother shattered my anticipation.

"I've invited Uncle Johnny to come on Friday," I overheard her telling my father. "Last week when I asked about his plans for Christmas, I discovered he hadn't any. Oh, he tried to say Cousin George had mentioned something back in the summer, but I have a feeling he was fibbing. He didn't want us to invite him out of pity. I said that since there'd be just the three of us this year, he'd be doing us a favor by helping us to eat that big turkey you bought."

"No!" Startling my parents, I burst into the kitchen. "No! No! No! He'll spoil everything with his shaking and drooling and dribbling! And he smells!"

"Gail, how can you say such dreadful things?" my mother said in dismay. "Uncle Johnny is a dear, old gentleman. He's kind and clever and…"

"I hate him! I hate him!" I yelled. "If he's here for Christmas, I won't come to the table!"

I stormed up to my room and slammed the door.

A half-hour later (my usual allowed cooling-off time), my father entered. I knew from his expression I was in deep trouble.

"You've hurt your mother's feelings," he said, his face grim. "I want you to apologize to her." He turned to leave, then paused.

"And if you refuse to share Christmas dinner with Uncle Johnny, Santa definitely won't be pleased."

Consequently, Christmas Day saw me seated in my usual place across from Uncle Johnny. As my mother placed the steaming, golden brown turkey on the table, he drew a small, awkwardly wrapped package from inside his suit coat. With a shaking hand, he extended it toward me.

"Your mother tells me you enjoy reading and hope to be a writer some day," he said, his thin, old voice quavering. "I thought you might enjoy this."

I stared down at the crumpled wrappings. Some tatty old thing not even wrapped in new paper.

"Open it, Gail." My mother beamed down on both of us.

Gingerly, I untied the wrinkled ribbon and spread out the paper. Inside was a book, *Emily of New Moon*, by L. M. Montgomery.

"It's about a young lady about your age who, much like yourself, aspires to be a writer," Uncle Johnny explained, a tremulous smile on his moist lips.

"How thoughtful, Uncle Johnny." My mother put an arm around

the shoulders of his worn jacket and hugged him. "Gail, wasn't that thoughtful of Uncle Johnny?"

"Yes." I was turning the book slowly over in my hands. Used. I liked fresh, new books. But Uncle Johnny had said it was about a girl who wanted to write. "Thank you, Uncle Johnny."

"You're most welcome, my dear. I hope it will inspire you."

Uncle Johnny passed away that spring, alone in his room at the boardinghouse. Few people attended his funeral. In his poverty and isolation, he and his past scholarly achievements had been forgotten.

I stood by his grave, clutching my mother's hand and *Emily of New Moon*, the book I'd come to cherish and whose author would have a major influence on my literary life. I knew I would never forget the man who'd given it to me or the fact that he was a scholar and a gentleman.

~Gail MacMillan

What He Taught Me

One father is more than a hundred schoolmasters.
~George Herbert

He was only fifteen when he hired on as a stringer for the *Long Beach Press-Telegram*. For more than forty years, my father covered sporting events, the news desk, and managed a daily newspaper. At fifty-six, while on assignment in London, he wrote his last line. His death was sudden and unexpected, and while his colleagues mourned the loss of a talented journalist and friend, I grieved for the man I had idolized as a little girl. To this day, I still long for what might have been had we been given more time together.

I'm not sure if I inherited my love for the written word from my father, but I am certain it didn't develop solely out of a desire to please him. He's been gone twenty years now, and I still can't shake the compulsion to prick my heart, let it bleed all over an empty page, and share it with total strangers.

For a man of many words, my father rarely spoke them. His only encouragement for my writing obsession came in the form of daily vocabulary drills after dinner and a nod when I signed up to take Latin three years in a row. "It'll help you with your writing," he'd said.

I'll never forget the first time I asked him to critique my work. I was in elementary school, and very proud as I approached him one afternoon while he watched one baseball game on the living-room television, and Howard Cosell's nasally voice blared on the portable radio beside him, announcing another game.

"What's this?" he asked as I handed him handwritten sheets of lined binder paper. He reached for the dial on the radio. Then he pointed to the television with his cigarette.

"It's for a short story contest," I said as I bounced across the room and turned down the sound on the television.

Dad set his cigarette in the ashtray and thumbed through all five pages before crossing his legs and reading the first line. I agonized as he took his time, perusing the first sheet before turning it over and placing it upside down in his lap.

Pans rattled in the kitchen, and I tuned out my mother as she prepared dinner. Outside, my sister yelled, and I wondered if the neighborhood game of hide-and-seek would be over before my father finished reading my masterpiece.

I fidgeted and must have made a sound. Dad glanced up over his glasses, and I dropped my hand to my side. My face flushed with heat. I'd been caught once again chewing my fingernails.

Finally, he finished. Pages rustled, and Dad stacked all five sheets together before handing them back to me. "Do it over," he said.

I stared in disbelief. Surely he didn't mean it needed more work? Hadn't I perfected it, written it over and over again, made sure I hadn't misspelled or scratched out a single word?

"Cut it in half." He reached for his cigarette and turned the radio back on. Then he gestured toward the television. I sprinted to the console and turned up the volume. Before he could see the tears spill over and run down my cheeks, I fled down the hall to my room.

I've often wondered how my father mentored those who worked for him. Surely he didn't toss back articles or feature stories with nothing more than a "Do it over" or "Cut it in half." But despite his proclivity for critiquing me without constructive direction, neither praising nor denying my talent, I persevered. My desire to master the craft of writing never waned.

In the ensuing years, I dabbled in journalism; worked as a television reporter, editor, and news anchor; authored technical reports;

and created a greeting-card ministry. Even as a grown woman, I never outgrew my hope that one day my father would mentor me with his journalism expertise.

Three weeks before his death, I showed him my latest masterpiece. My husband and I and our two boys had flown out for a visit. Dad stood at the kitchen counter, and I felt my heart skip in anticipation as he flipped through my spiral-bound report. Then, without a sigh, a smile, or even a word, he closed the back cover and walked out of the room.

I felt my jaw drop to the floor and my eyes sting with tears.

He returned a moment later with a spiral notebook of his own. He said nothing when he handed me *The Associated Press Stylebook*, and nothing when he left the room for good.

If my dad were alive today, I have no doubt I'd still show him my work, still seek his approval. I can't help but wonder if he would be proud of my younger brother and me, both of us now published authors. Or if he'd praise his grandchildren and great-grandchildren who show promise when writing their newspaper articles, short stories, and school reports.

Today, when my grandchildren show me their writing, I make a concerted effort to comment on the sensory pictures and the emotion their creative use of words evokes. I want to point out what is good in their writing, to help foster a belief in themselves as some editors and publishers, as well as my critique partners, have done for me in recent years. As they grow older, I'll correct their sentence structure and overuse of adverbs and adjectives.

My father may not have taught me much about the craft of writing, but I've since learned that success as a published author isn't based solely on talent, or merit, or writing with emotion while using good grammar. Books and writing workshops have taught me the writing basics, but I learned from my father that a writer must be tenacious, thick-skinned, and determined to persevere despite rejection.

I am a writer today not because I was born one, or am talented, or lucky. I am a writer because I have mastered the craft of perseverance. I push through mind-numbing and spirit-draining exhaustion while laboring over each and every word. Then I flay myself open and spill out my guts, not knowing if critics will applaud me or feast on my words like buzzards.

My heart may pump life-sustaining blood through my veins, but I am most alive when words flow through and out of me. I must write or die trying.

That's what my father taught me.

~Dawn M. Lilly

This Writer's Soul

As you start to walk out on the way, the way appears.

~Rumi

"Mom, I just saw a woman with information about writers on her T-shirt," says my daughter, Betsy, as she ends her jog around the park in Tennessee. "Let's go to the parking lot and talk to her."

I have been wanting a second career as a writer, after recently retiring from teaching. A few days ago, I flew from Florida to Knoxville to attend a writers' workshop near Betsy's home.

"Excuse me, I noticed your T-shirt. My mom's a writer," Betsy lies to the woman in the parking lot. "Tell us about yourself."

We learn her name is Margaret, and her shirt came from a writers' conference she attended. With Betsy's urging, Margaret offers me some advice.

"You should attend the Southeastern Writers Conference on St. Simons Island, Georgia. The deadline for registering and submitting manuscripts to be critiqued is a few days away. I have an extra registration form. If Betsy will give me her address, I'll put it in her mailbox later today, and you can send it off immediately."

By chance, I had e-mailed Betsy a story to edit because she's excellent at finding errors in manuscripts I'm convinced are perfect. I printed the essay and submitted it to the Inspirational Writing category.

When I arrived at the conference, I was struck by the beauty of St. Simons Island, accented with quiet marshes and century-old oaks bearded with moss. The setting was tranquil, but I felt anxious about competing with experienced writers. I reminded myself that I was there to learn, and for the next five days I attended classes and listened to dynamic speakers.

At the end of the conference, I was nervous when I met with Debra, the Inspirational Writing judge who had critiqued my manuscript. I cringed when I noticed several red marks on my pages.

"I like your story," she began. "You need to eliminate adverbs, words ending in 'ly,' and I've circled them. You have talent, so keep writing." She handed me the manuscript and added, "I'll see you at the Awards Banquet tomorrow night."

The next evening, Debra stood at the podium to reveal the three awards for Inspirational Writing. I picked at my salad as she announced the third-place winner, then the second-place winner.

"And now, the first-place award for Inspirational Writing goes to... Miriam Hill! Please come forward and receive your fifty-dollar check. Congratulations!"

My knees felt weak as I walked to the podium amid the applause. Debra smiled and handed me an envelope.

Later that night, I phoned Betsy and screamed, "I won first place!"

"Oh, Mom, I'm so proud of you!" she gushed. "I'll tell Margaret."

After the conference, Debra stayed in contact and urged me to submit a story for *Chicken Soup for the Bride's Soul*.

"I can write about having Betsy's wedding in our home while it was under construction," I decided.

I wrote it.

Chicken Soup for the Soul published it.

It was the beginning of my writing career.

Since then, my work has appeared in bestselling books, national magazines, and major newspapers. One of my stories received Honorable Mention for Inspirational Writing in a *Writer's Digest* writing competition that received more than 19,000 entries.

When I visit bookstores in the United States and foreign countries, I smile when I find my essays in nearly thirty *Chicken Soup for the Soul* book titles. Seeing the published stories I've worked hard to write, rewrite, and edit is an inspiration for this writer's soul.

~Miriam Hill

A New Direction

Get over the idea that only children should spend their time in study.
Be a student so long as you still have something to learn,
and this will mean all your life.
~Henry L. Doherty

"Your blood pressure is awfully high," the doctor said. It was exactly the news I didn't want to hear. I had big-time job burnout, but I was way too old to change careers. If I could make it just a few more years until I turned sixty-two, my husband Bruce and I could retire.

We had built our dream home in Wisconsin knowing the commute to our jobs in Illinois would be long and tiring. But driving together had made it easier, almost fun at times. I hated the thought of him making that trip alone. But Bruce knew better than anyone how stressed out I was. Worried about my health, he encouraged me to quit.

His aging SUV was beginning to deteriorate seriously, although he was determined to make it last one more winter. I knew he longed for a Crossfire convertible, but felt it too impractical. I searched for one, knowing it would make his drive more fun. And I assured him he could use my car on those few days when the weather was bad. Suddenly, he looked forward to going to work again, and my guilt abated.

In January, reality hit hard. The little yellow Crossfire sat snug and warm in the garage, while my SUV slogged through the slush to get Bruce to and from work. The storms came in an endless string, not allowing so much as a peek at bare ground. Unceasing winds swept the snow like sand dunes, topping our windowsills, drifting over our narrow country road several times a day. I always thought being housebound in a snowstorm would be romantic, but never planned on it lasting for weeks.

My brother-in-law Al was taking online creative writing courses. His enthusiasm made me curious. I hadn't taken classes in decades and imagined my brain looked like an enormous dried-up cornflake. The idea of creative writing, though interesting, felt scary. But at seven o'clock one morning, faced with another long day of listening to the wind howl, I turned on the computer and sat down to browse a writing website.

As soon as I pressed Enter, it hit me that I'd just registered. I jumped up from my chair, my arms wrapped tightly around my middle like a straightjacket. I began pacing furiously, our five-month-old puppy, Alex, at my heels.

"What have I done? I'll never be able to do this."

Alex looked up at me confidently, with the kind of sincerity only a puppy or a small child can pull off.

In all my adult life, I'd written only one story. With all the self-assurance in the world and not one ounce of training, I had sent it off to *Good Housekeeping* magazine. The form rejection letter made me cringe. I dumped it into the garbage and never mentioned it to anyone.

Despite my lack of education, I knew I could write decently. I was the person at work who wrote everyone else's correspondence and the departmental goals. And I'd been a major contributor to a couple of manuals on bar coding for food packaging. Business writing, boring as it was, came easily to me. I wasn't sure I had a creative side.

The class I chose was called Beginning Writer's Workshop, taught by Ann Linquist. It was held in an open format where all the students saw and commented on one another's submissions. That had its benefits and drawbacks. Knowing none of my classmates would ever see me or know my real name gave me comfort. Never having to see the pained boredom on Ann's face as she read my work made it easier, too. I still carried scars from critiques I got during watercolor classes in college. That instructor honed his ego by shredding ours. But Ann's critiques were so much kinder than I expected. "Feel free to write poorly" was her mantra, and she meant it. That advice helped me let go of my fear. I was surprised to find I looked forward to hearing what she had to say about my work. She gave me courage, and I could see my writing improving. I felt sad when the class ended.

Weeks later, Bruce noticed a call for essays in a small farming magazine and brought it to my attention.

"You could easily write about this kind of thing," he said.

I looked at the upcoming topic list, a different one for each month. Eager to try my new skills, I sent in an essay titled "Neighbors from Heaven." It was selected and published a month later. I remember feeling proud and excited when my copy arrived in the big white envelope that also included a nice check. But that was nothing compared to the way I felt when the neighbor I'd written about told me a friend in another state had read the story and commented on it to him. There was someone out there—a stranger—who had actually read my work! I was ecstatic.

I tried a few more writing courses from the same site, but found that all teachers were not alike. I missed Ann's detailed, thoughtful critiques. It was summer, and I spent long, hot afternoons on my porch swing pounding away at my laptop. I figured if I sent out a hundred submissions, I should be able to get at least one published. My luck turned out to be better than that. By the end of the year, I'd seen two more of my essays in print.

With a group of other students from one of my classes, I began contributing to an online writing group. When I suggested we try to help one another more by giving positive but helpful critiques and pointing out grammatical errors, I was told quite abruptly to leave. To my surprise and emotional relief, most of my fellow students were supportive and left with me to form our own group, but I had learned a valuable lesson. Not everyone wants to hear what they are doing wrong or not everyone writes with the goal of getting published.

The following winter, I found the University of Wisconsin-Madison's online writing courses and "Coach" Marshall Cook. Marsh's classes were different in that we communicated one-on-one via e-mail, so it was more like taking private lessons. Like Ann, he was encouraging and patient. Marsh took apart every single sentence I wrote. His class challenged me with a wide variety of assignments, and I liked that. When I found out he was planning to retire, I took as many of his classes as I could cram in before he left.

I'm still practicing and learning. And I'm still in contact with both Ann and Marsh, who generously offer guidance and support. I'll never get over the thrill of having a piece published. And I'll always be grateful for the series of events that pushed me in this new direction.

~Barbara Ann Burris

Learning the Hard Way

I am always doing that which I cannot do,
in order that I may learn how to do it.
~Pablo Picasso

Going back to college at age forty was torture. Not only had I forgotten many of my study skills and most of my algebra rules, but I had been diagnosed with rheumatoid arthritis, the kind that inflames the joints and cripples. My hands had already taken a beating. My secretarial days were over.

"We need to retrain you for a job where you can use your brain and let someone else do the typing," my advisor said. Immediately, I envisioned myself making PowerPoint presentations and giving orders instead of taking them. The thought was exciting. But the reality was, I had no choice. I had two children at home who depended on me to make a living, and I couldn't give up.

Getting prepared was a challenge. Years before voice-recognition software, I learned I could still peck out letters on a keyboard using a fat kindergarten pencil, eraser end down. My brain adjusted quickly. I couldn't type eighty words per minute with my damaged fingers, but I could still get the job done.

I was put through a series of tests in order to find my strengths and weaknesses. To my surprise, I had a mild learning disability involving short-term memory. Now I understood why I had to study harder throughout my school days for every good grade I received.

A lot of my friends could get by without studying, but not me. I would have to put in my time if I ever expected to get through college. When the results were in, I was advised to pursue a degree in Business or English. I had plenty of time to make up my mind while I got my general education courses behind me. Most of all, I felt my life moving in the right direction.

That first day of the fall semester, I left home very early, hoping all the handicapped parking spaces wouldn't be taken. No such luck. I would have to walk several blocks to my English class. The four-story brick building with tall white columns loomed in the distance as I held on to my mind-over-matter approach. The books on my back felt like a load of bricks. At 100 pounds, my small frame, inflamed by a relentless disease, was put to the test. My knees would hurt that night, but I wouldn't let it stop me as I motivated myself to continue. "You can do it, Linda. Just put one foot in front of the other."

The building was surrounded by students not much older than my own kids, all talking and laughing, so excited to be there. Even in my exhausted state, I couldn't stop smiling too. English 101 would require a lot of writing and I couldn't wait to get started. I had always loved to write. I could just imagine myself writing a bestseller someday.

I soon learned there would be no breaks in Professor Bruton's class. He lectured non-stop and assigned lots of reading before divulging the writing topic for the week. As we filed out, I overheard disgruntled students call him, "Brutus," and I was in complete agreement.

The day after our first papers were turned in, I arrived to find him pacing the floor, saying nothing the first five minutes. Shaking his head, he stopped long enough to stare at us like last week's garbage before he said, "You people make me sick. I've never seen such bad writing in my life."

As he began to pass out the graded papers, I told myself not to worry. I had put a lot of time in on mine. Those kids were probably out partying all night. Mine was pretty good.

The ranting continued, "I actually banged my head on the wall last night, wondering how I could have gotten such an incompetent bunch of students in one class. I can't believe it," he said, tossing mine on my desk as if it was just another piece of trash.

I glanced down at my paper, now streaked with red ink. My visions of making at least a "B" were gone. A big red "D" took its place. I had never made a grade that low in my life—ever. I had to fight back tears. I didn't understand how a man with this rude method of teaching had a job with a university of such high standing.

I was tempted to question why I had gotten such a miserable grade until I heard the grumbling of my classmates. At least my grade was passing; many of theirs weren't. So I bit my tongue. "You have one week to rewrite," he said as the final bell sounded, and we all left without looking at him. I was livid.

At home, I looked my paper over and read his comments. My spirits lifted to a degree. I could make the changes he wanted with a little time and effort. In my estimation, they were trivial—only a couple of misspelled words, a run-on sentence, and his note that my flow of words lacked rhythm were justifiable. Still, in my estimation, getting a "D" was pretty drastic for such minor errors.

After making the necessary changes, I felt good about my efforts, but the professor wasn't too pleased. I received a "C" on my rewrite. Now, reality hit and knocked my confidence to the ground. Maybe I was only dreaming. Just because I wanted to be a writer didn't mean I was cut out for it.

By final exam day, I had written so many papers for Professor Bruton that I was beginning to get it. If I ever wanted to please him, every paper had to be perfect. Every "i" had to be dotted, and dangling participles were out of the question. Despite my frustrations, he was making sure I was learning to do it right. I was averaging a "C," which I had come to accept. How I wished I had known about his ornery reputation when I was scheduling my classes!

That day, I walked in with my chin high, picked one of the three subjects he had written on the board, and spent the hour calmly writing my paper the way he had taught. Pass or fail, I would give it all I had left. If he wasn't happy, I couldn't help it.

He actually smiled and shook my hand as I turned in my paper five minutes early. I was suspicious. Was that his way of adding more humiliation to my already deflated self-esteem? *Give her some hope before she cuts her throat.*

In those days, your grade had to be delivered by mail, so it took a week. It was worth the wait. I had an "A," the grade I never expected in a million years. Now I knew what his humiliating, yet critical tactics were all about, and they had worked. I was on my way to becoming a writer.

~Linda C. Defew

Making the Story My Own

*It is only when you open your veins and bleed onto the page a little
that you establish contact with your reader.*
~Paul Gallico

In a former professional life, I was a journalist. My first job after college was at a small weekly newspaper in Indianapolis where I wrote obituaries, covered local art fairs and did "man on the street" interviews, asking a different question every week. From there I became a feature writer for a daily paper upstate, and then Lifestyle Editor for another. For years, I wrote a Friday column that profiled everyday people doing everyday things, and I loved the challenge of turning what my subjects might think of as ordinary or boring into a story others would want to read. "Why would anyone care about me?" I heard over and over.

I always followed a set formula: Start with an attention-getting lead, follow chronologically with the details of the story, and end with a wistful quote from the subject, capturing the lesson he or she learned. It worked every time.

Eventually, I gave up journalism for a career in public relations, but my writing still tended to be formulaic, and I remained under the strong influence of my two long-time friends: *The Associated Press Stylebook* and the inverted pyramid.

When I moved to Chicago in 2006, I went looking for a creative outlet, an opportunity to take a deeper dive into my writing. I wanted to go beyond the "who, what, when, where and why" that was so ingrained in my journalistic mind. I found a writing studio close to an "L" train stop and signed up for a class in memoir writing because of the challenge I knew it would provide me. I was a third-person writer, I told myself, more comfortable writing about others, telling someone else's story. Could I dig as deep within myself? Did I have the guts to tell my own story?

In my Introduction to Memoir class, I learned the importance of balancing scene and summary. I read excerpts from books by masters like Joan Didion (*The Year of Magical Thinking*), Frank McCourt (*Angela's Ashes*) and Mary Karr (*The Liars' Club*). I practiced sensory writing, describing smells, tastes and textures during impromptu writing assignments. I experimented with metaphor and dialog.

It opened up my literary world.

When I nervously sat down to begin my first piece for class, I had every intention of writing about my recent move to Chicago—the transition from suburban home to city condo, from mother to empty nester, from divorcee to newlywed the second time around. Instead, I ended up writing about my mother, whom I lost to cancer when I was twelve. I hadn't planned to go there, but the story came to life after I discovered an old stack of letters one weekend while unpacking some boxes following the move. In the pile was a small note I had written as a child to my mother during one of her long hospital stays. "Please get well and come home soon. I am waiting for you," it said. It had a pencil-smudged drawing of a sad face with tears. I felt a wave of inspiration to share that little girl's story.

I hadn't thought about that small child for years—decades really—and when I immersed myself in those memories I was afraid the first draft of my piece might be too sappy and personal to interest anyone else. "Why would anyone care about me?" echoed in my head.

As I wrote, however, my piece became more than just the story of my mother's long years of illness—the story I probably would have written in my newspaper days. It evolved into the story of how the rest of the family coped—our day-to-day survival. I reached deep within myself to unveil the ugly truth of how that little girl felt:

scared every time her mom had to go to the hospital. Overwhelmed by all of the well wishes and pity from others. Angry because she had to empty bedpans and be extra quiet around the house. Embarrassed that her family was different from the others on the block.

It was the hardest story I had ever written, and an even harder one to share with others.

After three or four rewrites—with plenty of feedback from my writing instructor and classmates—that piece became my first published work of creative non-fiction, when it was selected for inclusion in an anthology entitled *Wisdom Has a Voice: Daughters Remember Mothers*. My writing teacher had learned of the project and encouraged me to submit my work.

When I worked for newspapers, I never got tired of seeing my byline in print, even after ten years or so of reporting. It was always a thrill. When I received a copy of the *Wisdom* anthology in the mail and was able to hold the book in my hands, turn to my piece, and see my name at the top of the page, that feeling returned. With gusto. I felt accomplished, yes, but more importantly, I felt a sense of ownership. I hadn't just reported that story, I had lived it.

I don't have a formula for that.

~Diane Hurles

Perseverance

Most of us, swimming against the tides of trouble
the world knows nothing about, need only a bit of praise
or encouragement — and we will make the goal.
~Jerome Fleishman

It was 1985, and my life was at a crossroads. I was thirty-five and, after years of floundering about, I had finally found a job with the Canadian federal government that looked like it was going to be a long-term career.

My background as a trade-mark lawyer had landed me a position with the Trade-marks Opposition Board, a small administrative tribunal that rules on disputes over trade-mark applications. Conducting hearings and writing decisions made use of my acquired skills and, to some extent, satisfied my lifelong urge to be a writer.

But writing legal decisions was not going to sate that long-held desire forever. I knew that something more had to be done.

In years past, I had made the occasional attempt at writing fiction and non-fiction, but nothing much ever came from those attempts. Whether it was lack of confidence, motivation or possibly talent, I seldom followed through and actually produced a final written work.

Yet I still had a desire to be a published writer. So in the fall of 1985, I enrolled in an evening personal interest course at one of the local universities.

The course was called "Writing for Publication" and was taught by Linda Jeays, a local freelance writer. It turned out to be just what the doctor ordered for this writer wannabe.

This was not a creative writing course aimed primarily at those aspiring to write the great Canadian, American or possibly North American novel. Rather, it was a nuts-and-bolts approach to the business of writing.

Linda taught us how to format our work for publication. She gave us tips on submitting our work to various publications and on organizing our files so we could coordinate submissions and payments received.

Back then, I couldn't envision ever receiving an actual payment for my written work, but I took down the information just in case it came in handy some day. I also started writing.

Linda encouraged us to try all manner of writing exercise. She had us write letters to the editor of the local daily newspaper to see if we could break into print. She urged us to try our hand at everything from fiction to humor to feature articles.

As a bonus, Linda let us submit samples of our work, which she would critique. And that's where my writing career began.

One week, I submitted a partially written short story. Linda had lots of constructive comments about the half-written story. But her first written comment was the one that stuck; she said that I was a publishable writer.

That encouragement spurred me on to write more and to actually complete pieces. I started submitting essays and opinion pieces, now fully aware that rejection didn't mean I was a failure. Linda taught us that rejection was a necessary and frequent part of being a writer.

Before I knew it, I had an opinion piece published in the *Ottawa Citizen* followed closely by an essay in *Newsweek*. Both placements garnered me a check and, for the first time, I felt like a real writer.

From that point on, I plugged away fearlessly, writing and submitting and, most of the time, getting rejected. But in between those rejections, I had some acceptances, mostly in my local paper.

A few years later, I started getting the occasional piece published in other newspapers. Then I had another essay in *Newsweek*. More pieces appeared in the *Ottawa Citizen* and some in far-flung major dailies like *The New York Times*.

Over the years, my number of placements grew steadily, but not smoothly. Sometimes I would go weeks or even months without a publication. But I would keep writing and submitting.

And that was the key. Perseverance. For, more often than not, just when I thought I'd never get published again, a new acceptance would arrive in my e-mail or a new market would present itself.

A case in point is *Smithsonian* magazine. I tried for twenty years to crack their back-page humor column with no success. But then it happened; a few years ago, a piece of mine was accepted with several more to follow. Sadly, that back-page humor column is no more, but I have faith that I'll find a new market for my written work.

For the most part, my writing career has been a labor of love. I never make more than $10,000 in a year, but I wouldn't trade it for the world. The thrill of seeing my name in print and actually getting paid for something I love to do is unmatched.

For all that, I owe a debt of gratitude to Linda Jeays, the writer who gave me the encouragement I needed to keep on trying. And that's what I'd like to say to other new writers: keep on trying. Keep reading, keep writing, and keep submitting. Despite all the rejections, that next acceptance may be just around the corner.

~David Martin

Getting Started

Don't aim for success if you want it;
just do what you love and believe in, and it will come naturally.
~David Frost

I went to my local bookstore looking for something new to read. I left the store clutching a book and a flyer that described their upcoming events, including a two-hour writers' workshop every Saturday morning for the month of March. I wasn't familiar with the author who was the workshop instructor, so the book I carried was one of hers.

The following Saturday, the day the workshop was to start, I almost didn't go back to the store. I worried that I didn't belong in a workshop for "writers." I had finished the book I bought the week before, and it was good. Really good. Obviously not the work of a beginner, like me. I was a reader—but was I a writer?

I had written a few things for local charities—press releases and newsletter articles. But so far, my dream of taking my notebooks with scribbled story ideas from the idea stage to completion was still just a dream.

Luckily, the workshop was free. I figured I could sit in the back where no one would notice me. I had written to an author (and received a reply) when I was in elementary school, but I had never met a writer in person. It would be a thrill just to meet her and listen to what she had to say.

The store had set up rows of chairs in a semi-circle near the front of the store. Two people were already seated at the front. I sat in the back row. Then, a few minutes before the workshop was scheduled to start, I recognized the author walking toward us. Although her written words transported me out of this world, to a land of myths and legends, she was flesh and blood in a turtleneck sweater and slacks. She looked just like her photo on the back jacket flap.

She looked at our group, about a dozen in all. "Let's sit in a circle so we can get to know each other better," she said.

The chairs in front of me were swept away, and suddenly I was part of the group.

The author asked everyone to go around the circle, telling what we had written or hoped to write. Several people in the group talked about drawers full of completed manuscripts. When it was my turn, I said I wanted to write books for children, and described my notebooks.

No one laughed. In fact, they whispered words of encouragement. One woman passed me a slip of paper with her phone number and e-mail address so I could call her if I wanted to be critique buddies.

By the end of the first session, my reluctance to attend was replaced by impatience. I didn't want the workshop to be over. I felt as if I had been in a foreign country and finally came across others who spoke my language. I could hardly wait for the second meeting.

For the third week, we had the option to bring ten pages of a work-in-progress. Our instructor would take them with her, critique our work, and return the manuscripts at the final meeting.

Over the course of the next few weeks, I was surprised to see half of the original group drop out. Perhaps they weren't ready to share their work with the world yet. But I think everyone who came the third week brought manuscripts for review. It was daunting to have someone read my words, but it was exciting, too. Although our workshop group couldn't possibly learn every aspect of writing for publication in one month, one central lesson I took away was the difference between having story ideas and being a writer. I knew that I was only beginning my writing journey — and I wasn't producing

Newbery or Pulitzer award-winning material yet—but if I put words on the page, I was a writer. I desperately wanted to belong to that club.

When the author returned the pages the following week, I steeled myself to be greeted by a sea of angry red ink. Even though her ink was red, the sea was a welcoming, encouraging message. She told me she hoped I would complete the work.

I did.

It was my first completed novel. Although I never sent it out to be published, I am so grateful for the experience. Through the writing process, I learned the technical aspects of word count, plot points, voice and character, as well as the practical aspects of working alone and keeping my butt in the chair. The novel took me places I had never been before, places inside myself I needed to go before I was ready to say out loud to anyone who will listen… "I'm a writer."

~Wendy Greenley

Chapter 8

inspiration
for
Writers

Reflections on Rejection

*I take rejection as someone blowing a bugle in my ear to wake me up
and get going, rather than retreat.*

~Sylvester Stallone

Knowing When to Turn Off the Noise

There is no greater agony than bearing an untold story inside you.
~Maya Angelou

L ike most writers, I assumed that once I sold my first book, the second would be a piece of cake. No one warned me about the painful and demoralizing condition known as *Secundus Libri Puteulanus* or Second Book Blues.

My bout with Second Book Blues hit hard because my first book came easily. At age thirty-eight, I finally gave myself the permission to pursue writing, the passion I'd been discouraged from following because it wouldn't lead to a lucrative career. I promised myself that I'd get a book contract for my fortieth birthday. I achieved that goal two months after my birthday. Okay, close enough.

My first book, *Confessions of a Closet Catholic*, came out to good reviews and won the 2006 Sydney Taylor Book Award for Older Readers. But as much as I wanted to celebrate the success I'd dreamed of for so long, in the background my marriage was falling apart, taking with it my confidence in the future. I'd walked down the aisle thinking it was a commitment for life.

I also thought that when you sold a book and it earned out in the first royalty period and won an award, selling the next one would be a cakewalk. Most of the important lessons I've learned in my personal life have come from painful experience, so why should the ones in my writing life be any different?

Confessions was a middle-grade novel, and both my then-editor and agent were telling me to write more middle-grade because I "didn't have a YA voice."

My editor wanted me to write even younger—as a nine-year-old—something that didn't appeal to me in the slightest at that point in time. Because the stories inside me at that very moment, the ones waiting to be told, had to be young adult because of their subject matter.

There was another, deeper psychological issue at work. My reaction to being told I can't do something tells you exactly why I *am* a young adult author—because the more I was told I *couldn't* write YA, the more determined I was to do it. Because I would *show* them!

Unfortunately, "showing them" wasn't as easy as I thought. I'd work on an idea for three months, produce a synopsis and three sample chapters, and… "Sorry it's not working." Rejection.

Between the failure of my marriage and my failure to sell a second book, I started to wonder if my first book was a fluke. I started to wonder what was the matter with my writing and what was the matter with me. To make matters worse, I was on a listserv for published YA writers, and it seemed like every week someone on the list was posting about a two-book deal they'd signed on proposal. It didn't matter that I was a supposedly mature mother of two in my forties. It brought me straight back to that place of high-school angst about being a Loser with a Capital L.

When I turned up for my first-ever writing retreat, Kindling Words, in January 2006, I was desperate and demoralized. I was in year three of what I'd started to refer to as *The Never Ending Divorce* and was also approaching three years since I'd sold *Confessions* without a second book deal on the horizon.

I was sweating on an exercise machine at 6:30 A.M. with two other authors, Nancy Werlin and Sarah Aronson, in the Inn's tiny little workout room. In between gasps for air, I whined about my career woes. Nancy, one of the smartest people I know in the writing world, said, "You're showing them your writing too early." Sarah agreed. We got into a discussion about selling on proposal versus writing the whole book first, and that's when I realized that *published authors don't always have to sell on proposal.* Sure, there might be folks who got six-figure deals on a proposal, but maybe that didn't suit my process. Would that complicate my cash flow? Certainly. Was it more risky? Yes, unless I had a great relationship with an agent and editor who I could touch base with when I was writing.

But what is more soul-destroying? Beating your head up against a wall forcing yourself to work against type, or accepting your process and nurturing it?

I left Kindling Words having started the project that became my second book, *Purge.* I told my agent I was going to write most of the book before I showed it to her. I turned off the external noise, all the voices that made me feel inadequate and Loser-like. I unsubscribed to that listserv, for example. And I tuned in again to the voice inside. The one that loved writing for the sake of it, not because she was worried about selling another book. The one who had stories inside that were bursting to be told, if only I would listen.

With all the chaos in my life (navigating a contentious divorce, a part-time freelance job, and most importantly, the wellbeing of my two young children), I knew I had to set goals. I also knew that it would be counterproductive to set myself up for any more feelings of failure, so I had to make my goals realistic and achievable. I set a daily goal of 250 words and made a spreadsheet to track my progress. Every night, after I'd read my kids their bedtime stories, I'd climb into my own bed with my laptop and write. Writing every day kept the story alive in my head, and I would meet my daily goal and then some by the time *The Daily Show* came on at 11:00 P.M. It was incredibly satisfying to see my total word count growing toward a book.

Do you want to know the biggest irony? After *Purge* sold and I'd convinced myself I was an author who had to write the whole book in order to sell it, my next two books were sold on proposal in a two-book deal. Go figure.

~Sarah Darer Littman

Fun with Rejection Letters

There is little success where there is little laughter.
~Andrew Carnegie

Seriously? I was rejected by a children's magazine? Those kids can hardly even read yet!

That was my first thought as I deleted yet another rejection e-mail. I was a college junior studying writing, and our professors encouraged us to submit material to different publications. Sometimes the risk and research paid off... and sometimes it resulted in a few lines of rejection from some big-shot editor who didn't appreciate my literary genius.

I remember flipping through my writing textbook, looking for information on rejection. Mostly what I got was: It's going to happen. Brace yourself! Don't get discouraged. Keep going. All of that is great in theory, but not especially practical.

There had to be a solution out there somewhere. So I had a brainstorming session in my dorm room, trying to come up with ideas for how to conquer rejection.

First, I thought about all the brilliant authors whose famous works were turned down. (I think I saw this on an inspirational poster once.) That didn't help, mostly because I realized that for every best-seller that was rejected, so were a dozen poorly written manuscripts. Rejection is no guarantee of greatness. Or, as Carl Sagan put it: "They laughed at Columbus; they laughed at Fulton; they laughed at the Wright Brothers. But they also laughed at Bozo the Clown."

So I tried to persuade myself that I didn't care if my writing got rejected. You know, the psychological approach. "No problem," I'd say, squaring my shoulders as I came back from the mailbox with a fistful of rejection letters. "This is just making me into a better person." That worked for a while... until I realized that I was lying. Then I went right back to being frustrated.

This led me to the realization that there was a foolproof way of not being bothered by rejection: not caring about the things I wrote. I'd just have to send them out with as much apathy as the mass Christmas cards I mailed to all those distant second cousins who probably didn't even read them. If you've ever invested your time and energy in a writing project, you know how well that worked.

One day, as I was staring at the computer screen, experiencing writer's block on a new project, inspiration hit. I figured out a great way to cope with rejection: I wrote the worst rejection letter I could possibly receive. Then I decided that, until I get this letter from an editor, things could be worse. Here's what I wrote.

Dear Incompetent Individual Who Calls Herself a Writer:
Hello.

Unfortunately, the article you sent us does not meet our publication's current needs. And by "unfortunately," I mean that your article was the most unfortunate piece of writing I have ever read. And by "current," I mean that you should never try to submit anything to our magazine ever again or we will assume it contains anthrax and report you to the authorities.

Besides your clear lack of awareness of anything resembling style, voice, grammar, syntax, or any other vocabulary word related to the craft of writing, I will also assume that you fabricated all of your credentials and writing experience, as no editor in his or her right mind would print anything that you wrote, except possibly as satire.

In addition, we would appreciate it if you did not attempt to contact our publication again, or our sister publications, or any company remotely involved in the writing business within a 50-mile radius of us. Please note that we have caller ID, have flagged your e-mail address as spam, and have installed an electric fence around our premises specifically triggered by your DNA code.

Thank you for submitting to our publication, as I enjoy the sound our paper shredder makes when it tears worthless material like yours to bits.

Sincerely,
Really Mean Editor

It's amazing what a little perspective can do for you. Suddenly, those form letters I got in the mail didn't seem half bad.

At first, I just chuckled to myself and tucked the letter away in an obscure file on my laptop. Then I decided to share it with others. Sure, the letter wasn't much of a groundbreaking solution, and I'd never write a self-help book for writers based on it, but maybe it could do a little good.

I showed the letter to some of my writer friends, and they were able to laugh along with me. "Loved it," one said. "It can be frustrating sometimes when you keep getting rejected, no matter how good you think your stuff is."

To which I said, shocked, "You mean you get rejected, too?" People always say that rejection is common and everyone experiences it, but it sure feels like you're the only one. Get published, and the world hears about it on Facebook. Get rejected, and you cry alone.

As it turns out, satirical rejection letters can open up a topic that most writers like to keep hidden. I think I learned more from people's responses to the fake letter than I did from the process of writing it. Some people went for encouragement: "If I keep submitting bits now and then, I'm bound to have more items published than if I just let them collect digital dust."

Another mentioned my letter in a blog post about seven creative ways to deal with rejection. "I have to admit, getting rejection letters hurts," he said. "So, how do we maintain an outwardly professional demeanor while simultaneously satisfying our need for vindication? Simple: we keep our revenge mostly to ourselves. And we have fun with their rejection."

Ironically, in my quest to learn how to deal with rejection, I learned a lot about acceptance. As writers, we need each other. We know about the struggles that go along with the writing life that outsiders just don't understand. And if talking about it together can help us laugh a little, well, maybe there's an upside to rejection after all.

~Amy Green

Making a Killing

You don't get to pick the vic.
~Captain Donald Cragen,
Law & Order: Special Victims Unit

I'm not one hundred percent sure, and there's no way to really prove it, but I think I murdered some literary agents. I'm serious. I think some agents are dead, and it is indirectly my fault. I wasn't at the scene of the crimes. I had no ulterior motive. And I do not know what the murder weapons were, or if it happened in the library, the billiard room, or the conservatory. However, every time someone rings my doorbell, I think it's a homicide detective from *Law & Order* waiting to read me my rights, put me in handcuffs, and take me away to rot in some prison on an island in the middle of the Mediterranean. It is a very unpleasant existence.

It all started right after I finished writing my first manuscript. It had taken four years to get to this point. It might have taken less time had I not had a family, but that's another issue. This isn't about interruptions or responsibilities. This is about murder, and this is about guilt. This is about death.

Upon finishing my book, I anguished day and night over the all-important query letter, missing meals, appointments, and sleep in order to get each sentence focused on selling my project to a complete stranger. I purchased several how-to books and did a good deal of serious research selecting the first lucky recipients of my bestseller. I took tedious notes, looking for key factors in each descriptive profile offered about each of these literary agents. I developed a spreadsheet with a color-coded system, which was posted on the mirror in my bathroom.

"How am I supposed to shave with THAT up there?" my husband asked.

"Carefully," I answered him, knowing I had to get all the details right, knowing that he knows I tend to obsess about things a little too much sometimes.

Besides finding a literary agent with a successful track record, it was extremely important for my book to find an agent with a dry wit and an appreciation for humorous writing. A humorless agent would not do. I needed an agent who enjoyed the process of chuckling and spitting out soda. It had to be an agent who would not be afraid to shed tears from laughing so hard.

Initially, my plan was to send my package out to ten perfectly chosen agents. I neurotically created my list. With the writing part of my book out of the way and the business part of my book about to begin, I promised myself I would not go off the deep end as I tend to do with everything else. I promised I would not drive everyone around me nuts while I found the perfect agent. I would wade carefully in the shallow end. I would wear a floatation device. And I would not get my hair wet.

I found about forty agents who were perfect or near-perfect matches. Phrases like "love discovering new talent" and "I keep my eyes open for a sharp sense of humor" and "somewhat off-centered taste" put an agent right at the top of my list.

Needless to say (but I'll say it anyway), I got the packages together for Literary Agents Number One through Ten, prepared SASEs because I was going to do this via snail mail, printed sample chapters where requested, and got the first set of ten into the mailbox.

I also said some magic words over each package as I opened the mailbox and dropped it in. "Un gobbi gobbi. Walla walla bing bang. Oh please, oh please. Let someone love my book. And let me get rich. My kid gets his license in a year, and I don't want him to be the only kid who doesn't have a car. Thank you. Thank you. Amen." I thought deeply about these magic words and felt they incorporated the best of all known magic words with power... especially the "walla walla" part.

Then I went back to work—writing. I decided to approach the business part of writing as unavoidable. I was upset that I had to stop writing in order to sell my writing. I decided that I would not let it eat up too much of my writing time, even though it did anyway. So I went back to writing morning, noon, and night, in between carpooling, laundry, cooking, allergy shots, phone calls from my mother, and cleaning up after disgusting cats that have no respect for carpeting.

I did mark my calendar for eight weeks. I felt this was a fair amount of time for an agent to open the envelope, fall in love with my book, and write back or call me telling me to send the whole manuscript. This was going to be a piece of devil's food cake.

A week after the mailing ceremony, I received the first reply.

Across the front of the original envelope was stamped, in bold letters, "DECEASED."

I was devastated.

It was a sign.

My first reply, and she croaked. Dead as a doornail. Gone to the great Agent's Convention in the Sky.

I am often told that the problem I have is that I can never see the bright side of things. I saw this as the ultimate rejection. My mental image had her picking up her mail, looking at the envelope, seeing my name, and becoming so violently ill that she keeled over at the mailbox.

My son saw it more optimistically. His attitude was that she took one look at the project and died LAUGHING.

The truth is that she never even opened the envelope. She could have been dead for a year before my package even arrived.

But it was a sign to me—that I had to re-evaluate the magic words and change to a luckier mailbox.

I went back to my color-coded chart and found Literary Agent Number Eleven. I repackaged the whole thing and went to a new mailbox. "Shimmee shimmee cocoa pop. Hula hoop with a cherry on top. Please like my book. Please make me rich. Please. Please. Please. Remember my teenaged son who wants to drive a Porsche. It can be a pre-owned Porsche. Thank you. Amen."

A week later, the envelope was returned unopened.

Across the front of the envelope was stamped, again, in bold letters, "DECEASED." Another agent had died. I killed another agent. Poof! Gone!

I've since received the assortment of replies most writers receive when submitting manuscripts, ranging from the "we're not looking for new clients" to the "I want to sell you my book about how to write a book." I have also received a few requests for the complete manuscript. Only time will tell whether the magic words worked or not.

I'm just going on record as saying I had nothing to do with the deaths of the first two agents, and if there was any Black Magic involved, I was unaware of the consequences. However, if you are a literary agent, and you receive a package with my name and address on it, you might want to let someone else open it. Just to be safe.

~Felice Prager

Who's Arthur?

If you hear a voice within you say "you cannot paint,"
then by all means paint, and that voice will be silenced.
~Vincent van Gogh

I had to do something. With a baby on my hip and another toddling at my feet, I was about to go crazy. I loved being a stay-at-home mom, but I needed something just for me. I decided to retreat to an old passion: writing for children.

Each night after the kids went to bed, I dragged myself downstairs and tried to be creative. I spent hours typing and writing, researching and organizing. One night, it happened. I completed an article and was ready to mail it out. I realized the only way I could be published was to start sending out my material. But there was a problem. I was scared, and so the envelope sat on the desk for another week.

My husband picked up the envelope. "When are you sending this out?" he asked.

"I don't know. When my nerve is up," I said, grabbing it out of his hand. The truth was I wasn't intending to send it out. I couldn't be rejected if it sat on my desk. Rejection had happened too many times before in my life with friends, boyfriends, and jobs; it was just too much for me to handle. How could I spend hours on a story only to have someone reject it?

My stories were my babies. I loved and nurtured each one, and even though it was ready to be sent out, I couldn't let go. After all, what if it came back? The only way it would come back was if an editor sent it back with one of those form letters. I had no idea what those form letters said, but I knew they weren't good. I avoided mailing my submission. Soon, I had a stack of eight envelopes sitting on my desk, waiting to be mailed.

"I'm mailing these," said my husband, taking the pile off my desk one day.

"No!" I shouted. "What if they come back with a rejection slip?"

He turned and looked at me. "They probably will, won't they? It's hard to get published, isn't it?"

I slumped in my chair and sighed. "Go ahead. Mail them. I don't care. They've only been sitting here for three weeks."

Three weeks later, the first envelope was returned. I squeezed it to see how thick it was. My manuscript was returned with a rejection letter. "We are sorry to inform you that your manuscript does not fit our editorial needs at this time...."

Great, I thought, and tossed it to the floor. Over the next month, I got the other seven rejection letters. I wrote other stories and articles, put together more submission packages and sent them out. They all came back rejected! I kept writing, submitting and throwing myself at the mercy of the mailman to give me a good letter from a publisher. He rolled his eyes and smiled as he handed me my mail.

"I'm a stinky writer," I told my friend one day at lunch.

"No, you're not," she said, patting my shoulder. "You're a new writer. One acceptance is all it takes to get your foot in the door. One acceptance, and your self-confidence will return."

When my husband got home from work, I thrust the latest rejection letter in his face. "No one likes what I do!" I cried. "I write and write, day and night, and I still can't get published."

"Hey, you're a poet," he said, chuckling, "and you don't even know it."

I wanted to smack him. I dropped to his feet and moaned, "I can't do this anymore. It's killing me."

"Jenn," he said, picking me up, "you're giving up too easily. No one said it was going to be easy. It's just a letter." He waved the rejection letter in the air and then crumpled it up in his hand. "It's not personal." He tossed it in the trash. He was right.

Nearly a year later, after sending out many submissions, I was depressed. "I give up!" I shouted at the top of my lungs one night. I threw the rejection letters in a pile and stomped on top of them. I knelt down in the pile and put my head in my hands. "I give up," I whispered. Yet as I looked down, something caught my eye. In my fury, I scooped up a picture my daughter had drawn, and slam-dunked it to the floor with the rest of the rejection letters. It was a drawing of her as a mother, and it said, "I want to be just like Mom." She drew a picture of her writing in a book. On the bottom of the paper it said, "You are a good arthur. I love you, Mommy. Emma."

The next morning, after my shower, I wiped the fog from the mirror and looked at myself. Who was that person staring back? Was I seeing the real Jennifer or someone else? I looked hard. Remembering the picture my daughter had drawn, I smiled and said, "I'm not a quitter. I am an author!"

Every morning, this became my ritual. Every morning, I liked what I saw more and more. "I'm not a quitter. I am an author!" I said over and over. My positive attitude didn't stop at the bathroom door. I took it with me wherever I went. I started to believe that I was an author, a good writer, and that I would be published. I saw myself at book signings and reading in classrooms. I imagined school visits and talking at lectures and teaching others how to write for children. What was once a wish became a belief. I believed that my success as a writer was true. Instead of focusing on those rejection letters, I focused on what was to be.

One morning, I looked in the mirror as I did every morning, and said proudly, "I'm not a quitter. I am an author."

"Mommy," said my four-year-old son, Eric, peeking through the crack. "Who's Arthur?" He stuck his head in a little further as if to look for someone else in the bathroom.

I took his hand and stood him in front of me. We both looked in the mirror, a confused look on my son's face. "I'm an author," I said. "I'm not a quitter. I am an author!"

A month later, it came. I carried the envelope back from the mailbox. I didn't know if this was a Dear John rejection letter or a love letter from a publisher. My hands shook. I took out the letter and searched the envelope for my manuscript. It wasn't there. Slowly, I opened the letter, scanning it for the usual negative words. There weren't any. I read it more carefully, "Dear Mrs. Reed, We enjoyed your article about springtime in Japan and would like to publish it in our March issue. We found this to be delightful and well-written, and are pleased you considered us for this piece."

I read it again. "I've been accepted!" I shouted. Then I danced and ran to show my family. "I'm an author!" I said over and over. That one letter ignited the fuel in me I needed to pursue my passion of writing for children. I framed that first acceptance, and it is proudly displayed in my office. One thing is certain: If I did give up, I wouldn't be where I am today. And I wouldn't be called "Author."

~Jennifer Reed

Mommy

From our ancestors come our names, but from our virtues our honors.
~Proverb

I showed my two preschoolers a copy of my newly released novel, *Sirat: Through the Fires of Hell.* "It's my new book," I proudly told them.

"I know it's a new book, Mommy, but where did you get it?" my daughter asked.

"I wrote it. Don't you see my name on the cover?"

Both children stared intently for a moment. "Mommy, I don't see your name."

I pointed out the "By Tamara Wilhite" section. "It's right there."

"But, Mommy, your name is spelled M-O-M-M-Y! I don't see an M on there!"

"What does Daddy call me?"

"Mommy."

I realized then that my kids didn't know my name.

~Tamara Wilhite

Dear John

Ye shall know the truth, and the truth shall make you mad.
~Aldous Huxley

I've been writing and publishing my work for more than fifteen years, and I hope to go on writing and publishing for many more. But there was a time back at the beginning when I reached a crossroads and had to decide just how much I wanted to be a writer.

I got the writing bug very young. I was writing stories back when I was in my teens. I wrote a lot of fiction, stories about people and places and plots that were sure to dazzle and delight my readers, who at the time consisted of my brother and sister and dog. But I learned about how to submit to magazines and journals, and I decided I was going to be that rarest kind of writer: a published one.

It was no trick writing enough stories to send out to the editors and publishers whom I was sure would buy my stuff. I mean, I'd been writing by then for about a year, so surely I knew all there was to know about telling a good story. I had the drive. I had the imagination. I had a typewriter and the addresses of the editors of my favorite magazines. I was ready to go.

Or so I thought. The rejections came fast and hard and endlessly. I would go out to the mailbox every day, pull open the door and peer into the darkness, hoping to find an envelope with the official return address of one of the magazines to which I was submitting my stories. I'd rip open the envelope to find a letter thanking me for the fantastic story accompanied by a fat check. A little later, I'd receive a complimentary copy of the magazine with my story in it that I could add to the ever-growing library of my work. That was my expectation each time I peered into that metal darkness.

What I got instead was a bunch of manila envelopes bearing my own address written in my own handwriting. The envelopes held my returned stories along with a rejection note that often read: "We thank you for your story submission. Unfortunately, it does not meet our present needs."

My heart sank every time I read those mechanically written words. But I was a writer, and I knew that if this editor didn't want that story, then another might. So off it went in the next day's mail, and back I went each day to the mailbox to wait for the letter that would change the course of my life. I lived between moments of pure anticipation and pure misery.

Then one day I opened the mailbox, stuck in my hand, and pulled out a letter with the official return address of a magazine. It was addressed to me, and my hand trembled as I held it. I sat down on the curb, carefully opened the letter, and read what an editor had written to me, feeling myself edge into the world of published writers. It read:

"Dear John, I'm writing to tell you that I'm rejecting another of your stories. In fact, this must be the hundredth story you've sent me. It's time I was truthful with you. Your stories are terrible. I'm not saying you don't have an imagination, because you do, but you tell a story with no idea how to construct a plot, create characters we care about, build suspense or interest. Your persistence indicates youth. I suggest you enroll in a grammar course and learn how to write. Good luck."

Holding that letter, rereading those words, I felt like I'd been crushed. All my dreams evaporated. I balled up the letter, stuffed it in my pocket, and slinked back home. That night, as I lay in bed, I stared at the ball of paper, hating that editor because I knew he was right. I wasn't a writer. I wanted to be published, but I didn't know how to write.

An hour later, I flattened out the note and read it again. He'd told me to learn how to write. He hadn't told me to quit, although that's just what I wanted to do. I never wanted to write another word for the rest of my life. But he'd said I could learn to write, and if I really wanted to be a writer, that's what I needed to do.

The next day, I began to learn how to be a writer. I pored through grammar and writing books, wrote my stories and tore them apart, put them back together and revised them over and over again. I learned that writers work very hard to get their stories to where they might be able to share them with others, and I spent the next few years trying to learn all that I could while I wrote, read, and slowly got better.

Today, I am a published writer, and I've learned that good writing takes hard work. I also learned that reaching your dreams means never quitting. Writing is done step by step, by the numbers, and by going on to the next story, knowing just a little more than you did before. I'm so glad I received the advice from that editor. You wouldn't be reading these words if I hadn't been smart enough to follow it.

~John P. Buentello

What Happened When I Did the Right Thing

A bit of fragrance always clings to the hand that gives roses.
~Chinese Proverb

I had committed to a five-hour book signing at a grocery store to benefit the Juvenile Diabetes Research Foundation (JDRF). I set up my books and posters (one of which said that a portion of the proceeds would be donated to JDRF) at my table right outside the entrance of the grocery store. It was a brisk, but sunny, Sunday morning, and I eagerly awaited what this adventure would bring.

My first prospect—a woman—hurried by, clutching the handle of her purse, her shoulders scrunched up and her head turned away from me. No way to strike up a conversation with her! Another walked quickly by, looking straight ahead, no eye contact. A man glanced quickly my way, but kept on walking. Another man smiled and nodded as he picked up his pace and went into the store. Then, a woman reached into her purse as she approached my table, pulled out a one-dollar bill, placed it on the table and kept on going—not a word spoken.

Not even five minutes had passed, but I very quickly realized that this was probably not the greatest venue for a book signing. People are on a mission when they go to the grocery store, especially on a cold Sunday morning. They want to run in, shop fast and get out. And since the person at the table is probably asking for money, that person is often ignored, or perhaps gets a quick smile as the shopper rushes past.

I wondered what I had been thinking. Five hours of this? I thought about leaving early. But then I decided that I had made a commitment and I had to honor it. I had to do the right thing and stay for the entire shift.

Time passed and then a woman came up to the table and asked me the price of the book. I told her twenty dollars and she pulled out a twenty-dollar bill and gave it to me. Then, she pulled out another twenty-dollar bill and said it was a donation. I suggested she take another book, but she declined. I was so excited—I sold a book! I thanked her profusely for being so generous and for supporting juvenile diabetes research.

She said, "No, no, no. It is I who want to thank you!" Then, she lifted the hem of her shirt a couple of inches to reveal an implanted insulin pump, and explained, "When I was eight years old, I was diagnosed with juvenile diabetes. I am now in my forties, married and have kids. It's because of people like you, and the love you give, and the work that you do, that I am alive and standing here today. So, thank you!" My eyes welled up with tears and I didn't know what to say.

Up until then, this project was a rather abstract way of helping others. I was still amazed that I had written my first book, *Penelope's Cruise*, and that people would actually buy it and read it.

During this moment, I realized that selling just one book could contribute to saving someone's life. I only sold three books that day but that was okay. The money being donated from the sale of those three books could help save someone's life.

When I get stuck or I get rejected as I work on my mission to create products and events that give back, the first being *Penelope's Cruise*, I remember this experience and it inspires me to keep working towards my goal. And by the way, now when I go to the grocery store and there is someone at a table, I almost always take a minute and stop by to see and honor what they are doing!

~Dodie Milardo

70

The Challenge

Whether you think you can or think you can't — you are right.
~Henry Ford

W hat motivates me? The words "You can't!" As a sandy-haired boy growing up in a small town in North Central Texas, my rebellious statements of "Oh, yes I can" or "I'll show you" never failed to place me right in the middle of trouble. Because of my stubbornness, my mouth wrote several checks the seat of my pants had to pay. Now much older and somewhat wiser, my attitude doesn't get me into trouble as often; it just fills out bigger checks. This is how I discovered my desire to write, and in a small way it continues to drive me to succeed.

On a business trip in 2007, I made a point to stop at a small country cemetery near Eugene, Oregon, to pay my respects at the gravesite of a dear friend buried there the previous year. While there, I noticed several old marble gravestones mottled with moss and worn with years of weather. One grave marker had the name Belknap carved into the face of it. This caught my attention as it is my mother's family name. I recorded the information from the stone onto a piece of paper and carried it home. Researching reams of helpful genealogical records, I discovered a connection with a family member who had crossed the Oregon Trail in the 1800s.

The excitement of reading all of this research consumed me. Full of information and facts, I told my wife, "I think this would make a good story. I should write a novel about a family and their struggles to cross the country."

To which my wife replied, "You can't write a book."

"Yes, I can," escaped from my lips.

"You don't know how to write a book," she retorted.

The truth hurts sometimes. However, my pride plugged my ears and out of the whole conversation I only heard two words: "You can't."

Without hesitation, I shot back, "I bet I can have a manuscript ready to send to a publisher before you can."

"I accept that bet," she said.

My mouth wrote a check that I didn't think my wife would really cash.

Immediately, I began searching the Internet and found the Panhandle Professional Writers, a local writers' organization, and joined in order to gain some knowledge of how to write a book. With the help of many other writers, my critique group and, yes, my wife, I have published several works.

Today, as I continue to write and submit works to publishers, I get the dreaded rejection letters. I open them, read them and, no matter what the words might say, all I hear is, "You can't write." I slide the letters carefully into the plain manila folder next to the bright orange notebook with letters and contracts that say, "Oh yes, I can!"

~Rory C. Keel

71

A Writer's Vow

I have written a great many stories and I still don't know how to go about it except to write it and take my chances.
~John Steinbeck

As writers, we may not remember the worst sentence we ever wrote. But we may never forget the worst sentence we ever spoke. It's only three little words, but every writer has at least mumbled them under his breath: "I give up." It's so easy to give up our pursuit of publication because the writing life is so tough. Yet, quitting speaks volumes about what we believe about ourselves—and our work. "I give up" eventually becomes "I gave up," and that is literally a death sentence to any writer's dream of publication.

That said, when should you realistically give up on your first finished novel if it appears to be going nowhere?

Let's say your first novel absorbed three years of your life. You hired a freelance editor who once worked as an editor for a major publisher to make sure it was ready for publication. You expanded it, edited it and revised it again—then again. You proofed it with a recently retired English teacher, tested its impact with multiple readers, and had a few journalists analyze it. You analyzed it, dreamed about it, and virtually memorized it. Finally, you submitted it (or at least the first three chapters) to an agent—make that thirty-five agents. They showed some interest, but they all rejected it in the end. Reasons varied. Now what? Is it time to give up on your novel and move on?

Yes and no. Rejection may never happen that way to you. It happened exactly that way to me. How did I respond? First, I did what every self-respecting first-time novelist would do: I moped around the house for a week. Thankfully, I got tired of that, and then I reread all of my rejection slips. Yes, all thirty-five of them, and I looked for the silver lining. I was encouraged by what I found.

Several agents gave me insightful feedback that I didn't recognize at first blush because I was too emotionally invested in the work. Agents normally wouldn't take the time for this if they didn't believe the writing was sound. Many e-mailed me a few times to stay in touch and offer a few words of encouragement. And, yes, most sent a standard brush-off e-mail. One agent e-mailed me a rejection letter that started with "Dear _____." Even the space to drop in my name was left blank. A close friend affectionately refers to this as my "Dear Blank" rejection letter. Talk about feeling obscure. I felt like the poster boy for Rejected Newbie Novelists.

Yet, I clung to all of the encouragement I could squeeze out of those rejections. Next, I followed the advice of the one agent who cared enough to share detailed advice. I converted the entire novel from first person to third person omniscient narrator, refashioned the first chapter, expanded the story by ten chapters to develop the characters and enhance the transformation of the main character, and layered in multiple subplots to an otherwise linear story.

When I finished, I had a new novel ready for new agents. I sent it out again. How did the agents respond? Rejection. No "Dear Blank" letters, but rejection just the same.

Discouraged, I asked myself just how serious I was about this thing called "the writer's life." It's an easy question when things are running smoothly, but how do I respond when my work hits a brick wall? I realized that rejection, on any level, is a test. It challenges the depth of our convictions, the clarity of our call, and the intensity of our passion to write.

But rejection is nothing if not a great teacher, so I knew I must learn from it. Ironically, this all happened around my wedding anniversary, which, in turn, reminded me of my marriage vows—vows to never give up on my marriage despite the hurdles we would face. This got me thinking about creating a "writer's vow." Why not vow to never give up on my writing despite the devastating disappointments and setbacks of the writing life? So I sat down and vowed I would always work through rejection by writing through it. This was a breakthrough for me. I realized my status as a writer should not be measured only by the fruit of my labor, but by the labor itself. After all, with writing, the process is the end. This vow will keep me writing. And writing is the best way to get better.

Next, I wrote to the freelance editor who helped me reshape my book for advice. Her words were golden!

"It's unusual to write just one book and have it sell," she said. "You often need to get the hang of crafting a novel by writing several before you write anything that nears being publishable."

Then came the nugget that still rings in my ears.

"Most authors make the mistake of clinging too tightly to their first novel without continuing to write more. Publishers will want to see that you have a certain velocity to your writing and can consistently come up with plot concepts and craft them into manuscripts before they decide to invest in your first novel."

Have I made the mistake of clinging too tightly to my first novel? Have you? We must develop velocity to our writing.

So, what will I do with my first novel now? Give up? (There's that dreaded sentence again.) No, but I will give it a rest. In the meantime, I will write one or two more, knowing that my second or third novel may actually be the first one published. But that won't happen unless I fulfill my writer's vow.

Someday, when I have a novel published, I will return to my very first novel to see if it's as worthy of publication as my second book—or if it's worthy of a rejection letter addressed to "Dear Blank."

~James C. Magruder

inspiration
for
Writers

Finding Inspiration

You can't wait for inspiration. You have to go after it with a club.

~Jack London

The Story Behind "Second Watch"

We come, not to mourn our dead soldiers, but to praise them.
~Francis A. Walker

Sometimes it takes a lifetime to tell a story. J.P. Beaumont and I have been together as character and author for thirty years. A year ago at Thanksgiving, one of my sons said to me, "J.P. is getting a little long-in-the-tooth. Have you ever thought of writing a Beaumont prequel?" At that point I hadn't, but this summer when it came time to sit down and write Beaumont #21, the idea of doing a prequel was the only one that came to mind.

In order to write about Beau's life before that first book, I had to reread *Until Proven Guilty*, a book I wrote in 1982. The Beau books are all written in the first person through a middle-aged male homicide detective's point of view. In that story he mentions having served in the military in Vietnam. Just seeing the word in print sent my mind wandering down a long trail of memories.

I attended Bisbee High School in Bisbee, Arizona. A year ahead of me was a boy named Doug Davis. He was handsome, smart, and an outstanding athlete. He graduated as valedictorian of his class, went to West Point, attended Ranger school, and then went to Vietnam where he died on August 2, 1966, a few weeks before his twenty-third birthday.

When they brought Doug's body home to Bisbee to bury, I didn't attend the funeral because I didn't know about it until after it happened. I've always felt guilty about not being there. In the early 1980s when a replica of the Vietnam War Memorial came to Seattle, I took my kids to see it. While there, Doug's was the only name we looked up. Years later on a book tour in Washington, D.C., I had my escort take me to visit the real wall. Of the 58,000 names etched in black granite, Doug's was the only one I touched.

From second grade on, I wanted to be a writer. By the mid-1980s, my dream had come true; I was a published author. The Beaumont books are mostly set in Seattle; the ones featuring Joanna Brady are set in Bisbee. In the first of the Joanna books, *Desert Heat*, her murdered husband is buried in Bisbee's Evergreen Cemetery.

I was living in Seattle when that book was published. Diagonally across the country, a woman living in Florida, Bonnie Abney, picked up *Desert Heat* and read it. When she got to the funeral scene, her reading came to a dead stop. Doug Davis was buried in the "real" Evergreen Cemetery, and in 1966 he and Bonnie had been engaged to be married. For months afterwards, Bonnie carried that tattered paperback in her purse because she sensed there had to be some connection between the author of *Desert Heat* and Doug Davis.

Eventually, through the intervention of Bonnie's sister in Seattle, Bonnie and I met and became friends. This past summer, while reading about Beau's fictional tour of duty in Vietnam, I remembered Doug Davis. In a moment of divine inspiration, it occurred to me that perhaps I could write a book in which fictional J.P. Beaumont could cross paths with a real Doug Davis.

I immediately sent Bonnie an e-mail asking what she thought of the idea. The next day she signed on for the ride. My upcoming book, *Second Watch*, is the result of months of collaboration.

Over the next days and weeks Bonnie shared her remembrances of that time, including an essay about her first heartbreaking trip to Bisbee for Doug's funeral. Although his family was unfailingly kind to her, at the funeral, the flag from Doug's casket went to his mother—as it should have. His West Point sword went to Doug's younger brother,

Blaine, and after Blaine's death, as far as Bonnie knew, the sword was lost. She was left with her memories, Doug's medals, his letters, and a single precious photograph of the two of them together.

To forward the writing project, she sent along the letters of condolence that had come to her from Doug's commanding officer as well as from his fellow officers and West Point graduates. Gradually a new picture began to form in my mind, not one of the boy I had once known in high school but of the remarkable young man he became.

In *Second Watch* we meet Beaumont as a sixty-something curmudgeonly sort of fellow with a somewhat younger wife and a pair of knees badly in need of repair. We also see him as a young police officer at Seattle P.D., first on Patrol and later as a newbie detective in Homicide. In addition, we encounter him earlier still, in the last few days of July of 1966 when he first arrives in the Pleiku Highlands in Vietnam where Doug Davis is his platoon leader.

There are only a few fleeting glimpses of Doug Davis in the book, and yet I believe they capture the essential nature of that outstanding young man—his sense of humor; his love of reading and poker playing; his occasional use of salty language; his kindness. And it is through an act of kindness on Doug's part rather than heroism that J.P. Beaumont lives to tell the tale.

As it turns out, Beau's guilt is similar to mine for not attending Doug's funeral. In the book, Beau is charged with doing what he didn't do long ago when he first came home from Vietnam. As a returning soldier, he made no effort to track down Bonnie Abney and comfort her in her terrible loss. Now, almost fifty years later, finding her and comforting her becomes his mission. The scenes in which he does that and the manner in which that mission is accomplished are scenes that have moved my readers to tears, and writing those words moved me to tears, as well.

I write murder mysteries. My regular fans can be assured, there is a murder in this book—several in fact—and Beaumont does solve them, but as far as I'm concerned, Doug Davis's story is the very heart of the book.

Second Watch is a tale for our time and for our generation. When

Bonnie went to meet the freight train that brought Doug's casket home, she parked next to a waiting hearse on a deserted railroad siding somewhere between Bisbee and Benson. The train stopped outside of town because the authorities feared that delivering caskets of returning dead soldiers to train depots in town might attract protestors, and we all know there were plenty of those. Just thinking about that lonely desert homecoming breaks my heart, not just for Bonnie, but for all of us.

There are 58,000 names etched on that wall in Washington. That means there are 58,000 stories just like this one—the untold stories of countless guys, the unsung heroes of Vietnam, who went away to war and never came home. It's also the stories of countless wives, sweethearts, parents, and children—the ones who were left behind to live out their lives with someone they loved gone forever.

Then there are the guys who did come home—hundreds of thousands of them. They're the ones who didn't die, but who lost their youth, their health, and often their way by serving our country in a misguided war. They came home from surviving that terrible carnage, not to be honored or thanked for their service but to be spit upon, taunted, and despised. The vast majority of those guys quietly picked up the pieces of their shattered lives and went to work, never speaking about what they had seen and endured.

That's something I've learned while writing this book. It's no surprise that in the twenty books between *Until Proven Guilty* and now, J.P. Beaumont never said another word about serving in Vietnam, not to me and not to anyone else, either. Like so many others, he came home from the war, hid his well-deserved medal away, and never mentioned it again.

These days, whenever I'm traveling and encounter uniformed soldiers in airports, I try to speak to them, shake their hands, and thank them for their service.

I'm hoping that by telling Doug and Bonnie's story in *Second Watch*, due to be published September 10, 2013, that I will be able to offer that same kind of thank you to an earlier generation of soldiers and to their loved ones as well—a thanks they richly deserved and never received.

In writing this book I believe I've finally found what I've been searching for all along—from 1966 until now—forgiveness for missing Doug Davis's funeral. He was an unsung hero, and it is my honor to tell his story to the world.

~J.A. Jance

Something in Common

What the daughter does, the mother did.
~Jewish Proverb

A s I was flying home from Romania, my newly adopted daughter Andrea resting comfortably on my lap, I thought about all the things I would not pass onto her genetically. I wondered if someday we would have anything in common. I shed any expectation I might have for her on that flight to America. Oh sure, I wanted her to be healthy and happy, but I did not want to mold her into my image, or force her to live up to the monumental expectations of society. I wanted her to simply be, to grow, learn and develop on her own accord. However, once we were home, it became evident that Andrea needed a lot of medical help to grow, learn and develop.

Many wonderful doctors and therapists helped Andrea navigate through life, and she began to thrive after a few months. Andrea's talents began to emerge with a vengeance. The first gift that I noticed was her ability to smile and be friendly to those around her. She mastered her socialization skills early. Later, I recognized her ability to sing, act and entertain. She was blossoming before my eyes, and sometimes I daydreamed about who she would grow up to be.

Before she entered kindergarten, she underwent a myriad of tests to ascertain if she was emotionally and physically ready for school. When the speech therapist called me, I was alarmed.

"Andrea is a lovely child," Colleen, the therapist, began. "I don't want you to be concerned. Andrea's speech is on target."

"Oh, thank goodness," I stammered, feeling instantly relieved.

"I feel compelled to tell you something you might not know about your daughter."

"Oh?"

"Andrea is quite the storyteller," she said cheerfully. "We don't usually see children her age with the ability to tell such elaborate stories."

"Really?"

"Yes. Typically, I show the children a picture of an object and hope they can identify it using a partial or complete sentence," she said, pausing slightly. "I showed Andrea a picture of a bird. She adjusted her glasses, and then slapped her forehead when she saw it and said, 'It's a mockingbird, of course. It goes tweet, tweet all night long, perched in a cherry tree outside my mother's bedroom window, and it keeps her awake every single night. And that's not all. My mother wants to shoot it, but she knows she can't do that because it's against the law and we don't have a gun!'"

"Oh, my," I said sheepishly. "Andrea is a chatty and gregarious girl."

"In this case, it's a very good thing," Colleen said.

When I hung up the phone, I smiled, believing Andrea and I had something wonderful in common: We were both storytellers.

As she grew up, I enjoyed reading her essays, which brought rave reviews from her teachers. One day, Andrea showed me a story she had written. "I was asked to write something about bullying," she said softly. "Would you read it and give me your opinion?"

While she made hot cocoa to go with her chocolate-chip cookies, I read the essay. When I had finished her story, I could barely speak. My mouth hung open a few minutes before my brain could form the message I wanted to deliver. "This essay is phenomenal! You are a remarkable writer."

Andrea smiled humbly. "Thank you."

"Andrea, you need to enter this essay in a writing contest," I said, full of encouragement. "I know the perfect one." I shuffled through the papers that cluttered my desk. "I just know you are going to win."

"Really?" she squealed with excitement.

"Yes," I said matter-of-factly, "and the prize is fifty dollars!"

Andrea submitted the story and waited patiently for an answer, which seemed to take forever to arrive. We were excited beyond words the day the contest results were in. I could see the disappointment on her face as she read the letter. I felt responsible for her grief, and I blamed myself for setting her up for failure. I couldn't understand how her story didn't even rank an "honorable mention." I set her rejection letter aside and mulled it over a few days. Then an idea came to me.

I slid my arms around her tiny frame and reminded her how good her story was. "Do you know what I think you should do?" I asked.

"Try again?" she said awkwardly.

"Sort of," I began. "As a freelance writer, I get rejection letters all the time, but I do not take them personally. Neither should you." I sighed deeply as I wondered if I was making matters worse. "Trust me," I said. "You don't have anything to lose, but so much to gain by sending it out again." I swallowed hard. "Publishing this story could be the beginning of a wonderful career, but you don't know until you try."

Her jaw dropped open. "Are you kidding?"

"I think you should send it to Chicken Soup for the Soul. They are seeking stories for a new book dedicated to middle-school students. That's the perfect venue for your story." I powered on my computer and showed Andrea how to submit a story online. "Now, we wait."

The day her congratulations letter arrived, I ran down the street to meet her at the bus stop. I was waving the letter wildly, shrieking, "Andrea, you did it!"

She climbed off the bus wearing a quizzical grin. "Did what?"

"Chicken Soup for the Soul wants your story!" I yelled as I hugged her. She dropped her backpack, and together we jumped up and down like we had just won the lottery. "The reason you didn't win that contest is because your story belonged in a *Chicken Soup for the Soul* book." As I walked home from the bus stop embracing my fifteen-year-old daughter, my thoughts drifted to the day I brought her home, wondering who she would grow up to be. I felt dismayed that I couldn't pass along something of mine to her genetically, but God made sure it happened anyway. My little storyteller became quite the writer, just like me.

~Barbara S. Canale

74

It's a Poem

Alas for those that never sing,
But die with all their music in them.
~Oliver Wendell Holmes

"Ray, you seem to be having a difficult time finishing your novel," observed my wife. "You haven't written a word in a week."

"I can't seem to find the proper ending. I want my readers to enjoy the final chapter."

Later, as I stared at my computer, the phone rang. "I'll get it," Ellie said. She hung up and said, "It's hospice. We've got a new patient to see."

I turned off the computer. "Let's go then."

"What about your writing?"

"I'll work on it later."

Upon arriving at Bay Nursing Home, we asked for Harriet Gardner's room number. "I'll go and see Harriet while you call on our other three residents," I told my wife.

I entered Harriet's room and found a tiny, white-haired woman in her late eighties, sitting in a wheelchair and staring out the window. Her bent arthritic hands were folded in her lap.

"Good morning, Harriet. I'm Ray from Suncoast Hospice. They asked my wife and me to start visiting you if that's okay."

Quietly, she said, "Yes."

I spent the next fifteen minutes talking about the weather. "It's nice outside. Would you like me to take you outside to the patio?"

"Not really."

At this point, I realized it would take more than one visit to break the ice with this lady. "I'll say goodbye then. The next time I come, I'll bring my wife to meet you."

Upon our second and third visits, Harriet did not warm up much, neither to my wife nor me.

The next time, I took in a stack of magazines for her to read. She looked briefly through them. "Hard for me to turn the pages with my crippled fingers."

"I noticed that you seem to have a problem with your fingers so I brought you a rubber ball to exercise them."

Cringing, she forced herself to squeeze it. "That hurts a bit, but maybe it will help me to hold a fork better."

Then, out of the blue, she looked at me and asked, "What do you do to keep busy all day?"

"I write in my spare time. Right now, I'm trying to finish my first novel. I've been having writer's block for the past couple of weeks. Just can't seem to find the right ending for it."

She looked sadly down at her bent fingers. "I used to have beautiful penmanship when I was younger. Also, I used to write poetry."

"Do you have any of it handy that I could read?"

"No. After my husband died, I moved in with my sister. We had a fire in her house, and all my writings were lost."

With that, I excused myself and went to the office to get a pen and a pad of paper. I headed back to Harriet's room. "Look what I have for you." I handed her the two items. "Maybe you can try writing me a poem. I'll be back in a few days."

She picked up the pen in her gnarled fingers and gripped it between her fingers and thumb. "I'll try. And you finish your story."

"It's a deal," I said as I left.

All the way home, my mind was racing as I thought of the great effort that Harriet had to put forth just to hold the pen in her hand.

If she could write, then so could I. All of a sudden, the ending to my novel became clear to me.

It was three in the morning when my wife came into the study and found me still writing. "Don't you think it's time you came to bed, dear?"

I threw down my pen. "Finished. Please read the last chapter of my book."

She sat down and read it. Smiling, she said, "Someone gave you inspiration."

The next day, I headed to the nursing home, anxious to share my great success with Harriet. The door to Harriet's room was closed. As I started to knock, the Director of Nursing came out of the room. "If you're here to see Harriet, you're too late. She passed away early this morning."

I stood there, stunned.

"You're Mr. Weaver, aren't you? I saw an envelope on her night-stand addressed to you. You're welcome to go inside and say goodbye to Harriet before the funeral home comes for her."

Harriet was lying peacefully in her bed, her hands folded over her chest. Her face was relaxed, almost with a smile, and she appeared to be at peace.

I sat down and said a brief prayer for her. Before I left, I opened the envelope she had left for me. Inside was a sheet of paper covered with child-like writing. Apparently, it had taken Harriet a lot of time and effort to write her poem. It was about the end of life and how she was bravely awaiting it. The poem, "What Is God's Plan for Me?" moved me to tears, and I knew I would cherish it forever.

Two weeks later, my editor and publisher read my novel. "I just love it," she said, "especially the ending." She designed a beautiful cover, and it was soon in print.

A couple of months later, one of my friends, Wayne, who was also a writer, approached me with a flyer in his hand. "The local library where I teach seminars is having a poetry contest. Maybe you would like to enter it or know someone who would."

When I told my wife about the contest, she suggested, "Why don't you submit Harriet's poem?"

Two months later, I had a book signing at the local library. As I entered the building, the director approached me. "Ray, I just talked to Wayne, and he said you submitted a poem to our recent poetry contest for a friend of yours—Harriet Gardner."

"That's right."

"Well, I must contact her. She won third place in the contest, and I wanted to present her with a ribbon and a plaque."

"Harriet passed away after she wrote it, but I would be glad to accept them on her behalf and take them to the nursing home where she resided. They can hang them there in her honor."

After I gave a reading from my novel in front of the crowd in the library annex, I conducted a question-and-answer period.

One woman stood up. "Where did you get the inspiration for the beautiful ending of your novel?"

I held up Harriet's ribbon and plaque. "It came from a dear friend, someone who will inspire me to write until my dying day."

~Raymond P. Weaver

75

Ask, Listen, Write

The happiest moments of my life have been the few
which I have passed at home in the bosom of my family.
~Thomas Jefferson

Who inspired me to write? As I pondered this question, I found myself back in the eighth grade. A few years before, the miniseries *Roots* debuted on television. We had a very progressive English teacher named Mrs. Mouha, who used this series to inspire us to write our own family stories. The project spanned most of the year and required us to interview our parents and grandparents, listen to their stories, and then write about them in essay form. I loved that project! I remember sitting wide-eyed and eager around my Grandma Iachini's dining-room table with my pencil poised, as she and my aunts and uncles told stories of the "old days."

"Remember the time Gibbi set the basement on fire?" someone said. Laughter erupted as the story unfolded, each person interjecting their own memory until one story soon flowed into another and another. "And you know how your dad got that bald spot on the top of his head," my Uncle Richard said to me with a broad smile. "He thought it would be funny to carry a pot full of hot pasta into dinner on top of his head!"

"That explains mine," my dad yelled back. "How'd you get yours?"

Anybody with a large family knows what I'm talking about. I

grew up the youngest of five children, with twenty-two first cousins and thirty-plus second and third cousins who we saw regularly. Think *My Big Fat Greek Wedding*, only Italian-Irish Catholics. Throw in a bone disease that collectively has the fracture count in our immediate family at around 475 and a sister who is a stand-up comedienne, and you can see where humor, sadness, and life mix to make for great stories. Sibling antics, holiday memories, nuns praying for strength and patience till a certain family of children leave their tutelage... nothing too extraordinary, but in my family full of extended relatives, these stories abound and remain the sustenance of every Sunday and holiday dinner conversation.

"I remember da time..." my grandma stated slowly in her thick Italian accent, "there was a-no Christmas. No money... and a-no presents under da tree." The voices in the room quieted, and all eyes focused on her as she spoke. "Poppa... he finda little Victor under da tree just a sobbing an-a crying. 'Why did Santy Claus forget us?' I see your Poppa cry for da first time dat night," she said to her now grown children as she traced the rim of her china coffee cup with her finger. She was staring down at the table, her mind wandering in the past, her eyes showing a renewed sadness. "He say to me... 'Next year, Amelia... next year my kids a gonna have a Christmas if I hava to robba da store to make it a-happen!' He worked double shifts to make-a sure there was presents unda da tree for you kids," she stated matter-of-factly as she pointed her finger in their direction before tapping it on the starched white tablecloth. "Every year... every year... he was a gooda Poppa."

To me, listening to those stories was better than any television show I could recall. I wrote them down as well as a child of thirteen could. It was the first time that homework was fun, and I got an A on that project. When I graduated from eighth grade that spring, I was completely surprised to win the English award for having the highest grade in my class. I asked Mrs. Mouha later if it was a mistake. I knew I was a good student, but there were always students who were better. She said it was not a mistake, and then she told me that I was a "gifted writer." She told me to keep writing even if it was just for me. She inspired me, and I started journaling from that point forward.

In 1991, I gave birth to twin daughters prematurely. They were born at twenty-four weeks' gestation and weighed one pound, three ounces each. Hayley, my firstborn, lived for twenty-one days and nine hours before succumbing to pneumonia. Today, her surviving sister, Hanna, is a healthy, thriving young woman. Holding Hayley after she passed away moved me to write a story called "Angel in my Arms." I entered it into a local writing contest. Even though it didn't win, my family loved the story, and that was the only gold star I needed.

People used to ask me how I survived the death of my child. Writing that story was part of the answer. The other part of my healing came from an unconventional source. After Hayley's death, a co-worker gave me a copy of the original *Chicken Soup for the Soul*. "There's nothing I can say to you at a time like this," she said as she quietly laid the book on my desk, "but maybe this will help." A box of tissues later, I had read the book cover to cover, and I thought to myself, "If these people can overcome the challenges they've faced in their life, I can, too."

At the end of the book, the authors asked readers to share their own stories of inspiration. Immediately, my sister Debbie came to mind, and I sat down and wrote my second short story, "Imprints." Debbie had been confined to a wheelchair most of her life, but through sheer will and determination, she taught herself to walk again before she graduated high school. I submitted my story to Chicken Soup for the Soul and heard nothing for several years. About six months into that period, I remember thinking, "Well, I guess that's that… My writing must suck." However, I was not discouraged, and I continued to write for myself and my children through journaling.

One day, two years after I submitted my story, I got a call from D'ette Corona telling me they wanted to publish "Imprints" in *Chicken Soup for the Sister's Soul*. "Are you serious?" I shouted into the phone.

"Yes, we loved your story," she said with a laugh after her hearing returned. "And if you have any others, please send them in. We like your style. You have a gift for storytelling."

I screamed again into the receiver, but they still published my story, and six more after that! Since then, I've had my stories printed in other anthologies and some magazines. I've tried writing fiction, but to me, my best writing comes from the stories I see around me every day... the true stories of my family and friends.

So when you ask who inspires me to write, my answer is "everyone." Everyone has a story to tell; you just have to ask, listen, and then write.

~Jodi Iachini Severson

76

Accountability Partner

Authors like cats because they are such quiet, lovable, wise creatures,
and cats like authors for the same reasons.
~Robertson Davies

Nothing motivates a writer like an accountability partner. Right now, mine sits on my desk two feet from my elbow. From her spot, she has a lovely view out my office window to woods across the street. The sun gleams on her black fur, and I pause in my writing to admire her.

"Do you have any idea how beautiful you are?" I ask Naomi.

She blinks her round yellow eyes. "Meow," she says, which might mean "certainly," but more likely, "Get back to your writing." Or maybe, "Finish that story so you can read it to me."

Naomi, as foreman of our morning routine, is a harsh taskmaster. When the first summer light slips through the vertical blinds of the bedroom, she pads up my chest and presses her nose to mine. Never mind what time I got to bed the night before. "Mrrow."

I open one eye. I've been known, after a particularly late night, to tell her, "Not now, Naomi."

She answers by leaping off the bed and playing with her toys in a shoebox nearby for two or three minutes, jangling bells and scratching cardboard boxes. Then she springs back up. "Rrrrrrrow," she insists in her raspy voice.

I snake one hand out from under the covers, and stroke her

cheeks and the length of her back. This is my miracle kitty, seventeen years old and an eighteen-month cancer survivor. I can't possibly be cross with her. "Okay," I murmur, slip out of bed and tie on my robe.

"Meow, meow, meow." Naomi runs down the hall to stand outside my office door.

"Can I brush my teeth first?"

"Rrrrrow." Evidently not. Naomi stalks through the door and over to my desk. She's a drill sergeant disguised as a seven-pound feline. She's also right. The house will be quiet for another hour or two before my retired husband gets up. It's a perfect time to work on the story circling in my head.

I sit at my computer, and she leaps up to the water and food bowls I've put to my right. With a different accountability partner, one might offer coffee and donuts. My gift to her is an unlimited supply of kibbles and fresh water.

I'm tempted to start with e-mails. You know, warm up the brain. She glances at my computer. Can she actually see my inbox? She paces the length of my desk. "Meow, meow," she scolds in her imitation Siamese cat voice.

"You're a slave driver, you know." I stroke her silky cheeks. She's such a smart cat. I can do e-mails along with laundry when my husband is up. He'll be offering to make oatmeal, wanting to review plans for the day, suggesting a walk or a hike. Now is my opportunity for uninterrupted writing time.

When I am steadily working, Naomi jumps from the desk and takes up residence on the heater grate. Understandable. It's one of those damp, gray mornings in Portland. I've worked fifteen minutes when she gets up, arches her back in a cat pose perfect for a yoga calendar, and settles into the empty file-folder box near my chair. A few weeks earlier, I'd used the last of the folders and set aside the box for recycling. Naomi stepped delicately into it and snuggled down. The box is hers now. She especially favors it for morning naps.

She turns her head lazily toward me. "Meow," she says. I think she means, "Isn't this nice? You working away, me keeping you on track?"

It is nice. The ideas come easily, and my fingers dance on the keyboard for an hour. Then a story that started out charming turns into drivel. I'm not sure what to do next. Rethink the plot? Add a bit of spicy dialogue? "This is so not working," I tell Naomi, stretching my arms in front of me, fingers curled together.

She lifts her head to look at me. I see no sympathy in her eyes.

"I need a break," I tell her and head into the kitchen. Maybe if I spend a few minutes with the newspaper and a cup of tea, ideas will come to me.

As quickly as I'm out of my chair, Naomi is out of her box. She scolds me with a haughty flick of her tail and walks from the room. The word "quitter" reverberates in the air.

"I'm only going to take five minutes," I call over my shoulder as I retrieve the newspaper. I plug in the electric teakettle, spread the newspaper on the dining-room table, and open it to the crossword puzzle. Naomi sits alert on a chair beside me. "Every writer should do crossword puzzles," I explain to her. "Keeps the mind sharp."

"Rrrrrr." She flattens her ears.

"What a commando." I fill in a couple of words that quickly come to mind, then abruptly hit a snag. I look at Naomi. "8 across, 'carries things too far.' What do you think? 'Provokes'? That isn't quite right. 'Exaggerates'? Too many letters. 'Overdo'?"

"Mrrrow." She isn't helpful.

"I'm going with 'overdo.'" As I'm penciling in the word, Naomi leaps on the table and walks onto the paper, crinkling it with every step. She sits squarely on the crossword puzzle and lifts one hind leg to begin her morning ablutions.

"I had three more minutes to relax." There's a slight whine in my voice.

She lifts her other hind leg and continues to clean herself.

I think of the advice a writing teacher gave me in a workshop recently. "When you hit an obstacle, stay with it. The bigger the obstacle, the greater the triumph. Stay with it, and you'll get a major breakthrough."

He didn't mean a blank in a crossword puzzle. He meant that

issue I'm having with my story. "Okay, sweetie. You win." I sigh and chuck Naomi under her chin, take my cup of tea, and return to my office and my story. If Naomi can fight cancer, I can fight writer's block.

She follows me in and jumps on my desk with a throaty whir. "This is where we belong, isn't it?" she seems to say.

"Here's to a major breakthrough. And to the world's best accountability partner." I lift my teacup to her and catch her eye.

She stretches out a paw, softly touches my forearm, and purrs her agreement.

~Samantha Ducloux Waltz

Some People Do This for a Living

People tend to forget that the word "history" contains the word "story."
~Ken Burns

I f I told you that a life-changing revelation hit me as I rested my hand on the gate of a white picket fence, you'd probably think of small-town true love, right? No such thing.

I stood before a turn-of-the-century beach cottage, its shingled walls stained red to match the low roof and brick chimney. The cottage housed the local historical society of a Southern California community. The fence separated it from a public park, and the day was warm and sunny. I was a student at UCLA, led to this place by a history class assignment.

Correction: historiography class.

All history majors at UCLA were required to take a historiography seminar. Basically, the small classes made us think about how history got written. Who got to preserve their memories? What got forgotten? Important questions, if you like history.

I loved history. I also loved writing, and had a couple of unsold novels in my dresser drawer. In college, I learned that this love almost guaranteed me good grades, because most students hate writing and consequently avoid it. Their grades suffer for that.

Our assignment for this historiography class had been to interview an older person and write a paper about something in the interview we found interesting. I talked to Cathy, a friend of my late mother's, for an hour while the tape recorder caught every word.

Cathy told me a funny story about sneaking out to a gambling ship when she was in high school. This would have been in the 1930s, and the ship was anchored three miles from shore. Cathy and her friends paid a quarter to ride out in a water taxi.

To look older, Cathy wore a hat with a veil. She didn't gamble or order a drink. She and her friends strolled by the crowded roulette wheels and poker tables, hoping to see movie stars, or maybe gangsters. They didn't—at least, none that they recognized. Giggly but disappointed, they went home.

Great, my professor said. Now expand on your anecdote. Research it. Try to find other eyewitnesses. This will be your final paper for the class.

Although several gambling ships had anchored around Southern California in the 1930s, the classiest ship—the one Cathy visited—was the Rex. I threw myself into old newspapers and begged everyone I knew to ask grandparents and octogenarian friends about that ship.

I met a man who used to swim in the Ink Well—the only section of Santa Monica Beach open to African Americans—and he remembered seeing the lights of the Rex on the horizon. "The big boys used to dare each other to swim out there and try to get on board," he said. "I think some of them swam that far, but they never got on the ship. The men would lean over the rail and yell, 'Go 'way, you!'"

I talked to old musicians and dancers. I dug up pictures and memorabilia. I even read about the gambling ships in a Raymond Chandler mystery.

And I learned the story of how a young, gung-ho attorney general named Earl Warren (yup, the Supreme Court Chief Justice) shut down the Rex in a headline-grabbing standoff that Los Angeles papers called "The Battle of Santa Monica Bay."

All that brought me to that white picket fence. A docent of the historical society remembered the Rex and had some old pictures, and we had an appointment to talk.

I put my hand on the gate and looked up at the pretty cottage, with its low, sloping roof and brick chimney. My recorder was in one pocket, my camera in another. Five pens lined the bottom of my purse, and a notebook was in my hand. The sun was shining, life couldn't be better, and it suddenly occurred to me that some people do this for a living.

Every day.

They get paid to talk to people.

They get paid to write.

Have I mentioned that I was no young girl, but a woman in my late forties with a grown daughter? That I worked for a federal agency and had a great benefits package? That, although I loved history, I had no idea what I was going to do with a degree in the field?

Some people do THIS for a living!

That was it. That idea changed my life.

My first paid article is still online, all about the advantages of being an older student in college. The second? "The Battle of Santa Monica Bay," which appeared in *American History* magazine a year or two later.

After graduating, I never went back to my government job. I've written for blogs, encyclopedias, textbooks, magazines, and greeting card companies. I've self-published and have more books in me.

Income can be uncertain. The benefits package for a writer includes passion, not insurance.

But I love my life. I love it like I could never love the eight hours spent at an office working for someone else. I love writing.

Some people do this for a living. You can recognize them by the great big grins on their faces.

~Vickey Kall

I Knew I Could Do It

If there is a book that you want to read, but it hasn't been written yet,
you must be the one to write it.
~Toni Morrison

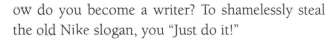

How do you become a writer? To shamelessly steal the old Nike slogan, you "Just do it!"

First of all, to call myself "a writer" is definitely stretching the definition of a glorious occupation. But for those of us who have actually opened that envelope containing our first published story, article, or even book, we can't help but feel privileged to join the ranks of writers, no matter on how small a scale.

As a teacher of literature and a librarian, I have always had an immense respect for authors. But I had always placed them on another plane, a rarified breed somewhat removed from ordinary, everyday humanity. All that changed back in 1995 when, based on a stellar *New York Times* review, my husband and I decided to see the movie *Babe*. We both had a long-standing respect for animals and had been semi-vegetarians for years. But that singularly outstanding movie tipped us into the category of confirmed non-meat-eaters and advocates for the humane treatment of farm animals. And, even more remarkably, it me made contemplate a whole new avocation.

My husband was a fifth-grade teacher. After being stunned by the power of the *Babe* storyline, he couldn't wait to order a classroom set of *Babe: The Gallant Pig* (by Dick King-Smith), the novel on which the movie was based, and start sharing it with his students. He had frequently used an excellent series of multi-disciplinary curriculum guides for children's novels and was hoping that *Babe* would be among the available titles. When he discovered that it was not, I suggested, almost without thinking and with uncharacteristic boldness: "Why don't we call the curriculum guide company and tell them that we would like to write a guide?"

My never-at-a-loss-for-words husband was speechless.

"Think about it," I continued. "We're both experienced teachers with specialties in language arts. I think our ideas are as good as anyone else's. And since we've both fallen in love with this novel, who better to entice students to fall in love with it, too?"

Now, I've never been an overly confident person. I'm basically introverted with many doubts about my abilities. But here's the thing: I had something that I wanted to say, a message that I considered important, and I knew that the way I could most effectively convey that message to the greatest number of children—children whose values were still being shaped—was by writing it.

And so bright and early the following morning, we called the New York curriculum guide company and presented our case to the editor. A couple of things were in our favor: The movie was a runaway hit at the box office. The editor had already received other inquiries about the availability of a guide. And our enthusiasm must have been palpable, even across the 900 miles of intervening phone lines.

So the editor gave us forty-eight hours to submit an Introduction and Chapter 1. Did I tell you that I work well under pressure? Less than two days later, my husband and I faxed our work to New York—and waited.

Before the end of that day's office hours, we received a phone call: "I'm putting a contract in the mail. But it must be completed and submitted in four weeks, so we can include it in our upcoming catalog."

We were elated—but four weeks? Is wasn't as though my husband and I could pack up and head for a remote cabin in the mountains to spend all of our time writing. We both had demanding full-time jobs! But the desire to call one's self an author is a powerful motivator. The vision of our names listed jointly in the following year's *Books in Print*, which occupied a place of honor in every library we'd ever entered, spurred us on.

I'll spare you the agonizing details, but we finished all eleven chapters on schedule. A few months later, opening that special-delivery envelope containing our authors' copies made it all worthwhile.

That was the start. After that, I knew I could do it. Through subsequent rejections and acceptances and still more rejections, I still know that I can do it. Early in my writing "career," I traveled to the University of Wisconsin to hear award-winning author Lois Lowry speak to aspiring authors. She told us one thing I'll always remember: "To be a writer, all you need is an envelope and a postage stamp." Fast forward fifteen years, and it's even easier. What could be more convenient than e-mailing submissions? But the message is the same. Anyone can do it. Now, it may be very difficult for the average would-be writers to put themselves in the same category as a Lois Lowry, so please allow me to put it in more down-to-earth terms: "If I can do it, you can, too!"

~Joyce Styron Madsen

79

A Word Can Paint 1,000 Pictures

The best things in life aren't things.
~Art Buchwald

I t was one of those sunlit Saturdays in spring, so fresh that even my three-year-old could feel the magic. I stood at the kitchen counter making sandwiches while he perched on a chair, swinging his feet, enjoying the feel of wearing the first shorts of the season. The plastic tips of his tennis-shoe laces clicked against the tile floor with a comforting rhythm. "Close your eyes, Mom," he said. He whispered, "It sounds like we're spitting watermelon seeds into the grass." He was so right. Just like that, the sound of those clicking laces instead became puffed-up cheeks firing glossy seeds, translucent pink pulp splattering the ground, juice oozing down our chins. His simple words painted the picture.

As a mother of toddlers, I was a consumer of writing, not a creator, but I soon found myself writing down the kids' extraordinary discoveries ("Those bugs fly slow enough that I can catch them! And their butts light up!") and endearing phrases ("So you guys are Santa? How does Dad make it down the chimney?"). The words painted the picture and brought me back every time I read them. I was onto something.

But it was someone else's words that inspired me to action. My mom asked me to transcribe my grandfather's letters from World War I. Written in pencil on fragile paper, they were fading with time and would soon be lost. I became engrossed in the picture of a Swedish farm boy with an easy smile and white-blond hair. A teen who had rarely left town, donning a scratchy wool uniform and traversing the ocean to a place called Germany. The picture grew to include the black-haired beauty who waited for him at home, knitting socks and mailing paper-thin sugar cookies to Red Cross stations on the French border. A picture of my grandparents' young lives and love emerged and grew into a book.

After that, I became attentive to the pictures that words invoked, and found inspiration everywhere. I found a tackle box in the garage scribbled with crooked letters, "Screwdrivers and Secrets." Oh, the places those two words took my imagination! (Never mind that my son said later, "You know that says 'Screwdrivers and Sockets,' right?") I began to carry a little notebook in my purse and scribbled in it when words painted a picture in my brain. My friend described his high-school job, in charge of mixing instant potatoes with a five-gallon bucket and a garden hose. A WWII POW from my church told me about the plane that was shot from under him, unluckily named "Borrowed Time." My husband reminded me of a desolate Nevada motel where the wake-up call was a sharp rap on the door.

I found that a word or phrase could paint that picture, and the game—the challenge—was to paint them into a story. Readers noticed, commenting that, "I felt like I could see it," or "After I read it, I was right there!" I learned the writer's lesson that words matter, and finding the right ones can be as easy as tuning in to the world around you.

I used to think that inspiration was big. A bombshell. An epiphany. But it is more like a wafting smell, just there to be noticed. Like watermelon, screwdrivers, mashed potatoes or a wake-up call. Waiting for the writer in you to sniff, smile and paint 1,000 pictures with your words.

~Gail Wilkinson

80

A Lifetime of Inspiration

*Cannery Row in Monterey in California is a poem, a stink, a grating noise, a
quality of light, a tone, a habit, a nostalgia, a dream.*
~John Steinbeck, Cannery Row

The summer I turned sixteen, I decided to become a writer.
The realization hit me when I read *Cannery Row* by John
Steinbeck. It was a beautiful story and extremely well-
written. When I finished the book, I sat on my bed and
thought about the places it had taken me. I had visited the Palace
Flop House and Lee Chong's Market. I had stood beside Doc in the
Western Biological Lab, sat by the old cypress tree where Hazel had
reposed, and gone frog hunting with Mack and Eddie and Whitey. I
had lived in Cannery Row.

I wanted to write a book like *Cannery Row* someday. It became
the standard of literary excellence for which I would strive.

Actually, I knew I wanted to be a writer long before that summer.
I loved English class and spent long hours at school reading Mark
Twain, F. Scott Fitzgerald and Ernest Hemingway. I did this as often
as possible and whenever I could get away from my father, who was
always harping on me to take up more masculine pursuits like fishing and hunting and football. It didn't matter that I wasn't the least
bit interested in the hook-and-bullet mentality, or that I considered
football to be about the most mind-numbing sport ever devised by
man. The secret to survival in a small town is to fit in. Don't rock the
boat or make waves. And if you do, watch out.

When Vern Bickle decided that he wanted to go to college, he was teased mercilessly by his schoolmates. Another kid, Tommy Dawson, asked his parents for a chemistry set one Christmas and was forever labeled a geek. Back then, people in small towns weren't exactly what you might call "tolerant." Or smart, either. Take my dad, for instance.

My father pulled green chain at the mill. That meant grabbing newly cut planks as they came off the big raw logs, while dodging the evil teeth of the band saw. Pulling green chain isn't exactly a mind-expanding experience. Dad was living proof of that. I didn't dare talk about writing with him. He read nothing but the sports page of the paper and struggled with the simplest mathematical calculations. The only confusion he allowed in his life centered on the remote control for the television.

I don't mean to sound disrespectful. My father was a good man. He worked hard and provided for his family. But he expected things of me, manly things. He wanted a boy who was athletic, competitive and rambunctious. I wanted to write short stories for *Harper's Magazine* and *The Atlantic*. He wanted a son who could fight and overhaul truck engines. Those activities repulsed me, but I did my best to keep the wraps on. A few fibs here and there, quite a few, in fact. And I kept silent about my writing because there aren't many men who want to hear that their son is an author.

Sometimes, I would hunt with my dad. We would drive up Twenty Mile Creek in the pickup and search for squirrels. He rode with a shotgun in his lap and would blast away at the poor animals as we cruised past. Sometimes, he would kill a dozen or more. As I drove, he would clean them in the truck. Tufts of fur would swirl around us as he skinned and gutted the little creatures, tossing their entrails into a bag he had brought along for just that purpose. The sight and smell of those dead squirrels always made me sick. I drove with my head out the window and thought about the satirical father/son hunting story I would one day write.

Other times, we'd go fishing. Actually, it was called gaffing, and it was fishing's spiritual opposite. Gaffing required a long, stout stick and a large hook. You tied the hook to the stick, stuck it in the water and snagged whatever ventured near. Gaffing was not particularly sporting, but I did it anyway to make Dad happy. I always kept a pencil and notepad in my coat pocket during those fishing trips, but never brought them out.

Once or twice a week, we would plunk ourselves down in front of the TV and watch The Game. My father thought football was just about the greatest sport ever invented.

"It builds stamina and character," he maintained. "It produces the qualities we look for in our leaders." As we watched the game, I would laugh inwardly, give a caveman grunt (also inwardly), and think about how much I wanted to make a derisive remark or two about bloodlust. I didn't care who won or lost, or even if the stadium collapsed at halftime. But my father certainly did.

When the game was over, I would rush to my room, pull my latest story or library book out of hiding, and once again life would be filled with the joy of words.

That was the sad story of my father and me. We were so far away from each other you could have fitted a couple of generations between us. I didn't blame him, though. What would be the point? There was a sense in which I blamed the logging town where I grew up.

Call me crazy, but I wanted more from life than a daily routine of schlepping lumber with a bunch of shallow, insipid, aw-shucks fellas who disappeared into the mill at daybreak and stumbled home at sundown. I wanted to be a great author known for his storytelling abilities. I wanted to write inspiring stories that millions of people would read.

I also wanted to keep my body parts intact. Ever notice how there's always something wrong with people who work in sawmills? You'd think the life of a mill worker would be a healthy one, with lots of fresh air and exercise. But I never saw a single man who wasn't maimed in some way: an eye gouged by a sliver of wood; a finger caught in a planer blade; a leg squashed by a runaway log.

I wanted none of that, and I didn't want to be around to watch it happen, either. But there I was, stuck fast in a mill town, and until I turned eighteen there was no way to escape this area of one-eyed, nine-fingered, broken-legged people. In the meantime, I zipped myself up in a cozy cocoon, wrote my stories and dreamed of Cannery Row, where seabirds wander the beach with sad, muted cries, and pelicans glided past and dipped low to the water, and brightly colored purse seiners and trawlers rocked gently in the harbor.

Forty-seven years later, *Cannery Row* remains my great inspiration. I'm still dreaming about the sparkling waters of Monterey Bay, the frantic clanging of cannery bells, and the lazy movements of fishermen casting lines along the shore. And, of course, I'm still writing. Thanks to John Steinbeck, I'll never stop doing that.

~Timothy Martin

81

Confessions of a Columnist

The thing that is really hard, and really amazing, is giving up on being perfect and beginning the work of becoming yourself.
~Anna Quindlen

Strangely, I can pinpoint the exact moment when I became a writer. It was March 30, 1964, in a darkened bedroom in a little Cape Cod home in a New Jersey suburb. I was overdue with our second baby, positive that I would never deliver, when I awakened to full-scale, no-nonsense labor.

Of course, my husband called our obstetrician, who told what he assumed was one more hysterical husband not to worry—we'd make it to the hospital.

Except he was wrong. I gave birth to our daughter Amy in our bedroom, and my husband, a lawyer by profession, became an instant obstetrician.

It was scary, crazy and wonderful to greet our daughter that way. And the obstetrician did ultimately arrive, along with a pediatrician and a couple of policemen who somehow had gotten the word that some couple had had a baby at home. This was, it must be noted, long before home births were in vogue.

For a few days, we became local celebrities. The local paper ran a headline that read, "Lawyer turns doctor..."

And then Vic went back to his law office, and I was left with a toddler, a new baby, and all those feelings.

One afternoon when both girls were sleeping at the same

time—a small miracle in and of itself—I reached for a yellow legal tablet and decided to "tell it"—the story of Amy's wild birth.

I'll never know what made me reach for that tablet, but it was almost as if the words were being channeled.

Then Amy, our newborn, needed attention, and so did her two-year-old sister. That chronicle of Amy's birth got stashed in a drawer and was promptly forgotten.

Some weeks later, I rediscovered those pages and took a leap of faith. I sent that longhand narrative to a very prestigious publication—the magazine that came with our diaper service.

One morning, when I was dusting the living-room coffee table, a voice on the phone asked for Sally Friedman, the writer. I was positive the guy had the wrong number.

But it turned out that the magazine had liked my account of Amy's birth and offered to pay me $12.50 for it—or give me the equivalent in diapers.

I'm a practical woman. I took the diapers.

That was back in 1964.

There was actually another birth that year in our little house. A writer was born, only I was the last to know it.

For the next crowded, exhausting years, and the birth of another daughter, I was just a mommy to Jill, Amy and Nancy. My own reading was likely to be Dr. Seuss, rather than something trendy on The New York Times bestseller list. I was far more conversant with Johnson's baby powder than Chanel Number anything.

But one September morning, I marched little Nancy, the last of the Friedman daughters, to "big school," dropped her off at the kindergarten gate, and wondered what in the world I'd do with the rest of my life.

There happened to be another of those legal tablets on the kitchen counter that morning—not unusual when there's a lawyer in the family—and again, almost on automatic pilot, I started writing on it. I "told" that tablet how it felt to watch Nancy walk off in that crooked kindergarten line without once looking back. How I was so scared—not for her, but for me…

Emboldened, I took those yellow pages and mailed them to the local daily in our community. I didn't know enough to write a decent cover letter, let alone present my work in typewritten form.

But that paper liked my honest tale of Nancy's first day of school and ran it. It was buried on a back page, a cinch to miss. But a woman in the supermarket told me that my story of Nancy's leaving had made her cry.

It was amazing to me. And habit-forming.

So I tried another personal essay, and another. And then a male editor at the paper told me he'd take one column a month, then two a month, then one a week. He warned me that these personal essays run their course, and this gig might last a year.

That was back in 1971. My weekly column, unabashedly personal, still runs weekly in the *Burlington County Times*, that same newspaper. And that kindergartener, Nancy, has three children of her own, one of whom is getting ready for the launch to college in a couple of years.

Yes, it's been a long run. It has changed my life forever, this writing thing. It has allowed me do what wonderful writer Anna Quindlen used to call "Living Out Loud." And that's what it is.

Over these long writing years, I've branched out into feature and profile writing, health writing, and even writing about the famous. And I've found that the famous come layered with PR types, and are often quite dull interview subjects.

When *The New York Times* bought my column about sending our first daughter off to college in 1980, I wept in gratitude. There have been more bylines in *The New York Times*, but that first one remains taped to the headboard of our king-sized bed—and there it will stay.

My daughter, and now my seven grandchildren, have come to understand that they are fodder for me. And my husband, a man who instinctively loves privacy, has been generous beyond belief, because he, too, is "out there" in my jottings for various publications.

I have loved these writing years more than I can shovel into words. Ironic for a longtime writer.

I have loved opening the door to my kitchen and my soul, and letting strangers in.

The Internet has changed everything—and nothing. There are more folks than ever who "live out loud," and evidently, there are readers who want to follow them. So much for the personal essay form wearing thin.

Writing has allowed me to share my life with others, and to remind them that they're not crazy or lost or alone. When I write about my fears, my joys, my tiniest and grandest moments, I often hear from them. "Me, too!" is what they are essentially saying. And that is such precious reward.

"Will you ever retire?" people often ask me. And for now, the answer is a resounding no.

For now, writing what I live is as natural as breathing. It's a little like taking your arm in mine and saying, "Let's walk together."

And what a journey we share.

~Sally Friedman

82

My Ideal Reader

The two most engaging powers of an author
are to make new things familiar and familiar things new.
~Samuel Johnson

I read a poem today called "Selecting a Reader," by Ted Kooser. In it, the poet reflects upon who would be the ideal recipient of his prose. It's something I've considered. I'm sure there are writers who write for themselves alone, just as there are painters who paint for their own pleasure. But I am not one of them. When I write, I know to whom I speak. I can see her there — nodding her head or slack-jawed with an it's-not-just-me revelation.

What does my reader look like? A lot like I did a few years back — a new mom up to her emotional armpits in motherhood, treading water in the simultaneous loneliness, joy, ecstasy, doubt, exhilaration, exhaustion, fear and awe I felt when my first three kids were born within five short years. Maybe it was because I ventured into motherhood so late — on the heels of my thirtieth birthday — that my perspective on everything morphed the second I discovered I'd conceived.

I was like a person with new glasses, suddenly able to see leaves and blades of grass where before there'd been only green. I spent nine months reevaluating everything in my life — and out of it. Things that never mattered to me were suddenly my business. Things that had been my end-all-be-all now seemed expendable.

As a kid, I'd hated the time "the news" took up on our family's

TV set. I didn't see the attraction of a bunch of depressing stories of other people's misery. When I grew up, I never came to a point where I felt like it was my turn to start watching the evening news or reading the newspaper. But as a mommy-to-be, I was waylaid by the very real problems of global warming, waning natural resources, trouble in the Middle East, and killer bees. (Remember those?)

Then came Haley O'Hara. Two years later came Molly, and Hewson arrived three years after that. And parenting became my god. Every minute of my day was taken up with teaching them, stimulating their minds, challenging their imaginations, watching them with awe and delight and panic. When they slept, I read parenting books or documented their day in journals or—I hate to admit it—stood over their cribs whispering affirmations into their sleeping ears. What little time I spent away from them was either sitting in a restaurant with their dad talking about how much we missed them or gathering with my mom friends comparing notes on what our babies had been up to.

My ideal reader is a woman who's still back where I was then, still up to her eyeballs in it and feeling all the elation, confusion and insecurity I felt. I picture her laying a little one down for a nap, picking up a magazine with one of my articles or essays in it, and finding a friend among my words, finding permission to be human, to doubt and worry and second guess herself. I see her there shaking her head, laughing and crying, thinking, *I know. I know.* My ideal reader loves her kids so much it hurts. She wants for them everything she didn't have and all the good things she did.

Once I was sitting in the OB's office and saw a pregnant woman pick up a copy of *American Baby* I knew to contain one of my essays. I watched her flip through the pages half-interested. She got closer and closer to my story, and I imagined watching her read it, seeing her smile and then laugh out loud. I'd casually mention that I wrote it, and we'd get into a lively conversation—maybe even exchange phone numbers—and I could be her mentor, someone she could call on the days when things were too much for her. She got closer and closer to my essay and then finally paused on my page. I held my breath. She glanced at the artwork, scanned the words, then flipped again. My heart sank. Okay, so she wasn't my reader — or maybe she was and didn't know it yet.

A few times, readers have e-mailed to say they enjoyed one of my essays and wanted to tell me how much they could relate. And some editors have been kind enough to pass along a compliment they've received on my stories — although the last one I recognized to be from my friend, Jeri. (Shhh, don't tell.)

You better believe I answer every one of them and have developed Internet friendships with a few readers. Sometimes, they're older women who write to tell me how my essay brought them back to a time when their kids were little and how much they miss it.

But the ones I love the most are from women who're still in the trenches. I want so much to let them know how precious this time is. It's like those old people at your high-school graduation who tell you, "Enjoy these carefree years" just when you think you're carrying the world on your shoulders.

But the credo of we writers is "Show. Don't tell." And that's what I'm hoping to do for my reader — show her that this time is golden, that she's not alone or a bad mother just because she stumbles sometimes. Yes, I know my ideal reader. In fact, she e-mailed me this morning and closed with, "I'd love to read anything else you wrote." She might be sorry she asked.

~Mimi Greenwood Knight

Chapter
10

inspiration
for
Writers

Try, Try Again

Never stop pedaling to power your dreams.

~Terri Guillemets

83

Write
What You Don't Know

In the spider-web of facts,
many a truth is strangled.
~Paul Eldridge

For a job title that traditionally doesn't require driving, writers sure encounter plenty of roadblocks.

In 2006, I embarked on what would become the most intensive research jag of my career. The book would be a picture book for all ages, and the first-ever book at all, on Bill Finger, the uncredited co-creator and original writer of Batman.

To a guy who binged on comic books and Saturday morning cartoons as a kid and grew up to be an author of books for young people, writing about a superhero—and the real person behind a superhero—seemed like the perfect fusion of passion and profession.

For a man who forged a character so iconic even people who have never read a comic book can identify multiple elements about him, it seemed paradoxical that few outside the superhero community knew a thing about Finger. They didn't know that the "created by" credit line on every Batman story is not true. They didn't know that the *main* mind behind the Dark Knight died poor, alone, and virtually anonymous in 1974.

That's because his onetime partner, cartoonist Bob Kane,

perpetuated the notion that *he* was the sole creator of Batman even though Bill Finger...

- designed Batman's distinctive costume
- wrote the first Batman story
- wrote many of the best Batman stories of the first twenty-five years
- wrote the debut stories of other popular characters, including Robin and the Joker
- named Bruce Wayne, Gotham City, and the Batmobile
- nicknamed Batman "the Dark Knight"

In effect, it was Bill who created our culture's ultimate champion of justice, yet he got little justice of his own. I wanted to change that. If anyone can sympathize with a writer who was cheated out of his legacy, it is another writer. I knew it wouldn't be easy. I thought I knew what the most likely obstacles would be. Those, it turns out, were not even the most interesting ones.

Some roadblocks were a test of stamina. Few people like cold-calling (whether receiving or making), writers being no exception. But if you're a writer of non-fiction, you're going to have to do it. No matter what you say to the strangers on the other end, some are going to think you're a telemarketer. My cold-calling highlight: trying every Finger in the Florida directory... approximately 500 numbers total. How many bore (this being Florida) oranges? Not a one. (And how many hung up on me? Only one!)

Some roadblocks involved overturning perception. At least a couple of editors said they didn't feel one could do a picture book about a writer. Their concern: it's hard to create spread after spread of compelling images of a person typing at a desk. I constructed the story so it'd be visually diverse, but their minds seemed made up. (For the record, out of the forty pages of art in the finished book, only one shows Bill at a desk.)

Another roadblock was really more of a mindblock. When I asked another comics expert if he knew of any photos of Finger beyond the same two that had been published and republished for years, he said, "Those are the only two photos of Finger that exist."

But that's just a defeatist way of saying, "No one has looked hard enough." After digging for months, tapping channels no one else had uncovered, I found Bill's 1933 yearbook photo—and ten more photos scattered among an eclectic group of people. The best of the photos was in the possession of a man who had lived five minutes away from my house for years.

One roadblock was almost philosophical. Finger is among the most tragic (and most beloved) figures in comics history; for decades, legions of fans have been clamoring for him to receive posthumous credit. Therefore, I did not expect anyone in the comics business to question my choice of subjects.

Yet a longtime comic book writer/historian asked me why I was focusing on Finger when so many *living* comics creators are struggling. I saw his point, but you don't defend a friend only when he's in the room. Besides, I wasn't writing the book only to validate Finger's role in Batman; I also simply wanted to disseminate a compelling story. Still, it gave me pause that such a respected figure in comics seemed to be disapproving of my comics-related priority.

And I ended up finding out that I could still help the Finger family, even if Bill is not here to see it.

The biggest roadblock: At the dawn of my research, I was told that no Finger family was left—in other words, no one who could legally go to bat for Bill. To be more precise, I was told that Bill had only one child, his son Fred, who was gay and who died in 1992.

For a few months of my research, it was my own perception that was a roadblock. I assumed, as did everyone else I asked, that Fred had no offspring. So I didn't try to find out otherwise. It was a total fluke when Bill's nephew (who was a challenge in his own right to track down) told me that, two years after Bill died, Fred *did* have a child... meaning Bill had a granddaughter.

Meaning Batman had an heir. A lone and previously unknown heir.

Athena knew who she was, but she had not established herself publicly as Bill Finger's descendant. While still a total stranger to her, I encouraged her to contact DC Comics, publisher of Batman, to inquire about royalties. Though Bill did not have a contract with DC, after he died the company did begin to pay Fred royalties for reprints of Bill's stories. When Fred died, that money went not to Athena but to Fred's manipulative partner Charles. And when Charles died, in 2002, the money went not to Athena, but to someone even more removed from the Finger family (and someone who lied and said he *was* family to get it).

This discovery of Athena and of the unjust money trail would have significant repercussions for both my book and for the Fingers. It was not right, of course, that imposters were getting Finger money for fifteen years; it was bad enough that it happened throughout Bill's twenty-five-year career. Yet this is a Batman story, which means it has a fight.

At first, Athena was hesitant to get in touch with DC. She felt the situation was too big, and in any case she was not motivated by financial gain. I understood, and admired that, but at the same time, I felt she owed it to herself (not to mention her young son and her unsung grandfather) to at least make contact to see what it could lead to. At that point, Athena had a change of heart. In only a month's time, she saw to it that this money—this birthright—was rerouted back to her family. I was beyond thrilled, but it's only the first step. It remains to be seen if Bill's name can officially be added to the Batman credit line. As I noted, one reason I wrote a book on Bill is because I thought it might help bring that about in some way. Awareness inspires action. Stay tuned, Bat-fans.

Bill was inspired by silent films, comic strips, and pulp magazines to create Batman. I was inspired by my longtime interest in superheroes to write about Bill, and further inspired during the research when I saw how a good story in print could help create a good story in real life. And Athena will now, I suspect, inspire others to embrace their heritage.

It's commonly said, "Write what you know." But for writers of non-fiction, it's far more thrilling to write what you don't know.

Because in your research, you may discover something that *nobody* knows.

~Marc Tyler Nobleman

You Gotta Be in It to Win It

If you have the will to win, you have achieved half your success;
if you don't, you have achieved half your failure.
~David Ambrose

Ever watch an Oscar speech and wonder who you would thank? I have. I am a stay-at-home mom who writes novels, screenplays, short stories and essays in moments purloined from time-challenged days. My collection of rejection letters could wallpaper a bedroom or two. Still, I keep typing.

Almost ten years ago, I entered the second year of Project Greenlight, a contest for amateur screenwriters and directors. The contest was the brainchild of actors Matt Damon and Ben Affleck. The winners got a million-dollar budget to make their movie, which Miramax Films would distribute to theaters nationwide. They also starred in a reality program about the making of the film for HBO. The winners committed a year of their life to embrace their dream.

I didn't enter the contest the first year, but I watched the HBO show. It followed a freshman filmmaker as he took his screenplay from page to screen. After each episode, I asked my husband, "Can you imagine if I won?"

"First, you have to enter," he said.

It reminded me of the lottery slogan, "You gotta be in it to win it."

When the second Project Greenlight contest was announced, I had four weeks until the entry deadline. What I didn't have was a finished screenplay.

But I had an idea.

Fueled by coffee and chocolate—a winning combination—I wrote day and night. In one week, I had finished a first draft. It was a story about three generations of women working in a donut shop. Several friends read it and gave me feedback. The story had some flaws. Over the next ten days, I did my best to fix them. Revise, revise, revise was the drumbeat that played in my mind. Finally, I declared my screenplay complete and e-mailed the entry three days before the deadline. I had never written anything that fast.

I read on the Project Greenlight website that they received more than five thousand screenplay entries. The first cut was a month away—they would announce 250 quarter-finalists. Bracing myself for possible rejection, I told myself there was no way I'd make it.

My optimistic husband said, "You never know."

When my screenplay was named a quarter-finalist, my husband and kids cheered. Family and friends called with congratulations. I was stunned.

The next cut was a few weeks away and would narrow the field from 250 down to a mere fifty. I told myself that if I didn't make it I should be satisfied with my accomplishment—but the more you have, the more you want. Friends joked about meeting Ben and Matt, walking the red carpet, and appearing in *People* magazine. When my screenplay made the cut down to fifty semi-finalists, friends and family rejoiced with me. We chatted jokingly about what we would wear to the premiere—pie-in-the-sky dreaming that suddenly seemed tangible.

The next cut would take the fifty semi-finalists down to ten finalists. These top-ten finalists would be flown to the Sundance Film Festival to be interviewed by Matt Damon and Ben Affleck. They'd appear on television. I checked the Project Greenlight website numerous times a day in case new information was posted before the deadline. Reality tempered my excitement. I fretted over how my husband and kids would get along for a year with me on location shooting a movie.

My husband said, "We'll cross that bridge when we come to it."

Meanwhile, Project Greenlight wanted a three-minute video about me and my screenplay. I also had to fill out a twenty-page background questionnaire. Had I ever appeared in a commercial nude? Had I ever been convicted of a felony? What were my five favorite movies of all time?

As the days of waiting ticked by, I hoped to make the cut, while praying for the strength to bear the disappointment if I did not.

The day the announcement was due, I waited by the phone, learning firsthand that a watched phone never rings. I did not make the cut to ten, and I wish I could say that I stoically shrugged it off. That was not the case. After locking myself in my bedroom, I wept as if someone had died. I was turning forty soon and had thought this was my time.

A few days later, a friend told me about a college professor he'd known in school whose first novel wasn't published until he was well into his sixties. It was a critical and commercial success. Then he asked me, "If you didn't get there for another twenty years, would you still keep writing?"

My answer was a definitive "yes."

And I didn't give up. I kept pounding the keyboard. I entered more contests, and wrote more essays, novels and short stories. Now, my brief writer's biography has a nice paragraph filled with publishing credits. In my writing life, I have overcome several hurdles, well aware that there are always more ahead. And I'm fine with that because I know how to jump. There are always new ideas swimming around in my head.

My husband supportively tells everyone, "She's my retirement plan."

Just like life and the lottery, you gotta be in it to win it.

After all, my Oscar speech doesn't have an expiration date.

~Sharon Kurtzman

A to Z

Fill your paper with the breathings of your heart.
~William Wordsworth

"W"e'll find something special to put between these," Ken said, weighing the pair of heavy black A- and Z-shaped bookends in his palms. "What a gorgeous gift."

The two of us toured the house, looking for a suitable spot to display this Christmas present from his youngest son.

"Maybe on top of the entertainment center?" I asked.

I always deferred to my husband about grouping paintings or positioning the potted plants and knickknacks that crowded the shelves and tables of our airy home. I'd often thought that with his unerring eye for spatial relations, Ken would have made a successful interior decorator.

"Sure. We can put them there now and figure out what books they'll hold later."

A few months later, I received notice that one of my stories had been selected to appear in an upcoming anthology, *Chicken Soup for the Soul: Celebrating Brothers and Sisters*. Subsequently, I received my contributor's copy—the first book I'd ever held that contained one of my bylined stories. I'd been published in periodicals dozens of times, but this was different. This was a book!

I handed it to my husband.

"Look inside where I stuck the bookmark. It's my story. I

know it's only one book, but can we put it between the A and Z bookends?"

"I've never heard of bookends holding only one book," Ken said, with a chuckle that sounded like a blend of snicker and snort.

"Oh, don't worry," I replied. "I'll soon have more."

I walked over to the bookends, tucked my book between them, and stepped back. It looked a little lonely there, like an orphan in need of a family.

"How many books do you think would fit up there on top of the entertainment center?"

Ken cast a professional eye in its direction.

"If they're all paperbacks, there's easily room for fifty. But even two or three would look better than one."

"Well, that one's pretty special, since it's my first. But I'll conjure up some companions soon. Fifty sounds about right."

Ken raised an eyebrow and chuckled.

"Didn't you say these anthologies want true stories, things that have actually happened? Do you think you really have fifty stories to tell that people would want to read about?"

"I don't know. I've got loads of memories I'd love to share. You're right, though. Fifty's a lot."

"Baby, make it easy on yourself. Try for a dozen."

"No… you said there's room for fifty."

Ken shrugged and walked away as I hunkered down at my computer.

So I wrote and sold a second story, and then a third. From time to time, Ken would ask, "How many books have you got up there now?" Sometimes I'd overhear him on the phone, bragging to friends that I'd placed yet another story.

I'd always read them to him before I sent them out.

He'd scrunch up his face in wonder. "How do you remember every word your mother said to you when you were six?"

"I don't," I confessed. "It's literary license."

"Aren't they supposed to be true?"

"They are," I insisted. "But I write what I think sounds like what Mama or my brother or you would have said."

Ken grinned. Unable to recall much about his own early days, he liked hearing about mine. So I continued to track down memories I could translate into tales.

One day, I noticed that Ken's skin looked sallow. He'd complained that morning of lacking energy. I made an emergency appointment for him with his doctor. Jaundiced, he had to be hospitalized for tests and an MRI, and the diagnosis turned out to be horrific: pancreatic cancer.

Throughout the next few months, I doubted I'd be able to continue to write. Sometimes I'd sit at my laptop, stare at the page, and wait for the words to come. Then I'd remember I promised Ken I would appear in fifty books, so I'd write another story. He'd nod approval as I read aloud.

By June 2009, when Ken died, eleven books were nestled between the bookends, a burgeoning family. On the actual date of his death, UPS delivered a box containing my copies of *Chicken Soup for the Soul: Tough Times, Tough People* with two stories about Ken and our lives together. Now the bookends embraced the neat dozen he'd suggested as a fair goal.

Still, I longed for that original fifty. At first, in my grief, I feared my muse had fled. Soon, however, I found solace in remembering more of our adventures, so once again I began to write and submit. I could still do it, even without Ken sitting in his favorite recliner waiting for me to read him my latest effort.

As I write this, I've lined up more than fifty bewitching books, with several more scheduled to be published over the remainder of the year. Now I've set my sights on seventy-five.

When I'm feeling lonely, it lifts my spirits to see the anthologies assembled between the A and Z bookends, bookmarks saucily inserted between the pages where my stories begin. While I used to begin my morning with a cup of tea and a chat with Ken, now I've substituted reading an anthology story as I sip.

Should I ever write an autobiography, I doubt I'd find an

interested publisher. I'm not a celebrity. My name's not a household word. Nonetheless, I'm blessed to have found a way to publish my life's story, chapter by chapter, through these collections.

A few months ago, I staged a workshop at my local library, "A Penny for Your Thoughts," on writing narrative essays. Sixteen people showed up, eager to learn how to put their lives on paper.

"Nobody gets rich writing for anthologies," I admitted. "But look at the other compensations. Writing puts zing into your days, zest into your life."

"Yeah," one man interrupted, "and you've got a published work!"

Later, I received a note from the librarian. She wrote, "It was such a treat to hear you read your stories… Your tips and experience in the field were so valuable. Your audience was completely captivated!"

I'd read two of my stories—one about my grandmother's funeral, and one about becoming a grandmother myself. The audience hung on my every word. And when I finished, they applauded. Even Ken, appreciative as he may have been, never did that.

What a gorgeous gift those bookends remain: A for applause… and Z for zing and zest!

~Terri Elders

A Real Writer at Heart

Never, never, never give up.
~Winston Churchill

Writers are a funny lot. I should know. I've been one for more years than I care to admit—whether I put pen to paper or not. As a child, my imaginative take on reality repeatedly got me into trouble.

"Why did you lie?" my parents would ask.

"I didn't," I'd insist over and over. Was it lying to tweak reality just enough to make it more fun, more palatable? More interesting?

Then, somewhere between childhood and my late teens, I lost my creativity—or buried it under the kind of sensible, traditional behavior that was expected of me. I fell in love, married, had kids and settled down. By the time I was forty, I was beginning to think my life was joyfully predictable. Boy, was I in for a surprise!

I got a catalog in the mail offering a college extension course on writing. It sounded appealing. Even better, it was to be held on a campus near my married daughter's apartment.

"We can meet for lunch every Saturday," I told her excitedly. "Like a girls' day out."

"What do you want to take a writing class for, anyway?" she asked. She might as well have added "at your age" or "since you have no special talent," although my latent imagination supplied the words for her.

"I just thought it might be fun," I kept insisting to myself and to my family. And it certainly was fun. I enrolled. I loved the class. And I started reading fiction voraciously again, reawakening my creativity. Eventually, I even began to dream of selling something I had written some day.

Truth be told, if I had known how hard it is to get published, I might have quit before I'd even explored the possibilities. But I was blissfully ignorant. Within a year of completing the class, I had written a novel, found an agent, and sold the manuscript. I was being paid for my work! What a concept. What a heady feeling. Until I found out that editors actually edit.

"They're sending it back," I wailed to my long-suffering husband after getting the news from my agent. "How can they do that?"

Well, they can, and they did. If you think getting bad marks in school is hard on the ego, try dealing with a panel of New York editors whose careers depend upon finding new talent and molding it to their publishing house's parameters.

"We love your book and want to buy it," one gushed when we finally spoke.

Before I could stop hyperventilating long enough to thank her, she went on. "However, we'll need a different opening, changes to the chapters, and a totally new ending to make it fit our guidelines. I'll be sending you a detailed revision letter."

Deflated, I hung up and wept. If they loved my writing, why were they so determined to change it? I'd sent them my very best work. How could I possibly do any better?

Then I haunted my mailbox, awaiting her dreaded revision letter. Yes, that was in the days before e-mail and blogs and instant gratification—or instant rejection. Back then, we had to pick up every letter or self-addressed, stamped, return envelope, and tear it open before beginning to rant and rave and insist that no one was smart enough to appreciate our talent. These days, an author's fragile ego can be crushed electronically—in less time than it would take to make a phone call!

So, that's the way it was—and is—my friends. You work. You

sweat. You pray. You hope. And in the end, if you succeed, your precious manuscript may be torn apart and reassembled in a way you didn't expect. But it just might become a better book. And the effort is well worth it.

If you can dream, if you feel compelled to put your ideas on paper, no matter who does or does not ultimately read your work, you are a writer. And if you can't imagine not creating new worlds peopled with amazing characters, you just might see yourself published some day.

The secret, if there is one, is perseverance. I've had dry spells of years at a time when I didn't sell a thing. The last time one of those disastrous hiatuses ended, an editor told me, "We're going to give you a contract because we like your work—and because I can see from our records that you never gave up. You kept sending in ideas even when we didn't buy anything from you for a long time." She shook my hand and made my day when she said, "We can tell you're a real writer at heart."

I sure am.

~Valerie Whisenand

A Pat on the Back

*A pat on the back is only a few vertebrae removed
from a kick in the pants, but is miles ahead in results.*
~Ella Wheeler Wilcox

I had taken a vacation day off work to spend some time writing. The page on the screen was as empty as my coffee cup, even though I'd been sitting there trying to write for an hour. I turned away from the screen and looked at my desk. The dust on the desktop was gone; the pencils were all sharpened and facing the same direction; and the Post-it notes were neatly stacked according to size and color. If they were giving a medal for an organized desk, I'd win it for sure.

The problem was that I wasn't hoping for a clean desk award. What I wanted was a check. Or maybe PayPal. What I wanted was to write and get paid for it. Oh, I wasn't looking for a three-book deal or anything earth-shattering. I was just hoping for enough to buy dinner or go to a movie.

For as long as I can remember, I've been writing. My basement bookshelves are filled with evidence of my passion. Construction-paper-backed fairytales are written in round pencil letters and stored in boxes. Spiral notebooks contain trite schoolgirl romances, and high-school ring binders hold deep, non-rhyming poetry that makes sense to no one—including me. Then we entered the computer age, and the magic of a dot-matrix printer shows itself in my college term papers and literary themes, which are now barely readable on green bar paper. After college, I began to save my writing on my computer, so it is harder to account for the past twenty years of submissions. But they are there on the electronic bookshelf, gathering digital dust with a few floppy disks thrown in for good measure.

I'd written tons of words over so many years and sent them off to editors near and far, and yet I'd never received payment for a piece of my work. Plenty of pieces in newsletters, online blogs and other places where editors gobbled up content like trick-or-treaters eating candy bore my byline, but nobody had ever paid me.

I kept telling myself it didn't matter. I loved to write, and it was my passion for the written word that mattered. I told myself that just having someone read my work was the real payment, not the money.

All that was true, but, well, it wasn't an acceptable answer to the inevitable question your friends asked when you told them you had a piece accepted. "So, how much did they pay you for it?"

To most people, you are not a writer unless you get paid. And that hurts a little after all the work you've put into something. Plus, there is something rewarding about the idea that someone cared enough about what you wrote to recognize you with a payment of some kind.

While still pondering what to write next, I started chaining my paperclips together. I didn't have any great ideas yet, but I had chained together twenty-three paperclips when the doorbell rang.

Writing, or trying to write, can be a solitary pursuit, and the thought of speaking to another human was such a rush that I ran to the door. I saw through the glass that it was my mailman bearing a package and a clipboard. I couldn't for the life of me remember ordering anything.

"Glad you were home, Shawn. I need you to sign for this package." He gave me the clipboard, and I scribbled my name.

"Thanks, Rick. I have no idea what this is." He handed me the package, which was heavier than it looked.

"Don't know, but it feels like a book to me. Have a good day!"

I stood in the doorway as he drove off in his truck. There was no return address label on the package. I felt the contents through the brown envelope. It did, indeed, feel like a book—a square, thick, paperback book.

A good five minutes must have passed while I held that package. It never occurred to me to go ahead and open it; it was much more fun to wonder what was inside. Finally, my cat decided if I wasn't going to do anything but stand there, it was time for lunch. He came over to the door and meowed at me.

I went upstairs and put the package on the kitchen counter while I dished out the cat food. And then I remembered I had laundry to put in the dryer, and I forgot all about the package until I came into the kitchen three hours later to start dinner.

I was pretty happy with myself that I was able to put a few thousand words on the screen about planting my herb garden, but I couldn't believe I had forgotten about the package. I grabbed a pair of scissors and carefully snipped off the end.

The package did, indeed, contain a paperback book. It was an anthology of stories of family life and food. Inside the book, I found a check for twenty-five dollars and a thank-you note from the editor for my story called "Summer Salad." She called it "a classic family story filled with emotion." Wow.

My hand shook as I held the check. I didn't quite remember submitting a story about salad to anyone. What an odd topic. I checked the table of contents and turned to the page it listed. There was my name and my story!

As I read the story about how my mother used to make me iceberg lettuce salads with Thousand Island dressing when I was young, I remembered writing the story on my steno pad during a long, boring meeting at work. I checked my submissions list and found that I had sent that story off nearly two years earlier and never heard a thing about it. I figured it had been discarded as not good enough.

But here it was, in print, with my name on it. And I had a twenty-five-dollar check with my name on it, too—my first real payment for writing something. It had finally happened! I was a paid writer. Now I could tell everybody that the little story I wrote in a few minutes during a boring meeting had paid off.

And the truth was it did feel good to have that payment, to use it to celebrate with a dinner out. I told all my friends, and some laughed at the small amount, but others treated me a little differently, with a little more respect. I felt validated and appreciated as a writer in a way that none of my non-paying jobs had made me feel.

Since that time, I've received quite a few checks, some of them a good deal more than twenty-five dollars and some less, but every time it still feels like a pat on the back for a job well done. It is that recognition that keeps me writing day after day.

Sometimes, when it's been a while since I've sold a story, I will pull out that first book—and the copy of that first check I keep tucked inside—as proof to myself that I can do it, that I have done it, and that I will do it again.

You never know when the story you are about to write will be the one the editor just has to have. Every piece you write is a new chance to impress an editor and excite a reader. The possibilities are endless if you just stick with it.

~Shawn Marie Mann

From Dream to Reality

If you can find a path with no obstacles, it probably doesn't lead anywhere.
~Frank A. Clark

When I left the office after twenty-five years with the telephone company, I announced, "I'm going home to write a book." I had written the story in my head while driving to and from work over the years. I planned to document my journey during our daughter Susan's illness with a brain tumor and after her death at nine years old. She had inspired many. This would be my gift to the many people who had supported our family at that time. But writing an entire book, I realized, was much different from penning a short story.

While our son's Shar Pei slept at my feet, I wrote feverishly. I had hardly started the story when my mom fell ill. Dad needed help driving her to a city hospital. I dropped everything and devoted months to my parents, who had always been there for me.

By the time I returned to the book, I had lost my place and started revising. My writers' group encouraged me to take each chapter individually and not worry about the book as a whole since it might seem overwhelming, so I tried to finish one chapter each week.

Joy mingled with sadness while I recaptured memories. One minute, tears streamed down my cheeks, and the next minute I'd be laughing aloud at some of our daughter's antics. Using scribbled pencil notes, journal entries and medical documents, I filled pages, moving from scene to scene, reliving each moment. The telephone ringing would startle me and bring me back to the present.

When our daughter, Kristen, needed a babysitter for her two girls, Steph and Jess, again I walked away from the computer in hopes of one day picking up where I left off.

After a few months, I climbed the stairs to my home office, pulled up the story on the computer, and cast a critical eye at my work. I went back to revising several chapters for the fourth time.

In distress, I confided in my friend. "I'm having second thoughts. Maybe I should just give up the whole idea of this book."

Sharon listened. She, too, had lost a child and she understood my diligence. Knowing how much time I had devoted to writing, she said, "Don't do any more revisions. Take the manuscript to a printer."

Regaining my confidence, I painstakingly organized the chapters. The following week, I visited a printing company and showed the manager the finished product formatted in Microsoft Word. I glanced down at the pages in a box and proudly said, "I need to order fifty copies of this manuscript. What will it cost?"

Instead of seeming impressed by my work, the man said, "We don't take orders for less than five hundred books."

"How about one hundred?" I asked, hoping to change his mind.

The manager said, "Maybe a friend of mine will do this. He does special projects." He picked up the telephone and, after a brief conversation, handed me a paper with the cost per book and total for one hundred copies — enough for everyone on my list and some left over.

The order arrived just in time for Christmas. I remember the thrill of holding my memoir in my hands for the first time. My friend, Brenda, had designed and hand-painted the beautiful cover with a scenic view and pathway.

I placed each book in a gift box with tissue paper and a personal message to each of my loved ones before wrapping it and attaching a bow.

On Christmas morning, the recipients called with requests. "I need four... five... eight copies of your book." The phone calls came in for weeks. Orders for the memoir mounted. I considered ordering another one hundred copies until a friend asked for a large order for her nursing class. I was moved to think someone would use my book as a tool to teach students. I placed the order for an additional five hundred copies.

After the orders were fulfilled, I counted twelve boxes stacked against the wall. "What have I done?" I asked myself. "I can't leave these here to gather dust."

I never believed it would take years to finish one book, but it had, and now lying in bed that night I wondered how I would distribute the remainder of the books. In my heart, I believed God had answered my prayer to see the book completed. Would He also guide me to find a way to distribute them?

With renewed joy and purpose, I rose to this new challenge. Pounding the pavement with a canvas bag packed with books, I spoke to business owners in my local area and surrounding towns about selling the memoir. Gift shops, craft centers, bookstores, beauticians, and fitness centers readily offered to sell copies. Within two years, I found homes for nearly all the books.

Our daughter's story continues to be read, and the books are passed on from friend to friend. Today, I recall those days when I might have given up.

I continue to be amazed when I meet new acquaintances and hear how our Susan's story is helping them. How happy I am that I did not allow obstacles to hinder the memoir's completion.

~Phyllis Cochran

Nothing Ventured; Nothing Gained

If you never take risks in life, you'll never see anything new.
~Blake Lewis

I n 1990, I sent a letter to the editor at *The Dallas Morning News*. I was a young mother with strong opinions, and I thought my local newspaper would be the perfect outlet for whatever was bugging me or blessing me at the time. Never mind that hundreds of other readers had the same idea. I figured: Nothing ventured; nothing gained.

When my letter was selected for print, I was beyond thrilled. Although it was only three paragraphs long, seeing my words in a major newspaper was a huge reward, and I determined it wouldn't be my last.

One letter led to another, and after almost a decade, I had a bushel of printed letters about a myriad of things. Around 1997, the Letters to the Editor section launched *The Dallas Morning News'* Golden Pen Award. Here's how it worked:

At the end of each month, a printed letter was selected for clarity and writing style. It was then reprinted in the Sunday paper, along with a short blurb about the writer's accomplishment. I really wanted to win the award. Not only would it solidify my abilities as a writer, it would give me the confidence I needed to pursue bigger things.

However, I didn't want to "write to win"—that's never a good idea. So I resolved to keep expressing myself about topics that affected me and let the words fall where they may.

Imagine my shock a few months later when I opened Sunday's paper and saw that my latest letter had, indeed, won the Golden Pen Award. Within a day or so, a delightful *Dallas Morning News* coffee cup arrived in the mail. It was love at first sight, and you'd have thought I won the lottery. Fifteen years later, the cup still brings me cheer.

While that's all well and good, I'm really writing to share what happened next.

Winning the Golden Pen Award was a defining moment in my writing journey. Not only did it give me that boost of confidence I needed, it propelled me to do something I had always dreamed of doing: write an op-ed piece.

For those of you unfamiliar with the term "op-ed," it is abbreviated from "opposite the editorial page" (though often mistaken for opinion-editorial), and it is a newspaper article that expresses the opinions of a named writer who is usually unaffiliated with the newspaper's editorial board.

I was an avid reader of op-eds and had my favorite writers. Not only did I follow them faithfully, but I dreamed of being one of them—of seeing my words next to theirs, of sharing my thoughts and having people "listen." For the first time in my life, I felt my dream was within reach.

Of course, writing a full-fledged column would require lots of research, editing and time—much more than a letter did. And the competition would be fierce. But no matter the odds, I had to pursue my passion. Nothing ventured; nothing gained.

I remember exactly where I was the day the Viewpoints Editor called to say that my article would be running in the Sunday paper. I had seen this man's name in print for years, and here I was speaking with him on the phone, listening to him say gratifying things about my writing, and giving me goose bumps, head-to-toe.

Needless to say, I didn't sleep a wink Saturday night. As soon as the paperboy threw the paper in the front yard, I was out the door and all over it.

That was the first of many published op-eds, I'm happy to report—years of op-eds, in fact. And it began a writer/editor relationship that I draw strength from even now—all because I wrote a letter to the editor, once upon a time, and had the chutzpah to mail it in.

I can't guarantee where your writing journey will take you, of course, but you'll never know if you don't start driving. Nothing ventured; nothing gained.

~Gayle Allen Cox

From Rejected to Bestseller

Find a need and fill it.
~Ruth Stafford Peale

I'll confess to it now: In 1996, I sneaked into the Association of American Publishers' American Book Exposition (now BookExpo America) at the vast McCormick Place in Chicago to pitch my unpublished book. My goal was to talk to the second-tier publishers who had received the proposal from my agent but not yet replied. I felt a moral imperative: My readers were desperate for the information in my book. And I had done the math: Despite twenty-some rejections from the big New York houses, my research had shown that *Stop Walking on Eggshells (SWOE)* would be a bestseller that any publisher would be lucky to have.

As my husband followed me around, carrying copies of the proposal, I ignored the circus-like atmosphere of the place with the hope of talking to acquisitions editors about mental illness. In as few words as possible, I needed to explain a complex mental illness—borderline personality disorder—which causes those who have it to see people and situations as all good or all bad; to feel empty and without an identity; and to have extreme, blink-of-an-eye mood swings.

Once I identified the right people, I swung into my elevator speech. I said that there was zilch on the market for the family members of people with BPD, who were the frequent target of their wrath. I confided that I had lived with someone with BPD and knew how much this book was needed, and that hundreds of people on the Internet had told me they would buy a book about it.

One editor talked to me for thirty minutes before confessing that his brother was married to such a person. (This publisher, like many others, eventually rejected the proposal because the book's audience was "too small and too hard to reach.") Another editor couldn't take her eyes away from romance-novel model Fabio, who was standing a few feet away. A long line of giggling women waited to get their picture taken with him. An editor from a psychiatric press dismissed me right away because I used the word "borderlines" instead of "people with BPD."

Finally, I arrived at one of the smaller booths, New Harbinger Publications. Standing there was the publisher himself, a psychologist who had cofounded the Oakland-based company in 1973 to offer self-help books that offered "real tools for real change."

"I know this book will do well," I said. "I guarantee it."

The mustached publisher, Matt McKay, paused for a minute. "Borderline personality disorder is a hard one," he said. "There's not much in the way of treatment."

I countered, "But *Stop Walking on Eggshells* is for the family members, not the people who need treatment. For every person with BPD, there must be three or four people whose lives they affect—some 24 to 34 million people. This book will tell them how to cope."

Matt believed me. A few months later, he bought the book, which came out in 1998. Today, *Stop Walking on Eggshells: Taking Your Life Back When Someone You Care About Has Borderline Personality Disorder* (with Paul Mason) has sold more than 500,000 copies and been translated into twelve different languages. *SWOE* is one of New Harbinger's top bestsellers. Since then, I've written three other books, two for New Harbinger.

I learned that when there is nothing out there on the topic of your non-fiction book, and you KNOW people need it, document the need to the best of your ability. Some publishers won't take it precisely because "there's nothing out there" and they don't want to take a risk. But it only takes one publisher to believe in your book.

~Randi Kreger

91

Paying the Price to Be Published

For every hope that you entertain, you have a task
that you must perform. For every good that you wish to preserve,
you will have to sacrifice your comfort and ease.
~Walter Lippmann

As a U.S. Army medical evacuation helicopter pilot during the Vietnam War in 1969-1970, my crews evacuated over 2,500 patients from both sides of the action to aid stations and hospitals in 987 combat missions. Seven times my helicopters were shot up by enemy fire, and I was shot down twice, with crewmembers wounded. Back when I was six years old, the second son of a small-town Protestant minister in Iowa in 1948, this was not how I imagined my life would turn out.

The first dreams I distinctly remember at this tender age encompassed three major goals: becoming a pilot, an army officer, and a writer. A yellow, single-engine airplane that often flew low over our metropolis of 125 souls — so low I could see the pilot wave back when I waved — may have been a contributing factor. Critics might say that being this specific so young isn't credible, but they'd be wrong.

Fast-forward to 1965 when I graduated as a second lieutenant from Officer Candidate School at Ft. Benning, Georgia. My first dream was accomplished. Four months later, my unit was activated by the governor of California for six days during the Watts Riot in

Los Angeles. That was my initial exposure to deadly violence. A year later, I was once more activated for three days due to the Hunter's Point Riot in San Francisco.

After two-and-a-half years of college, and with the Vietnam War heating up, I saw another opportunity. Since I was now an officer, I applied for rotary-wing flight school. In March 1969, I graduated at Hunter Army Airfield in Savannah, Georgia, as a U.S. Army helicopter pilot. Dream number two had become reality.

While in flight school, I'd already volunteered for an active duty assignment to Vietnam as a medical evacuation pilot. Three months after graduation, I was in Da Nang, South Vietnam, now a captain and operations officer for the 236th Medical Detachment.

I was twenty-six years old, just married, and twenty-two of my articles and short stories had already been published in a variety of national magazines. In college, I'd submitted stories to religious, military and young adult magazines. The subjects I'd written about included being a preacher's kid, becoming an aviator, the Watts Riot, and teen sports serials, among others. Dream number three had been accomplished.

What was amazing about my beginning freelance career was that the first three articles I sent out sold to the first three magazines they were submitted to. This gave me confidence to keep submitting. But, beginning with article number four, rejection slips started to appear consistently.

Wanting to do my part in America's war effort, I had decided to make the military a career. If I survived my tour of combat duty, I figured there would be plenty of missions and experiences to write about afterward.

My fellow pilots and crewmembers provided more than enough action and memories to whet my scribbler's appetite. On every mission, injustices of war lay in bloody heaps on my cargo deck. The outrageous suffering I witnessed could have made even horror-movie villains wince. By the end of that traumatic year, my initial hunch was correct: I'd accumulated enough adventures and material to last a lifetime. In fact, more than forty years later, I'm still publishing articles and short stories based on these experiences.

In war, you learn to live with what combat truly is, not what you want it to be. And everybody's afraid. It's okay and reasonable to be frightened when you're being shot at. Fear is good because it makes every sense sharper. Your mind works faster and better. Nothing is wrong with fear unless it rules you. Whether flying or writing, I've learned that it can't be allowed to keep me from completing my mission.

My time in Vietnam inspired my writing life beyond the page itself. The most fundamental technique of storytelling is placing the reader in the mind and heart of your protagonist. My main character in combat was the patient. His condition was paramount and far more pressing than my anxiety about the prospects of being blown out of the sky. Similarly, confronting a blank page with only your imagination takes courage when you know fear and rejection may be lurking nearby.

Numerous times, I thought my aircraft was about to become a metal pretzel in some sewage-filled rice paddy. But I never gave up, even with death staring me in the face. And I learned that writers must have this attitude, too, if they want to persevere in the literary world.

Combat taught me to do all I could, while I could, before it was too late. This has served me well as a military retiree, after twenty-seven-and-a-half years of service on three continents, nineteen years as a pilot, being a newspaper managing editor, columnist and freelancer. Since Vietnam, I've published more than 800 articles and short stories in 286 publications in 130 countries. This includes *Reader's Digest*, *Positive Living*, *Soldier of Fortune* and Frontier Airlines' magazine, *Frontier*. My work has also been featured in twenty-five book anthologies. I owe it all to the lessons I learned to challenge my fear of failure, to have dreams and to work to make them come true.

My recommendation for potential writers is to be turf-tough. Face your individual fears of never being published, of feeling unworthy, or of being rejected. Use the talents you've been given to impart knowledge and information, share experiences, and bring hope and enjoyment to others. Your varied experiences in life—like exquisite jewels or fine paintings—can inspire, bring joy and provide insight to fellow travelers. And don't be afraid to challenge yourself by being a risk-taker in fulfilling your dreams.

At one point in *The Flamingo Kid*, I recall that the father tells his son, "There are two things you have to find in life: what you are good at and what you love. And if God is smiling at you, it'll be the same thing." That's what flying and writing have been for me. On a combat mission or in an article or short story, you never know whose life you will step into or who will step into yours. That's what makes life interesting, adventurous and worthwhile.

If what you write is important to you, there's an excellent chance it will be interesting and of value to others. And if it's good enough, there will always be a market for it somewhere. I equate this to attempting to hit the ground when my helicopter's Lycoming jet engine is shot out at 1,500 feet. You can't miss.

~Robert B. Robeson

92

African Adventures

Where there's a will, there's a way.
~English Proverb

Twelve years ago, I moved to Botswana, Africa, as a missionary. One hundred people agreed to pray for me while I was there.

I was lonely on the other side of the world. I found great comfort in knowing that through writing prayer letters, I could share my adventures with my friends in America. At first, I felt I should only share the positive, life-changing things that were happening to me. I feared rejection or judgment if people viewed me as a complainer. However, one day I dared to share my honest struggles and hardships. Contrary to my suspicions, people related and truly encouraged me. From that point on, I found the prayer team acted like a therapist, allowing me to vent, to share joys, to ask questions, and to praise God with them.

Over the past twelve years, friends began forwarding my e-mails to others, and our group grew. It is now in the thousands, and recipients live on every continent. Interested readers replying from all over the planet have inspired me to reach deeper in trying to pen my thoughts and life lessons.

When I went into labor with a healthy baby boy and a doctor's mistake rendered him severely brain-damaged for life, it was only natural that I share the journey with my prayer team. Over the first year of his life, I shared my tears, my smiles, his milestones, doctors' reports, and how we overcame our bitterness toward the doctors and trusted God to bring something good out of an awful situation.

Throughout the year, various people wrote and said, "You should write a book about this." Initially, I shrugged it off. However, one day I received an e-mail from a publisher on my team saying he thought this story had the makings of a great book. As a stay-at-home mom of two small children, it was crazy to think I could find the time to write a book, so again I laughed at the idea. But the publisher suggested I sit down and start writing to see how it flowed.

Once I sat down and started typing, it was like a dam within me broke open. The story flooded out. Thanks to my detailed prayer letters, rereading them took me back to each step of the past year to relive it, enabling me to write with the same emotions I felt in those moments.

Finally, the book was complete. I sent it off to the publisher and anxiously watched my inbox. When I got his response, two points stuck out: He liked the book, and he wanted to know when I could go to America to promote it. I had already scheduled a month-long trip home in December for Christmas, so I thought this would be perfect timing. He responded that promoting a book took months and would require extensive travel. As a mother of two small children, a dedicated wife of a busy businessman, and a permanent resident of Botswana, I knew this wasn't possible. Despair and frustration filled me at the thought I had written this entire book for nothing.

Weeks went by as I questioned why God had so clearly enabled me to write this story if the only purpose was for it to sit in my saved documents. I looked into other publishing options, but they all had long waiting lists and the likelihood of them even reading my manuscript looked slim. Furthermore, most of the "fine print" stated that I would need to do most of the legwork promoting the book, and I wouldn't make much money. It didn't seem worth the sacrifices.

One day, a thought hit me: What if I could just pay a printing company to print the book for me and then promote it via the prayer team and sell it myself? After hours of research and enquiries with different companies, I realized I needed to put my book in a professional format to even submit it for printing. Having little patience for technical matters, I needed help. In its current form, it was too big to attach in an e-mail, so I needed someone local to help me format it. Could such a person be found in my small city in Botswana?

After fruitless searching, I finally stumbled by accident onto a printing house. There I met a graphic designer who agreed to format my book and properly position my pictures. His employer could then print the books for me. I was elated! The excitement quickly dissipated when I heard it would cost the same as our car to print 1,000 books!

Later, as my husband and I did the research and math, we realized that after selling 400 books, we would cover all our costs. But would 400 people be interested in buying the book to make the breakeven point? I thought we should ditch the project; it was too risky. But my husband believed in me and wanted me to go for my dream. We signed the contract and printed the first thousand books.

A local negligent medical case involving an innocent newborn quickly received loads of media attention and, within months, we had to print 500 more. As my upcoming December trip to America drew closer, I wrote my prayer team asking if anyone wanted to buy a book. Four hundred orders filled my inbox. Four hundred books would consume our entire airline baggage allowance, so it made more sense to just print copies in the States. Now my book was in a professional format so it was easy to submit, and soon I had ordered a thousand more copies for the States.

In a little over a year, we have sold about 2,500 copies in Botswana and the States. It has taken countless hours of e-mails telling friends about the book and posting the book cover on Facebook to spread the word. I keep copies on me at all times and take advantage of any opportunity to show people, whether in a line paying a power bill or at a play date with other moms. I have spoken on radio stations and at church gatherings. It has been a lot of hard work, but in the end we have made enough money to cover our initial investment and make a significant contribution toward our son's medical bills. I can finally say I am a published author!

~Ashley Thaba

Chapter
11

inspiration
for
Writers

Writing Changes Lives

Books can be dangerous. The best ones should be labeled
"This could change your life."

~Helen Exley

Writing My Way to Love

Why not go out on a limb? Isn't that where the fruit is?
~Frank Scully

My friend Gail was the one who convinced me that I could write fiction. I met her when we were both working on a healthcare project for a government contractor. We became friendly, and one day she showed me a story she had written. Although I had been an editor for my high-school newspaper and majored in English and History in college, I had never been able to write fiction. I was entranced.

Gail invited me to join her writers' group and encouraged me in my efforts. Soon, I found myself bringing forth a story and creating characters who became very real to me. My protagonist was a troubled lawman embroiled in a mystery from his past. He returns to his North Georgia roots and meets a woman who helps him find his way. I didn't know whether I wanted to love him or to be him, but I felt very close to him. Maybe all new writers are infatuated with the heroes they create.

I came down with a bad case of bronchitis that winter that had me down for almost three weeks. As I lay on the sofa recuperating and channel surfing, I stumbled upon reruns of *The Waltons* and started watching. I happened to see a few episodes that featured the sheriff, Ep Bridges, and I could see qualities in him that dovetailed with those of the lawman I was conjuring up in my story. I became intrigued with the actor portraying the sheriff because he was clearly the one who had breathed life into this role and made it his own. The actor's name was John Crawford.

Sitting at my computer, I searched for him on the Internet and found to my genuine surprise that he had appeared in many other shows and movies that I had enjoyed throughout my life. There was a quality and depth to his acting that touched me, and I found him very endearing. I sensed from watching him perform that there was much more to him than met the eye.

After a fan site came up in my search, giving an address for him and reporting that he responded positively to fan mail, sometimes with a phone call, I made up my mind to write to him. Mind you, I had never done anything like this in my life, but I felt my guardian angel sitting on my shoulder, nudging me along. Here's what I wrote.

Dear Mr. Crawford,

I am a huge fan of yours for your compelling portrayal of Sheriff Ep Bridges on The Waltons. *When I did a web search on you, however, I was amazed to discover that you were also one of the stars of my very favorite episode of* The Twilight Zone, *titled "A Hundred Yards over the Rim." I'm sure that without my realizing it, that was one of the reasons why I loved the episode so much. When I watched it again online, I knew for sure. It was a great story, and you were wonderful as Joe, the café owner. I would love to know if that show was as much fun to make as it was to watch, and where it was filmed.*

On the Internet, I found your contact information and a lot of positive comments from fans who had written to you, so I thought I'd take a chance. I'm 53, and I've never written a fan letter to anyone in my life! I just wanted to let you know that I think you are a very gifted and talented actor; you made the character of Ep Bridges real, and I found myself wanting to know him better. I really liked the episode where Ep proposed to Sarah; your sensitive, subtle portrayal of Ep as a man beyond the role of sheriff was right on the mark. The restraint that you exercise in your acting makes your performances all the more powerful.

When I originally watched The Waltons, *I was the same age as the kids on the show, so I had a completely different take on it. Now that I am watching the reruns on the Hallmark Channel as an adult, I see your character as a peer, and I find him very attractive; I definitely see Ep as a romantic character, mostly because he doesn't try to be one. It's interesting how a role that you played thirty years ago can continue to impact people throughout and even beyond your lifetime, so your art lives on forever to touch many more people than just the original viewers. I just wanted to share that with you and thank you for enriching so many lives like mine with your fine acting. If you want to write me back, I would love to hear from you and hear any interesting stories or comments you might want to share about your work on* The Waltons *or* The Twilight Zone.

I signed it, "With all good wishes," and included my name, address, telephone number and e-mail, to cover all my bases.

I waited a day before I mailed it, and even then, as I stood in front of my mailbox debating my decision, I had the strangest feeling that I was setting something in motion that would change my life. I finally opened the mailbox door, set the letter carefully inside, closed the door and put up the red flag. My heart was pounding as I walked back to the house, but I felt compelled to reach out to this stranger who felt so familiar to me.

Three days later and three thousand miles away in California, John Crawford received my letter and called me that same evening to thank me. I actually missed the call because I had company and it went to voicemail, but I called him back at midnight and we talked until almost 2:00 A.M.

Soon we were talking every day, sharing each other's lives and racking up enormous phone bills. He made me laugh. He made me think. He touched my heart. I was a widow with two school-aged children who had lost my husband to cancer nine years earlier and had never so much as gone out on a date since then. He was much older and had been married and divorced, in true Hollywood style, six times. Neither of us was looking for love or thinking that romance would ever come into our lives again, but we were wrong.

What followed were the sweetest eighteen months of my life, falling in love with John Crawford and getting to know him, visiting him in California and learning about the life of this remarkable and accomplished man.

John was a writer as well as an actor, with an award-winning screenplay and a book to his credit. I confessed to him that I had named my main character "Ep" in honor of him. Without hesitation, he told me to change it; the protagonist had to be my own, not an imitation of someone else. John listened to me, supported me in my writing and allowed me to index his book that was about to be published. He always gave me good advice. I was honored that he shared his triumphs and tragedies and so many wonderful stories with me until his death in 2010.

As for that first novel, I'm still working on it. I've published several short stories and have embarked upon other projects, but I'll always have a soft spot in my heart for my first protagonist, the one who came to life from my imagination and revealed himself to me through my writing.

That troubled North Georgia lawman led me to the greatest love of my life.

~Elizabeth S. Kline

My Daughter Helped Me Become a Writer

Act as if what you do makes a difference. It does.
~William James

"**I**s this a mid-life crisis?" I wondered aloud, as I drove home from teaching an ESL class at a local college. It was a crisp autumn day, and I opened the windows to enjoy the scent of the woods as I drove home, but it didn't improve my mood. I was frustrated by the college's refusal to allow me to teach a different class. Five years teaching the same class of beginners was getting old. I enjoyed my students, who were adult immigrants, but the material was so basic. I taught them to say, "Hello, my name is _____." It was hard to stay motivated.

Otherwise, my life was fulfilling. My husband and I lived two blocks from the beach in a house with weathered cedar shingles near the fashionable Hamptons on Long Island. Cottage gardens blossomed in our sunny yard. I had three daughters, the youngest of whom, Christina, was in preschool. Christina was born with Down syndrome. While her disability took us by surprise, I found that though she required more assistance than her sisters, the irresistible joy in her smile was a gift to our family. We had so many in our circle of friends that the girls' backyard birthday celebrations looked like block parties. Life was good.

Yet, I was seeking something more. I always wanted to be a

writer, and it seemed that I would never realize that goal. Add to that my growing frustration at the stereotypes of individuals with Down syndrome, which I encountered in the media. Either they were portrayed as absolute angels or unsupportable burdens; both were far from the experience our family had with our vivacious but fully human four-year-old. I attempted to contact healthcare professionals in my area to offer my services as a companion to new moms of babies with Down syndrome in the hospital. No one seemed interested, yet I knew the need was great to provide positive information to new parents.

When I gave birth to Christina, the hospital staff avoided me, unwilling to have a frank discussion about what lay ahead or answer my burning questions. I was told that plastic surgery was available to "fix" my daughter's face, and a nurse asked me angrily why I hadn't had prenatal testing. No one addressed the emotional turmoil my husband and I were experiencing or offered support as we adjusted to life with a special-needs baby. We were given the phone number for Early Intervention and nothing more. It was deeply disappointing.

Fortunately, my pastor called me in the hospital and asked if I wanted to speak with a fellow parishioner, Margaret, the mother of ten, the youngest of whom was a twenty-year-old with Down syndrome. From her patient and good-humored responses, I was delighted to learn that her daughter Kristen had a wonderful life; she graduated high school, walked to work at the local bakery each day, was godmother to three of her nieces, and had an enviably long guest list for her pending twenty-first birthday party. My fears were relieved by our chat, and hope dawned in my heart that my daughter could also have a fulfilled life. It was that hope which I wanted to share with other parents coming to grips with their child's Down syndrome, and it bothered me that no one understood how important peer counseling could be to a new parent.

To my great surprise, both of my frustrations found a common solution. My husband, an Internet specialist, was encouraging me to become more familiar with the Internet, and my mom knew that

I had always wanted to be a writer. So to make them both happy, I began to surf the net.

Soon I discovered how easy it was to comment on the various blogs and articles I found about Down syndrome, and I was encouraged when my letters to the editor were published. My confidence increased, until one morning, when, while reading someone else's blog, I clicked on the "Create a Blog" button, and began my own blog. Negative thoughts assailed me. "Who am I to start a blog? What do I have to contribute?" But I remembered how much I wanted to share my positive experiences raising Christina. No one could argue with the validity of my experience, and I felt driven to use my writing talents.

I called my blog "Cause of Our Joy" because that is the meaning of my name, and it seemed to be an apt description of what Christina was to our family. Later that day, at a family party, my male cousins scoffed at my blog, saying, "Who would read your blog?" Discouraged, I stopped blogging for three months, but my mother and a writing friend encouraged me to begin again, faithfully leaving comments to assure me that someone was reading my posts.

My blog visitors list grew, I was mentioned in a bloggers' guide, and I was asked to contribute to online support groups for parents of special-needs children. I found my voice as a writer and an advocate for children with Down syndrome. I became part of a budding movement of parents whose children had Down syndrome and wanted to tell the world what a blessing they were. I published articles to periodicals, and soon began to collect stories for a book. I was developing a reputation as a writer, and I felt more fulfilled than ever while making the world a more welcoming place for those with special needs. When I was first interviewed on the radio, I invited my co-workers to listen in. Several of them have purchased my book.

I began to write full-time. I stopped teaching and moved to the peaceful countryside of Connecticut to finish my book. I made many new friends online, and together with one of them, Eileen Haupt, I formed "Keep Infants with Down Syndrome" to tell the world that those with Down syndrome bring much joy to their families. I now appear on radio and TV, write for various periodicals, have written stories for books and won two writing awards. I travelled to New York, Washington, D.C., and Hollywood to support a positive image of those with Down syndrome in the public arena. I reviewed books and films for several periodicals. My dream of becoming a writer was accomplished in six short years.

Now Christina is ten and attends our local elementary school. She is learning to read and write and ride a bicycle. She is featured in my book, *A Special Mother is Born*, which contains thirty-four stories from parents whose children have special needs. Christina is a happy, healthy girl, who is the heart of her family, and her mother's inspiration. When I attended the United Nations first-ever celebration of World Down Syndrome Day on March 21, 2012, and sold my book to Down syndrome advocates from all over the world, I thought about how much my little girl, whom the world sees as disabled, inspired her mother to use her talents and start to change the world.

~Leticia Velasquez

From My Heart
to the World

Forgiveness does not change the past, but it does enlarge the future.
~Paul Boese

I stared at the computer screen through a blur of tears and deleted every word of the only paragraph I had written all day. Words that my therapist had encouraged me to write. Words that were supposed to be healing.

"What happened to you and your family is a tragedy, Diane," she said tenderly during our last session. "I think since you've been a writer your whole life that perhaps putting the story in book form would help to close the wounds. Even if you never do anything with it, just put your thoughts and feelings on paper as if you were telling the world how unfair life can be."

My husband, my best friend and father of my two children, took the thirteen years we had been "happily" married and turned them into an unfathomable nightmare. I didn't believe he had a mistress even after all the teasing hang-up calls and the time she actually spoke and confessed she was bedding the man I lay next to each night. I didn't really believe it when John's hours as a retail manager kept getting longer, and more clues began to appear. The reality came on August 13, 1996, when she called and introduced herself by name, and then described everything about my husband that only a secret lover would know. I hung up and called my husband at work in hysterics, wanting answers. He told me he'd be right home, that we'd talk and I'd understand, but John never came home. Instead, he hunted down his mistress and shot her to death in the parking lot of her college. He would spend his life behind prison bars, and two families would serve life sentences of broken hearts that would never heal.

"What good can possibly come from my sharing this story?" I said out loud to the walls around me. My daughters, Mariah and Vanessa, were in school, moving on with their pain and scars. I supported us by writing features for magazines out of my home office. But a book was something I didn't know how to tackle, even if it was never going to be seen by anyone but me. It meant replaying the life I had so dearly wanted to erase and revisiting the grave of our past.

"So, how is the writing going?" Linda asked me during our next therapy session. She sat back in her chair with a pad of paper on her lap, ready to jot down anything of importance.

I shrugged. "It's hard. I don't know why it would help when every time I begin to relive it all, I end up having stomach issues and sleeping problems."

The pen danced across the page. I must have said something monumental. "You are bound to have those feelings, but I think it might help to slant the book in the direction of what we were talking about last week. Do you remember the breakthrough we talked about?"

I flashed back to a night when I couldn't sleep and ached inside for something in life to feel right. The man I thought I knew and loved with all of my being was a lie. He murdered a young girl and destroyed so many people, including his own innocent children. I remembered wishing for that moment when I could just shut down and breathe my very last breath. That it was me who had died and was free of the pain. It was then I heard a whisper to my soul: Forgive, and your pain will be set free. Forgive and find healing. Instantly, I began to feel the knot in my stomach unwind. I realized the only way for me to be the best mother to my girls and to open the door completely to a new and better future was to forgive what John had done to our lives and let go of the horror of the past. Like a butterfly in my cupped hands. Just make the decision to set it free.

"Are you saying I should make the book about forgiving what John has done?" I asked, swallowing hard after the words made their way past my lips. "I was writing a true crime book about what he did and the hurt he caused. I thought that was what I was supposed to capture."

Linda shook her head and raised a brow. "What good is writing the negative when you could now center on the positive? If you take this story and embrace what you have already begun to do and forgive the pain from your past, this book won't just be an exercise you did for yourself in a counseling session. It could be a book that could actually be published one day and help countless others who need to learn to forgive and let go, too. That is true healing, Diane. When you can take a tragedy and turn it around to help others, that is when you know you have survived the storm."

One year later, *Prison of My Own… A True Story of Redemption & Forgiveness* was published by a Christian publisher that believed in its message. To my amazement, it went worldwide and was published in several different languages, touching lives in countries as far as South Africa and Australia. I began to get letters from my readers saying, "Thank you for the courage you have shown to bare your hurts and write this amazing story. It changed my life and taught me how to go on after all I have endured." Another letter was from a young mother who had planned her own suicide. "I was going to end my life because of my husband's affairs. Then I found your book in a store and read it all in one night. I knew then that there was hope for me, and I could let this go and move forward into a new future."

What started as an exercise in healing given to me by a very insightful therapist resulted in a book that ended up in readers' hands all around the globe, inspiring them and giving them the will to go on. I never dreamed on that unthinkable day when our world shattered to pieces that any good could possibly come from it. I never thought I could write a book about something so painful, yet let the topic of forgiving be the focus, leading other thirsty and hurting souls to drink it in. But today, as I cherish the hundreds of letters from readers, and now that the book has been translated into Braille and audio, I know that anything is possible as long as we pour out our hearts onto paper. Our life story can move mountains if we share the lessons we learned with those who need to learn them, too.

~Diane Nichols

Finding
Aricia Fleurimond

Speak up for those who cannot speak for themselves,
for the rights of all who are destitute.
~Proverbs 31:8

I knew in grade three I wanted to be a writer when my poem won a prize in a county fair. The blue ribbon on yellowing foolscap still hangs framed on my office wall. As a journalism graduate, I accepted a staff writer's position with a local newspaper and then, several years later, plunged into freelance writing.

That decision eventually led me to a foundation that works with the Canadian government to help establish and support agricultural co-ops in rural Haiti with the poor.

My position as public engagement coordinator and writer involved occasional travel to Haiti. Of all the stories I've covered during my career, Aricia Fleurimond's is dearest to my heart.

In partnership with a well-known magazine, I was assigned to write an article on the foundation's globally recognized work. It was a daunting project that involved travel to Haiti, interviews in remote areas, interviews with Haitian professionals and officials, translation services, photography and a pressing deadline.

I arrived in Haiti, and the misfortunes began. While exploring a roadside display of art, I fell down a set of cement steps and wrenched my back and ankle. My eye and ear became infected.

Sunburn resulted in an outbreak of cold sores on my face. A few days later, Montezuma's Revenge and a fainting spell with a racing heartbeat occurred. It hardly seemed possible to encounter so many challenges in one week, but there was no time to feel sorry for myself: A deadline loomed, and an article had to be written.

With my ankle wrapped in an elastic bandage, ointment smeared on my cold sores, and a generous supply of Tylenol and toilet paper, I huddled in the back of a pickup truck with my colleagues and began the lengthy trip up through the mountains to interview Aricia Fleurimond, who would be the centerpiece of my article.

Wearing a pair of men's dusty loafers, Aricia stood four feet, five inches tall, hardly what I'd expected. Her blue skirt and red blouse were laundered to an almost translucent thinness; her white purse was child-sized. She didn't look like someone who had ousted a corrupt co-op president, but her language was passionate, and a fire burned beneath her calm exterior.

It was unseasonably cool; Aricia and I and our translator shivered in the mountain air. Typical of Haitian hospitality, co-op members had enthusiastically dragged rickety wooden chairs behind their silo for us. The small rectangular building constructed of cement blocks and roofed with tin provided shelter from the wind. Just beyond our feet, the narrow lip of land where we sat dropped away sharply.

At the age of six or seven, Aricia went to work in the gardens and fields with her father. Often, the whole family went; Aricia, her three sisters and brother would labour until nightfall in the fields and their mother would cook meals there. Lack of proper nutrition contributed to her small stature.

Aricia worked as part of a konbit, a team of workers who hired themselves out to prepare, till and plant each other's land. Every day was filled with countless hectares of backbreaking labour for her.

She knew intimately, in a way I never would, the reality of abuse and vulnerability; in this land of bewildering contradictions, she represented countless women filled with resilience, faith, creativity and pride. Each one of them painted shining pictures of hope upon dark pages. I felt the weight of transcribing such a significant message.

When I asked Aricia what she would like to say to the women of Haiti, she said she wished them to be courageous and that they deserve the same wages as men to do the same work.

"My Land, My Voice, My Future" appeared in the summer 2005 issue of *Homemakers* magazine. Reader response was overwhelming; almost a year later, the foundation was still receiving e-mails from people moved by Aricia's story and eager to help.

One woman wrote to the editor: *Your article in the summer 2005 issue of* Homemakers *on Aricia Fleurimond in Haiti really touched me. I have not been able to stop thinking about her. She is certainly an incredible woman. I would like to be able to help her in some way, but I do not know how to go about it. How can I obtain more information?*

When I sat on a mountain in Haiti with Aricia, I discovered another facet of my destiny. Suddenly, I better understood the deeply passionate longing that drives me as a writer and haunts me with a strangely restless ache. It's the call to tell the stories of the marginalized — to give dignity and voice to the voiceless, to show what otherwise might not have been shown, to share a vision beyond this world. Each human being has a purpose, and I believe this is mine.

Recently, I was at my mentor's eightieth birthday celebration. I regard him as accomplished; he's written a number of books and worked for many years as an editor. He happened to remark that when he writes, he struggles to express his experiences and emotions. I disbelievingly asked if it happened once in a while, like writer's block. No, it's every time I sit down at the typewriter, he replied.

His admission took my breath away. This call to write is at times terrifying; it's an awesome, humbling responsibility to capably and with integrity translate the intangible. Yet as unworthy and unqualified as I often feel, I cannot ignore the summons to put pen to paper and record life as it unfolds around me; to not do so would cause my spirit to wither within me.

Aricia and I may never meet again, yet hers is probably one of the most important stories I will ever tell and one of the greatest influences on my work as a writer. I am privileged indeed to have met this woman and to have been entrusted with her mighty words.

Mèsi anpil, Aricia. *Anpil, anpil.* Thank you so very, very much.

~Rachel Wallace-Oberle

Lessons Learned in Writing My First Novel

Nobody can go back and start a new beginning,
but anyone can start today and make a new ending.
~Maria Robinson

I'm the type of guy who believes you can achieve anything you set your mind to, as long as you give it your all and don't give up. So when I decided to write a novel, it didn't matter to me that I had never done anything like that before. What did matter to me was that I had a great story in my head, a story that needed to be born. With no experience, training, or education in creative writing, I figured I'd pick up the skills along the way, which is exactly what happened. Besides, I thought, how hard could it be to write a book? Well, I'd soon find out.

What I thought would take a couple of months, took a couple of years. After five months of writing everyplace and everywhere, I finally reached the "finish line"—that magical day when you type "THE END." Okay, so I wrote a manuscript; now what? The first thing I did was to copyright it, followed by sending it out to all of my friends who read a lot, to get constructive criticism. This worked out great. Then it was back to rewriting the story, and when I was done, I rewrote some more. Next, I hired a professional to critique the story, who gave me great advice, which of course meant more rewriting. I soon learned Lesson One in writing: writing is rewriting. There'd always be room for improvement.

By this point in time during this process, I felt that the story had risen to a level of brilliance. But what about my writing style and voice? It needed to be just as good as the bestselling authors' because they don't put an asterisk next to your name along with an explanation about your education. So I spent months combing through the manuscript, trying to bring the level of writing up to the level of the story.

When I felt the time was right, I tried soliciting literary agents with a one-page query letter, synopsis, and whatever their submission guidelines called for. Oh, did I mention the Catch 22 in traditional publishing? Apparently, you need a literary agent to get traditionally published. However, in order to get a literary agent, you need to have already been published. So it's nearly impossible to get an agent unless you're a famous celebrity, politician, sports figure, etc. Certainly, they'd give me more credence if I had a BFA or MFA in creative writing, which I had not. Like all roads to success, this one's paved with rejection. So after tons of rejection letters from literary agents, I had a choice to make: give it up or step it up. Since giving up is not really in my vocabulary, I stepped it up.

I hired an editor, and the first thing she did was cross off 5,000 unnecessary words. For instance, you shouldn't write "run fast." You should simply write "run," because obviously if you're running, it's fast. Who knew? Besides copy-editing, my editor did developmental editing, too, telling me where the story needed to be improved. It was kind of like digging for treasure—she'd tell me where to dig, and I'd come up with something invaluable, as if she knew I had it in me before I ever did. I learned a lot simply by reading her edits and comments, and I became a better writer for it.

I had rewritten the manuscript time and time again for a period of two years, and in the process, I learned how to write. Looking back, I had no idea how long it was going to take or how hard it was going to be. Writing the manuscript, however, was the easy part. Navigating the way to a successful book, now that's the hard part.

After getting the go-ahead from my editor, I decided to self-publish my first novel, *Sand Dollar: A Story of Undying Love*. Now it was time to find out how good it really was. So I set up a website, SebastianColeAuthor.com, entered contests, gave away free books to reviewers, and waited for the reviews to start coming in.

And the results? Well, the reviews have been mostly outstanding, with an average rating of 4.6 stars (out of 5 stars) on Amazon with over sixty reviews. People who have reviewed *Sand Dollar* have even called it the best love story they've ever read, with many of them comparing me to Nicholas Sparks. I was also a finalist in ForeWord Firsts debut literary competition for first-time authors. Who knew?

But my greatest reward lies not in any number or rating. My greatest reward lies in the effect I've had on the lives of others through my writing. People who've read *Sand Dollar*, especially those who have lost a loved one, feel that the book was written just for them, as if the author expressed in words what they have always felt. One person wrote that the story "touched the very depths of her soul," and that she'll "cherish the book forever." She loved the book so much that she even had it made into earrings! Another person wrote that *Sand Dollar* was her "lighthouse in the storm"—this coming from a woman who had just survived Hurricane Sandy. Another woman was moved to tears as she finished the book on Veterans Day, missing her father, a veteran. And the list goes on.

But having great reviews hasn't translated into sales. What I need is exposure. But how do I do that? It would be great if I had a YouTube video with millions of hits, or if Oprah were to mention my book, but neither is likely to happen at this point. So I sent out press releases and got a couple of articles written about me in local newspapers. I've done several book signings and talked at different venues about my experiences. Despite all of my success, my book is currently only available online, not in bookstores, and very few people have ever heard of me.

So it's back to the literary agents I go. I've somehow made it full circle. But will I have a different result now that *Sand Dollar* has gained traction? Stay tuned to find out. Regardless of whether or not *Sand Dollar* ever makes it big, touching the lives of others through my writing has been the single most gratifying thing I have ever done in my life. And pursuing my dreams has made all the difference. Life's a journey. I can't see what lies ahead, but I know one thing for sure: when I look behind, I see the things that I've accomplished... and I smile with pride.

~Sebastian Cole

Anastasia the Adventurer

It is only in adventure that some people succeed in knowing themselves—
in finding themselves.
~André Gide

I admired the strong, courageous woman. She was an ordinary wife and mother, like me. But she had a penchant for travel. She embarked on exciting adventures zooming across the continent, down the Amazon on a raft, up the Himalayas with a Sherpa. I thought of her often, and could relate to her as a wife and mother. But the rest; those were things I never dared to do.

Those were things I only wrote about.

I work at my computer, writing books about pets. I publish blogs and articles about pet care and nutrition. Sometimes, I write inspirational tales about my little spaniel, Kelly, and our rescue dog, Brooks.

But I also like to write fiction. This time, the story I was working on was about an adventurer named Anastasia. I was not so bold as to call my character by my own name, Peggy. She had to be something strong, even exotic. I took Anastasia off on a heroic mission, knowing she'd come through triumphant. I smiled with satisfaction as I sent her off to face raging rapids. Of course, Anastasia was up for the challenge. My heroines were always brave.

But me—I was anything but. I didn't enjoy thrills. Some people talk about the fun of an adrenaline rush. Not for me! Sure, I went places with my husband Mike and the kids. But nothing risky and adventurous. That was for books. I preferred the safety of my little desk in the corner of my at-home office.

One day, a friend invited me on a weekend camping trip. It sounded fun until she started in with the details. "We're going to go rock climbing, and there's a big waterfall we can jump off."

What? Jump off a waterfall? I shuddered.

"We could even try the white-water rafting expedition!" she continued.

"Oh, I'm so sorry. I don't think I can," I said, my voice shallow. "I have too many deadlines."

It was true; I did have deadlines. But they could have waited. A few days wouldn't have made that much difference.

The next day, as I typed away, I thought about my friends packing and making plans together. And I was missing it all.

"Why don't you go?" my husband Mike asked, leaning over my shoulder. "You'll have fun."

"Nah," I said. "I have work to do."

"You can work any time. I think you ought to go."

I tried to forget all about that silly camping trip. Instead, I sat at my computer and worked on my story about Anastasia. She was about to face her horrible nemesis, the one who had locked her up and kept her away in the dungeon of a castle. I stared at the keys, but my thoughts froze. Try as I might, I couldn't get her out of that dungeon.

I went back and read over my words. "I'm trapped, Anastasia thought. It's too dark out, and I don't know what lurks behind that door." My fearless heroine was having doubts. How could she prevail with thinking like that?

Immediately, I deleted those thoughts and typed in a new scene. Anastasia formed a plan, tricked the guards, and escaped to freedom.

If only it was that easy to delete my own negative thoughts! But, maybe it was. All I had to do was write a better attitude in my own mind. I glanced out the window at the sunny skies and the birds fluttering around the feeder. I might not know for sure what the day would hold. It could be something scary… but it might be something good. Maybe I can do it, I thought. I even went back and deleted the word "maybe" from my mind. I could do it!

I reached for my cell phone.

"Changed your mind?" Mike asked.

"You know, I think I will give my friends a call and meet up with them. I don't know how I'll feel about rock climbing and jumping off waterfalls, but I could give it a try." Who'd have thought that writing fiction could influence my real life?

There was a little Anastasia in me after all.

~Peggy Frezon

Changing My Fate

The indispensable first step to getting the things you want out of life is this:
decide what you want.
~Ben Stein

I became pregnant with my first child at age seventeen, and I had my second child at nineteen. After having my second son, the harsh judgment I received from those around me only worsened. As a teen mother, the statistics were thrown at me—I wasn't going to succeed. I was going to live a life of poverty, struggle constantly, and never amount to anything. For a while, I believed these predictions.

That was until one day when I sat on the floor playing with my boys. I took a good look at the life we were living. It wasn't horrible. We had everything we needed. Although it wasn't the best of circumstances, we were okay, and we were together. But I knew there had to be more to life. Then, it hit me: Just because I was a teen mother, I didn't have to accept those statistics. I could make something out of my life. I could change the fate of my family.

For a while, I pondered what I could possibly do to improve our lives. My husband was working as hard as he could to provide for us, but it just wasn't enough. While unpacking some boxes after one of our many moves, I came across an old, tattered notebook. It contained short stories, poems and other writings from my high school years. I began browsing through them and thought, "Man, these are good. Too bad they are just sitting here."

On a whim, I submitted one poem to an online site and forgot about it. A few days later, I received an e-mail notifying me that my work had been published. I sat in front of my computer in shock. I had something published! How weird was that? A few days after my poem was published, I received a comment from a writer, who told me she loved my poem and how much potential I had. She encouraged me to keep writing because I had talent and could make a good living. Little did I know at the time, but this stranger on the other end of the computer would later become my business partner and the foundation of my support system throughout my writing career.

After reading the comment, I had an odd realization. From a very young age, I had always been told that I should be a writer, but I had always brushed it off. I thought nothing of the remarks from my past until this one comment from a complete stranger. Maybe there was something to this writing thing. Maybe I should give it a try. So I did.

I began submitting articles to online sites, known as the dreaded content mills, and received such positive feedback that I finally had my "a-ha moment" in life. This is what I was meant to do. Writing is what I was put on this earth to do. Writing is my gift, my potential in life, and it's the very thing that just might change the fate of my family.

I dove into my writing career with full force, but was scared. As a teen mother, I was also a high-school dropout. If anyone found out I didn't even graduate high school, my career would be over. This was my biggest obstacle to overcome, and the biggest thing holding back my success.

A couple of years after I began writing full-time, I met a writer who makes six figures a year just from writing, and she has no formal education. That was my second "a-ha moment." Putting words on paper to intrigue others is something that's instilled in you at birth. No school or training could give me that. I already had it. That was the moment I knew nothing was going to hold me back from living up to my life's potential, not even a high school diploma. I pushed myself even harder into my writing, and in my spare time, I read every grammar and writing book I possibly could to refine my talent. My hard work eventually paid off.

I've been freelance writing professionally for four years now. In that time, I co-founded Wakening Media with the woman who inspired me to follow my life's passion. She's not only my business partner, but has also become my best friend and my unfailing support system as I tread the waters of the publishing industry. I've also published a book, and I'm a contributor in four others. My little hobby has now turned into the main financial support system for my family.

I'm living my life's potential. I'm following my dreams and building a successful and lucrative career. Most importantly, I beat those statistics. I proved everyone wrong. My children now have the life they deserve, the life everyone said they couldn't have because I was a teen mother. By following my life's purpose as a writer, I changed my family's fate. Not only has writing changed my life, but my children's lives as well, and there's no greater satisfaction than knowing I did this. I followed my dream despite the odds against me.

I'm no longer defined by the fact I'm a teen mother. I'm a mother and a writer, who followed my dreams to make a better life for myself and my children. Everyone has potential; you just have to discover your talent and run with it.

~Alyssa Ast

Blow Them Off Their Feet

You must have control of the authorship of your own destiny.
The pen that writes your life story must be held in your own hand.
~Irene C. Kassorla

I've always been a writer. For as long as I can remember, I've been creating elaborate stories of all kinds, adventures, romances, dramas, mysteries. The only problem was that I never finished them. Not once have I ever completed one of my projects. Every time, after the "newness" of the storyline has worn off, it becomes a chore instead of a pleasure, and I procrastinate.

To be fair, with three kids and a full-time job, I don't have that much free time. But the truth is, despite how much I like the characters I create, after a while, they bore me. I can't get myself to care enough about them to put in the work to continue their stories. I've left one woman travelling across France in search of herself. Another one is on a cruise ship with her kids, and if only I could write a bit more she might meet the perfect man. A teenager is stuck trying to cope with high school, an annoying mom and a missing sister. One woman has actually been kidnapped—I care about her least of all.

And yet I call myself a writer?

Every New Year's resolution has involved some kind of commitment to writing. But time passes, and the woman in France has eaten more croissants than she cares to admit, the cruise-ship passenger has been sitting by the pool watching her kids for months, the teenager should have graduated two years ago, and the kidnapped woman is still sitting in the empty room. (At least she got the ropes off; give me credit for that.)

And then something happened. Something transformative and terrible.

My four-year-old son, Elliot, was diagnosed with cancer.

Yes, here in the Real World, nothing made up about this. Kidney cancer. We were thrown into a whirlwind of emotions, treatment, panic, chemotherapy, fear, surgery and, finally, remission.

It was during the month leading up to his third CT scan that I started to write again. The first scan had found the cancer. The second scan, two months into the treatment, had confirmed that the treatment was working. The third scan would tell us once again that everything would be okay. But the cumulative stress, the equivalent of holding on tight with your eyes closed as you speed downhill on a roller coaster, had become unbearable.

This time, I wrote about myself, and for myself. I wrote about what it was like to sit in the chemo ward with other parents and kids, all getting their doses, all holding on to hope. I wrote about the funny side to cancer treatment, the things nobody realizes, the strange realities of life. I wrote to release all the emotions I felt, but also to feel something other than raw fear. My stories were always uplifting, even though they dealt with such a difficult subject. I'm not sure why, because a lot of the time I was terrified inside. I think I was writing to myself. Telling myself it would all be okay. Explaining to myself that despite everything, life was good. Looking for the silver lining.

I didn't show my writing to anyone. After all, who would be interested in reading about life in the children's cancer world?

And then one day, out of the blue, I decided to start a blog. I have no idea where this idea came from. Maybe the France traveler, cruise-ship passenger, teenager and kidnap victim joined forces and snuck the idea into my thoughts while I slept that night. In any case, I suggested the idea to my husband. Martin is a techno geek. Those are his words, not mine. He was thrilled with the idea, and immediately launched into setting up a blog for me, explaining excitedly about the domain name and blogging options and other Internet things I didn't understand. I had created a monster. It all seems like a blur now, but I do recall I had to take out my credit card at some point. In any case, next thing I knew, nicolescobie.com was up and running.

I posted one of my cancer stories and told a few friends. Then waited.

There's a cool feature on a blog that lets you see how many people have visited in a day.

Oh, how exciting! Someone read my blog! A few minutes go by. *Oh, another!*

It was addicting. Grab a cup of coffee and sit in front of the laptop, watching the stats. *Oh! Another one!*

It's a bit like fishing, waiting for the line to move.

Motivated, I posted another story a few days later. The fish kept biting. The fish even posted comments! They liked my stories!

I had found my motivation. Writing about myself, my special situation, was interesting enough to keep me going. I liked my main character (me), and cared enough about her to finish each story. Sometimes, she annoyed me, and I wrote about that. I gave her the chance to figure things out, and when she couldn't, I was honest about it, and my readers didn't mind. Many of them could relate to what she was going through, so they would give me advice to help her out. I also knew that a new adventure was always just around the corner, so there would always be something to write about.

One day, I might amalgamate all these separate stories into a book. But there's no rush. I don't need to make a fortune on this. In fact, any revenue so far has been donated to children's cancer charities. I don't feel right making a profit from my son's cancer. But I definitely don't mind funding the research and support that has made all the difference in the outcome for Elliot.

I've stopped watching the blog stats. The number of readers keeps growing, but that's not important to me anymore. I once saw an interview with John Lennon where he described the early years of The Beatles, before they were "discovered," when they would play half-empty bars while on tour in Hamburg. He said because they loved their music, and loved performing, they decided to play for that handful of people as if they were royalty, to give them the best show they had ever seen or heard, to "blow them off their feet."

I'm writing for my handful of people. If I manage to blow them off their feet, I'll be thrilled, but in the meantime, I'm happy with the most recent comment I received. It was from a mom whose daughter was just diagnosed with leukemia. She said that my writing has given her hope and made her feel less alone.

It is payment enough to know that I have connected through my writing with one person, and made a difference. Sorry, France traveler, cruise-ship passenger, teenager and kidnap victim, you're on your own. I'm busy with my most recent story about how to hide mint-tasting medicine in toothpaste so your kid won't spit it out. Now, who isn't going to be blown off their feet by that story?

~Nicole Scobie

Bonus Points

Inner feeling, or inner knowing, is the silent voice of inspiration.
~Walter Russell

I was a twenty-two-year-old junior varsity boys' basketball coach and I was required to speak about the team and certain players at the end-of-season awards banquet, in front of about 300 people. I decided to talk about our team manager, Peter Boutros, who had overcome much adversity that season and achieved a long-time personal victory that inspired us all.

I got a mixed reaction to my speech. Some parents didn't like it at all, but I still felt like it was a valuable story to tell, that it really could inspire people. A few weeks after this feedback, Pat Williams, author of more than seventy books and the senior vice-president/co-founder of the NBA's Orlando Magic, mailed me a letter about an upcoming *Chicken Soup for the Soul* book he was putting together. He was looking for uplifting non-fiction basketball stories. Even though I had been shaken, I still believed in the value of Peter Boutros's story. So I sent in that story and another story I wrote about Coach John Wooden.

In February 2009, *Chicken Soup for the Soul: Inside Basketball* was released nationally, and inside that book are both of my stories. In March 2010, I received a letter from a seventh-grader at Reidland Middle School in Paducah, Kentucky. His teacher gave his class an assignment where they had to write to their favorite *Chicken Soup for the Soul* author. Jonathan chose me because, sure enough, the Peter Boutros story got to him. He wrote: "I read about five other stories, and I loved yours best. I understood how Peter felt throughout the story because I was kind of in his position in sports as well."

I was stunned! I thought back to that night four years earlier when I was writing Peter's story and almost scrapped it, and then the night after the speech when I almost bought in to the negative feedback. Then I became overwhelmed with joy that I stayed true to myself and trusted my writer's instinct.

The young boy from Kentucky ended his letter with these words: "If you could, please write back as soon as possible because I will get 75 bonus points, which can help out my grade by a ton." I wrote back to him and ended my letter with, "May your life be full of bonus points." I had Peter write him a letter, too.

All writers have what I call an "inner knowing," a story or message that is tugging at you to share with the world. When you trust that inner knowing, your influence can expand in every direction, even across the country to places you've never been. Writers are searchers and speakers of truth. We read stories to develop a greater understanding of our own story, and we write so that others may be liberated from their fears, insecurities, and ignorance, and be transported to their truth.

Belief begins the process of becoming, so you must believe in your writing, even when others don't. Some of those same people who mocked Peter's story when I first shared it as a twenty-two-year-old high-school basketball coach asked me to sign their copy of my *Chicken Soup for the Soul* book when I was a twenty-four-year-old nationally published author.

I've continued to trust my inner knowing as a writer and have been nationally published seven times: three times in *Educational Leadership* magazine, *Chicken Soup for the Soul: Inside Basketball* and *Chicken Soup for the Soul: Tough Times for Teens*, and in the books *A+ Teaching: 180 Ways to Enhance Your Success as a Teacher* and *Hey Leader, Wake Up and Hear the Feedback.*

I write a monthly column in *Fountain Valley Living Magazine*. It is a motivational column geared toward high-school students about developing themselves as leaders. I have also written for various local newspapers and I give motivational speeches. Just recently, I spoke at the University of California Irvine to about fifty young people in the On Track program, which helps children who have one or both parents in prison get to college. Whenever I speak, former players usually accompany me.

At the age of twenty-eight, writing has given me much fulfillment and allowed me to uplift many lives that otherwise I would not be able to reach. Other than receiving letters like Jonathan's, one of the greatest rewards for me as a writer is to see young people quote my words. High school and college students have quoted me on Twitter, Facebook, and Instagram. I have received letters from people who have motivational articles I have written hanging on the walls in their rooms and in their dorms. Students keep my Levels to Leadership chart in the cover of their binders at the high school where I teach. I've had young people, ranging from fourteen to twenty two, say they read a story from one of my books every morning as inspiration to start their day, or every night as a reminder on how to live before they go to sleep. A stark contrast to the callous feedback I received when I first started as a writer.

I share these achievements not to say, look at *me*, but to say, look at *you*. Anything I've done, you can do, and even greater things. You need to read every day, and whenever the words start tugging at you, write them down immediately. When you write them down, you give others permission to live them out. You never know who is hanging your words on their wall, or hanging on your every word at a speech.

You're going to have critics and people who mock you. Keep practicing your craft and believe in your work. If you have detractors, it means your work is creating traction; that's a good thing. The true master knows you've never mastered writing, but are in the perpetual process of mastering it.

Writing is strenuous and frustrating, but also exhilarating. The next time you are thinking about giving up, think about the little boy in Kentucky who is longing for your words to let him know he is not alone, or that he is enough, or it will get better.

~Steve Schultz

Meet Our Contributors

Jim Alexander has contributed a humor column, entitled "Notes from Downtown," to the *Montecito Journal* since 1996. His non-fiction stories have also been published in the *Los Angeles Times* and the *Santa Barbara News-Press* and his short story "Community Service" was published in 2012 by *The Whistling Fire*.

Christopher Allen, a corporate trainer in Germany, is the author of *Conversations with S. Teri O'Type (a Satire)*, published in 2012. His fiction and non-fiction work has appeared widely both online and in print. In 2012, Allen was nominated for both the Pushcart Prize and Best of the Net. Visit his blog at www.imustbeoff.com.

Alyssa Ast is a mother to four wonderful children and a wife to an amazing man. Alyssa is a freelance writer, journalist, and a SEO, SEM and social media marketing specialist. She is also the co-founder of Wakening Media, author of *The Fundamentals of SEO for the Average Joe*.

Jessica Ball is currently studying computer animation at Missouri State University. She enjoys storytelling and art, and with these she hopes to inspire people. She also hopes that her memoir, *The Camera and the Calculator*, available as an e-book on Amazon.com, will be an inspiration to others.

T. J. Banks is the author of *Sketch People*, *A Time for Shadows*, *Catsong* (winner of the 2007 Merial Human-Animal Bond Award), *Derv &*

Co., Souleiado, and *Houdini,* a novel that the late writer and activist Cleveland Amory enthusiastically branded "a winner." She is a Contributing Editor to *laJoie.*

John P. Buentello writes stories, essays, and poetry. He is the co-author of the novel *Reproduction Rights* and the short story collection *Binary Tales.* Currently he is at work on a collection of short stories and a new novel. E-mail him at jakkhakk@yahoo.com.

Barbara Ann Burris, her husband Bruce and their dog Alex live in a log cabin in Wisconsin. Her work has appeared in magazines and anthologies, both in print and online. Find other stories by Barbara in *Chicken Soup for the Soul: My Dog's Life* and *Chicken Soup for the Soul: Food and Love.*

Carisa J. (Wyrwas) Burrows is a previous contributor to *Chicken Soup for the Soul: Say Goodbye to Back Pain!* and the *Pittsburgh Post-Gazette.* She enjoys traveling and spending time with her husband Ralph. She started writing after several surgeries as a way of healing through humor. E-mail her at carisaw@hotmail.com.

Robin A. Burrows is a writer and poet from Arkansas. She discovered she could create stories like those she loved to read when her third grade class had to write a story using their spelling words. Robin writes fantasy and children's books. Learn more at www.robinaburrows. com.

Barbara Canale is a freelance writer and columnist for *The Catholic Sun* in Syracuse, NY. She has been published in ten *Chicken Soup for the Soul* books. She is the author of *Our Labor of Love: A Romanian Adoption Chronicle,* and *Prayers, Papers, and Play: Devotions for Every College Student,* by Liguori Publications.

Lorri Carpenter, along with her mother, writes under the pen name HL Carpenter. A mother/daughter duo, they admit to having way too much fun writing together. Their most recent book, *The SkyHorse*, is a young adult e-novel published by Musa Publishing and available on Amazon. See more of their work at www.TopDrawerInkCorp.com.

Beth Cato is an active member of the Science Fiction & Fantasy Writers of America, and a frequent contributor to *Chicken Soup for the Soul* books. She's originally from Hanford, CA, but now resides in Buckeye, AZ with her husband and son. Learn more at www.bethcato. com.

Emily Parke Chase began writing in 1995 and now has six books in print, including *Help! My Family's Messed Up* (Kregel, 2008). Her newest, *Standing Tall After Falling Short*, will be released in 2013. She encourages new writers by speaking at writers' conferences and doing one-on-one critiques. Visit her at emilychase.com.

Linda S. Clare is an award-winning author of five books, including *A Sky without Stars*, due out in 2014. She teaches writing for a community college and as an advisor for George Fox University. She lives in the Northwest with her family and three criminal cats. Visit her blog "Linda Clare's Writer's Tips" at www.lindasclare.com.

Phyllis Cochran has been writing and publishing stories for over twenty years. She has run writers' workshops and taught classes on "Writing for Publication." Phyllis enjoys visiting friends and family and traveling with her husband, Phil. They often care for their children and grandchildren's dogs. Her memoir, *Shades of Light*, was published in 2006.

A true romantic, **Sebastian Cole's** life is defined by following his heart and pursuing his dreams, which is why he has become a novelist. Sebastian writes from the heart, believes in true love, love at first sight, and finding the one person in life you're meant to be with. Learn more at www.SebastianColeAuthor.com.

Harriet Cooper is a freelance writer and has published personal essays, humour and creative non-fiction in newspapers, newsletters, anthologies and magazines. She is a frequent contributor to the *Chicken Soup for the Soul* series. She writes about family, relationships, health, food, cats, writing and daily life. E-mail her at shewrites@ live.ca.

Gayle Allen Cox is an award-winning writer from Texas. She has written op-eds and essays for various newspapers and magazines and is a returning contributor to *Chicken Soup for the Soul*. E-mail her at gayleacox@att.net.

Michael Damiano is a non-fiction writer and journalist who writes in English and Spanish about art and history. His first book, *Porque la vida no basta*, was published in Spain by Anagrama (and by Empuries in Catalan) in 2012. He is working on his second book, in English, about Easter Island. He is a 2010 graduate of Georgetown University.

Linda C. Defew began writing ten years ago. She has gone on to write articles for *Christian Woman*, *Kaleidoscope*, *Kentucky Explorer*, *The Writer*, and this is her fourth story published in the *Chicken Soup for the Soul* series. She has formed a writers' group that serves as a great source of inspiration. E-mail her at oldwest@tds.net.

Although blind, **Janet Perez Eckles** has been inspiring thousands to see the best in life. She is an international speaker, writer and #1 bestselling author of *Simply Salsa: Dancing without Fear at God's Fiesta*. Her mission is to ignite in you a passion to overcome and reach success and excellence. Learn more at www.janetperezeckles.com.

Terri Elders, LCSW, lives in the country near Colville, WA. A lifelong writer and editor, Terri's stories have appeared in dozens of anthologies, including multiple *Chicken Soup for the Soul* books. Contact her at telders@hotmail.com and read her blog at atouchoftarragon.blogspot.com.

Shawnelle Eliasen and her husband Lonny raise their brood of boys in Illinois. Her stories have been published in *Guideposts, MomSense, Marriage Partnership, Thriving Family, Cup of Comfort* books, numerous *Chicken Soup for the Soul* books, and more. Visit her blog, "Family Grace with My Five Sons," at shawnellewrites.blogspot.com.

Melissa Face lives in Virginia with her husband and son. She teaches high school English and spends countless hours editing student work. She is a stickler for details. E-mail Melissa at writermsface@yahoo.com.

Victoria Fedden received her MFA degree in creative writing from Florida Atlantic University in 2009. She is a stay-at-home mom who enjoys writing, cooking, and reading. She has just completed a memoir about life in South Florida. E-mail her at victoriafedden@gmail.com.

Peggy Frezon is author of *Heart to Heart, Hand in Paw* and *Dieting with My Dog*, pet columnist, writer for *Guideposts* magazine and *Be the Change for Animals*. Find her at peggyfrezon.blogspot.com and peggyfrezon.blogspot.com/p/pawsitively-pets.html. Facebook: www.facebook.com/PeggyFrezonBooks. Twitter: @peggyfrezon.

A longtime personal essayist, **Sally Friedman** is a graduate of the University of Pennsylvania. Her work has appeared in *The New York Times, Ladies' Home Journal* and in many regional and local publications. Her most important work is family: husband Victor, three daughters and sons-in-law, and seven astounding grandchildren.

Valerie Frost lives in San Diego, CA. She and her husband Terry are parents of three grown children. They have nine energetic grandchildren, and two turbo-charged Jack Russell Terriers, named Rocket and Daphne. E-mail her at tvfrost@aol.com.

Kathleen Gerard is an award-winning writer whose work has been widely published and broadcasted on National Public Radio (NPR). Her novel, *In Transit*, won Best Romantic Fiction at the New York Book Festival 2011. Learn more at www.kathleengerard.blogspot. com.

Jenna Glatzer is the author or ghostwriter of twenty books, including the authorized biographies *Celine Dion: For Keeps* and *The Marilyn Monroe Treasures*, and the memoirs *My Stolen Son* with Susan Markowitz and *Unthinkable* with Scott Rigsby. She's also mom to the world's coolest kindergartener. Visit Jenna at www.jennaglatzer.com.

Arlene Rains Graber is an award-winning freelance writer and author of one devotional book and three novels: *Devoted to Traveling*, released in 2010, by AWOC Publishers; *A Plane Tree in Provence* and *Angel on My Shoulder*, both released in 2011; and *The Cape Elizabeth Ocean Avenue Society* in 2012. Learn more at www.arlenerainsgraber. com.

Amy Green is a senior professional writing major at Taylor University. She is the author of a juvenile fiction series, the *Amarias Adventures*, published by Warner Press. Amy enjoys playing board games, talking to interesting people, baking cookies, and saying funny things, some of which she blogs about.

Wendy Greenley earned a master's degree in microbiology from the University of Delaware and a J.D. from the Villanova School of Law. Wendy is a SCBWI member, writing picture books and middle-grade novels. Her writing has won awards in both local and national competitions. E-mail her at wbgreenley@gmail.com or visit www. wendygreenley.com.

A freelance writer and editor, **Sarah Hamaker's** stories have appeared in previous *Chicken Soup for the Soul* books. Sarah lives in Virginia with her husband and four children, and is a certified Leadership Parenting Coach. Visit her online at www.sarahhamaker.com, where she blogs about parenting issues.

Wendy Hobday Haugh's stories and articles have appeared in dozens of national and regional magazines, including *Woman's World*, *Highlights for Children*, and *Saratoga Living*. She is inspired by the antics, wit and wisdom of her three grown sons and her soon-to-be four delightful grandchildren. E-mail her at whhaugh@nycap.rr.com.

Miriam Hill is a frequent contributor to *Chicken Soup for the Soul* books and has been published in *Writer's Digest*, *The Christian Science Monitor*, *Grit*, *St. Petersburg Times*, *The Sacramento Bee* and Poynter Online. Miriam's manuscript received Honorable Mention for Inspirational Writing in a Writer's Digest Writing Competition.

Diane Hurles has studied creative non-fiction for the past five years. A former journalist, she received a Bachelor of Arts degree in English from Hillsdale College, Hillsdale, MI. She has worked in public relations and financial development for the YMCA for more than twenty-five years. E-mail her at dianehurles@yahoo.com.

Kelly James-Enger has been a full-time freelancer and author for sixteen-plus years. She's also the lucky mom of two children — Ryan and Haley — through open adoptions. She lives outside Chicago with her family, and her latest book is *Writer for Hire: 101 Secrets to Freelance Success*.

J.A. Jance is The New York Times bestselling author of forty-five contemporary mysteries in four different series. Born in South Dakota and raised in Bisbee, AZ, she now divides her time between homes in

Tucson, AZ and in Bellevue, WA. *Second Watch*, her forty-sixth novel, will be published in September 2013.

Beckie Jas, an environmental media specialist in Southern Ontario, creates education campaigns for children and adults. Her third children's book will be published in 2013. She writes for the Restless Writers: www.restlesswriters.ca, and has received awards for publication excellence, including a 2012 Gold Quill Award. She also writes young-adult fiction.

L.S. Johnson lives in Northern California, where she currently works in book production. She has written short stories, interviews, and essays, and has recently completed the first book in a trilogy set in the 18th century.

Vickey Kall is author of the novels *Death Speaker* and *The Boomer Book of Christmas Memories* (a collection of toys, trees, and trivia from the 1950s and 1960s). She loves to write about history and pop culture, often under her real and unpronounceable name, Kalambakal. Her blog is at www.VickeyKall.com.

Rory C. Keel has served as an Evangelist since 1989. Ordained as an Elder in 2007 with the Amarillo Church of Christ. He is actively involved in writing with the Panhandle Professional Writers, IWA! and OWFI. Rory writes inspirational, historical and Christian fiction. E-mail him at roryckeel@gmail.com.

Brenda Kezar is a short story writer living in North Dakota. She enjoys fishing, camping, and spending time with her family, including her dogs, Abby and Roscoe Pascal. Someday she's going to make the leap to novelist! Visit her at www.BrendaKezar.com.

Elizabeth Stark Kline earned her B.A. degree with honors in English and history from Vanderbilt University in 1977. A medical biller by day, she continues to write fiction and enjoys metal detecting, crafting, and keeping up with her two kids, four cats and a dog named Linus.

Mimi Greenwood Knight is a freelance writer living in South Louisiana with her husband David and four spectacular kids, Haley, Molly, Hewson and Jonah. She enjoys knitting, gardening, Bible study and martial arts. Mimi is blessed to have over 500 published articles and essays, including stories in two dozen *Chicken Soup for the Soul* books.

Randi Kreger is the author of *Stop Walking on Eggshells* (with Paul Mason), *The Stop Walking on Eggshells Workbook*, *The Essential Family Guide to Borderline Personality Disorder*, and *Splitting* (with Bill Eddy), about divorcing someone with borderline or narcissistic personality disorder. Visit her at BPDCentral.com and psychologytoday.com/blog/stop-walking-eggshells.

Sharon Kurtzman's writing has been published in *All Things Girl*, *moonShine review*, *The Scruffy Dog Review*, *Airplane Reading*, *Still Crazy* and Raleigh's *The News & Observer*. Her novel, *Cosmo's Deli*, was published by Boson Books. In 2012, she ran her first marathon, after which she checked it off her Bucket List.

Cathi LaMarche is the author of the novel *While the Daffodils Danced* and has contributed to numerous anthologies. As a composition teacher, author, and writing coach, she spends most of her day reveling in the written word. She resides in Missouri with her husband, two children, and three dogs.

Dawn M. Lilly's inspirational writings have appeared in devotionals, anthologies, and DaySpring Cards. This is her third story published in the *Chicken Soup for the Soul* series. She and her husband live in Seattle where she gardens, spends time with her grandchildren, and is working on her first novel. Contact her at www.dawnmlilly.com.

Sarah Darer Littman is the author of *Confessions of a Closet Catholic*, which won the 2006 Sydney Taylor Book Award; *Life, After*, a 2011 Sydney Taylor Honor book; *Purge*; and *Want to Go Private?*, a 2012 YALSA Quick Pick for Reluctant Readers, and an award-winning columnist for CTNewsJunkie.com. Contact her at sarahdarerlittman. com or Twitter @sarahdarerlitt.

Gail MacMillan is an award-winning author of twenty-seven published books and numerous short stories both in North America and Western Europe. She is a graduate of Queen's University and lives in New Brunswick, Canada with her husband and two dogs.

Catherine Madera is an award-winning writer based in the Pacific Northwest. Her work has been widely published and includes two novels. She also serves as editor of *The Northwest Horse Source* magazine. Catherine enjoys horseback riding and spending time with her family. Learn more at www.catherinemadera.com.

Joyce Styron Madsen is a librarian/educator who has done corporate and medical research. She is an animal welfare advocate, foster mom for rescue dogs, Wisconsin Humane Society volunteer, and mother to four former puppy mill dogs. She's also very proud to say that she's a writer. E-mail her at joycestyron@sbcglobal.net

James C. Magruder is an award-winning advertising copywriter and executive speechwriter. He has had articles published in *Writer's Digest*, *Writers' Journal*, *Marriage Partnership*, *HomeLife*, *Christian Communicator*, *Today's Freelance Writer*, and *The Art of Self-Promotion*. He blogs about the writing life at www.thewritersrefuge.wordpress. com.

Former newspaper journalist **Diane Majeske** has published three books—*Death on Deadline*; *Magic, Miracles & Mistletoe*; and *Mom Tales: Stories of Parenting, Potties and Post-Partum Panic*. She lives in

Michigan with her husband and two children, and is a writer for the University of Michigan.

Shawn Marie Mann is a freelance writer and geographer living in central Pennsylvania. She is currently studying the history and people of her hometown for future writing projects. Contact her at www.shawnmariemann.com.

David Martin's humor and political satire have appeared in many publications including *The New York Times*, the *Chicago Tribune* and *Smithsonian* magazine. His latest humor collection *Dare to be Average* was published in 2010. David lives in Ottawa, Canada with his wife Cheryl and their daughter Sarah.

Timothy Martin is the author of numerous young adult novels and screenplays. His work has appeared in over a dozen *Chicken Soup for the Soul* books and several literary journals. E-mail Tim at tmartin@ northcoast.com.

Dodie Milardo's decision to take a cruise to celebrate her fiftieth birthday completely changed her life. From the corporate world, she is now author of roman à clef novel *Penelope's Cruise*. She also hosts radio talk shows and has raised more than $60,000 for charities to date. Learn more at www.penelopescruise.com.

Suzan Moyer has been enjoying teaching for the past twenty years. She is currently a middle school Learning Center teacher in Kansas. Now that her four sons are grown, she enjoys gardening, reading, playing the piano, and spoiling her grandchildren. E-mail her at suzanmoyer@att.net.

Diane Nichols has been a worldwide journalist for twenty years with more than 300 magazine and newspaper features in print. She is also the author of *Prison of My Own: A True Story of Redemption & Forgiveness* available at Amazon.com. E-mail her at diane@dianenichols.com.

Marc Tyler Nobleman is the author of *Boys of Steel: The Creators of Superman* and *Bill the Boy Wonder: The Secret Co-Creator of Batman*. Outlets including *USA Today*, NPR's *All Things Considered*, *Forbes*, and MTV have covered his work. Marc is invited to speak at conferences, schools, and other venues nationwide.

Novelist, blogger, and award-winning food writer, **Perry P. Perkins** is a work-at-home dad, and the owner of www.hautemealz.com. He has written for hundreds of magazines, and his inspirational stories have been included in many *Chicken Soup for the Soul* anthologies. Perry lives in the Pacific Northwest.

Mary C. M. Phillips is a writer of narrative essays and short stories. Her work has appeared in numerous anthologies including the *Chicken Soup for the Soul* series, *Cup of Comfort* series, and *Bad Austen: The Worst Stories Jane Never Wrote*. She is blessed with a loving family and resides in New York.

Felice Prager is a freelance writer and multisensory educational therapist and the author of five books: *Waiting in the Wrong Line*, *Negotiable and Non-Negotiable Negotiations*, *TurboCharge Your Brain*, *SuperTurboCharge Your Brain*, and *Quiz It: Arizona*. Her essays have been published locally, nationally, and internationally. Learn more at www.WriteFunny.com.

Anna Redsand is a retired educator and counselor. Her YA biography, *Viktor Frankl: A Life Worth Living* (Clarion, 2006), has received four awards. Her work has appeared in *Third Coast* magazine, *Friends Journal*, *Fireweed*, *Rockhurst Review*, and other periodicals. She lives in Albuquerque and writes full time.

Jennifer Reed has been publishing for both children and adults since 1990. She has over twenty-five books published for children and a slew of articles and stories in various magazines. She has her master's degree from Vermont College of Fine Arts. Visit her at www.jennifer-reed.com for more info.

Amelia Rhodes is the author of *Isn't It Time for a Coffee Break? Doing Life Together in an All-about-Me Kind of World* and a contributor to *Chicken Soup for the Soul: Here Comes the Bride*. Amelia lives with her husband and children in Michigan. E-mail her at amelia@ameliarhodes.com.

Tammy Roark-Proctor recently retired from a twenty-four-year newspaper career. The former executive editor and writer has interviewed thousands of people, all who have a story to tell. Leaving Ohio for the warmer climate of North Carolina, she is currently a full-time grandmother and freelance writer.

Robert Robeson is a professional member of the National Writers Association, the Distinguished Flying Cross Society and the Military Writers Society of America. He retired from the U.S. Army as a lieutenant colonel, has a BA degree in English from the University of Maryland and has completed extensive graduate journalism work.

Sioux Roslawski is a third grade teacher in St. Louis and a teacher-consultant for the Gateway Writing Project. She is a proud member of the infamous WWWP (Wild Women Wielding Pens) writing critique group; her favorite genre is memoir. Read more from Sioux at siouxspage.blogspot.com.

Hank Phillippi Ryan reports for Boston's NBC affiliate. Winner of twenty-eight Emmys, former U.S. Senate and *Rolling Stone* magazine staffer. She is president of national Sisters in Crime and MWA board member. Author of six novels, winner of two Agathas, the Anthony and the Macavity awards for crime fiction.

Steve Schultz is a teacher who has been published in *Educational Leadership* magazine and four other books: *Hey Leader, Wake Up And Hear The Feedback*, *A+ Teaching*, *Chicken Soup for the Soul: Tough Times* *for Teens*, and *Chicken Soup for the Soul: Inside Basketball*. E-mail him at personalbest22@gmail.com.

Nicole Scobie is a Canadian mom to three great boys, wife to one great Dane, living in Switzerland. She describes herself as a "Cancer-Mom instead of a Soccer-Mom." Her stories about life in the cancer world are sometimes heart-wrenching but also uplifting and inspiring. Read more at www.nicolescobie.com.

When **Sophfronia Scott** published her novel, *All I Need to Get By*, with St. Martin's Press, one reviewer referred to her as potentially "one of the best writers of her generation." Her work has appeared in *Time*, *People*, *More*, NewYorkTimes.com, *Sleet Magazine*, *Numéro Cinq*, and *O, The Oprah Magazine*.

Jodi Iachini Severson resides in Wisconsin and was raised in Johnstown, PA. Her large Italian-Irish-Catholic family (as do her co-workers) provides a constant source of humor and inspiration for her short stories, many of which can be found in other *Chicken Soup for the Soul* books. E-mail her at seversonjl@gmail.com.

Dayle Allen Shockley is an award-winning writer whose byline has appeared in dozens of publications. She is the author of three books and a contributor to many other works. She and her husband (a retired fire captain) enjoy traveling RV-style, enjoying God's handiwork. Dayle blogs at www.alittleofthisandthat2.blogspot.com.

Deborah Shouse is a writer, speaker, editor and creativity catalyst. Her writing has appeared in magazines, newspapers and *Chicken Soup for the Soul* books. Her book, *Love in the Land of Dementia: Finding Hope in the Caregiver's Journey* (Central Recovery Press: November 2013), focuses on finding the blessings in the Alzheimer's journey.

Michael T. Smith lives and works in Idaho with his beautiful and loving wife Ginny. Michael works in the telecom industry and writes inspirational and sometimes humorous stories for himself and readers of his newsletter "Hearts and Humor." You can subscribe to his newsletter at visitor.constantcontact.com/d. jsp?m=1101828445578&p=oi.

Diane Stark is a former teacher turned stay-at-home mom and freelance writer. She loves to write about the important things in life: her family and her faith. She is the author of *Teachers' Devotions to Go.* E-mail her at DianeStark19@yahoo.com.

Tsgoyna Tanzman's career spans from fitness trainer to speech pathologist, to memoir teacher to life coach. Writing is the ultimate "therapy" for raising her daughter. Published in numerous *Chicken Soup for the Soul* books, her essays and poems can be read online at More.com and mothering.com. E-mail her at coaching@changeitup. me.

Prudy Taylor-Board has twenty-four published books—two mysteries, three horror novels, eighteen regional histories, and a book about writing and selling your first novel. She is a member of Mensa, president of the Writers' Network of South Florida and a project editor with Taylor & Francis.

Ashley Thaba is a missionary and mom of three small children in Botswana, Africa. The highlight of her day is their nightly 10k walk. She pushes one child and her husband pushes the other two. The proceeds of her book cover her son's medical expenses. E-mail her at ashleythaba@gmail.com.

Leticia Velasquez is the editor of *A Special Mother is Born*. She contributed to the award-winning *Stories for the Homeschool Heart*, and *The Encyclopedia of Catholic Social Thought, Social Science and Social Policy*. She is currently writing her first novel. You may reach her at marysjoys@yahoo.com.

Pamela Walker is a mother, a wife and an observer of life. She loves old things and heirlooms, farmhouses and her husband. She enjoys spending her days on her Midwestern farm avoiding housework, homeschooling her three little chickadees, writing whenever she can and occasionally baking the world's best caramel apple pie.

Rachel Wallace-Oberle has an education in journalism, as well as broadcasting. She is currently working on a degree in communications and is senior marketing writer for a software company. Her work has been featured in *Reader's Digest, Homemakers, Canadian Living, Woman's World, Today's Parent*, and numerous other publications.

Samantha Ducloux Waltz offers people inspiration, courage and a fresh perspective on life as the writer of more than fifty creative non-fiction stories published in *Chicken Soup for the Soul, Cup of Comfort* and other anthologies. Naomi, her feline accountability partner, keeps a close eye on her.

Roz Warren and Janet Golden are a Philadelphia-based writing team. You can reach Roz at www.rosalindwarren.com or Janet at golden.rutgers.edu.

Ray Weaver, of Clearwater, FL, and his wife Ellie have been married for fifty-four years. They have two children and six grandchildren. His novels, *Tightrope to Justice, Miami Justice* and *European Justice* are available on Amazon and B&N. *Justice 4 Willis* will be released in the summer of 2013. E-mail him at raymondellie@aol.com.

Valerie Whisenand is the author of many Christian fiction novels, written using her maiden name of Valerie Hansen. These books are available as both paperbacks and e-books. When she moved to the Ozarks she found fresh inspiration, as well as a beautiful atmosphere filled with loving, caring folks. E-mail her at val@valeriehansen.com.

Mary Z. Whitney has written an inspirational fiction book and is a regular contributor to the *Chicken Soup for the Soul* series as well as *Angels on Earth* and *Guideposts*. When not penning praises to her creator, she can be found gardening, walking her dog Max or spending time with family and friends.

Tamara Wilhite is a mother, author and technical writer.

Gail Wilkinson loves writing stories, and is a third-time contributor to *Chicken Soup for the Soul* publications. She is the author of *Alice & Frosty: An American Adventure*, highlighting rural Midwestern life in the early 1900s. She enjoys traveling, people, family, and all the stories they tell. E-mail her at books@gailwilkinson.net.

Josie Willis received a master's degree in English from Southwest Missouri State University. A full-time writer, she is currently completing a book of grief poetry, after which she plans to write children's books. She shares her home with her two "parrot" muses, Nacho and Taco. E-mail her at josiewillis2000@yahoo.com.

Dallas Woodburn's work has appeared in *Nashville Review*, *Monkeybicycle*, *Prime Number*, and the *Los Angeles Times*; her plays have been produced in New York City and Los Angeles. Her manuscript, *Woman, Running Late, in a Dress*, was a finalist for the 2012 Flannery O'Connor Award for Short Fiction.

Amy Zhang is an exceedingly average junior in high school. She edits the school newspaper, plays tennis, and occasionally texts during class. Secretly, she is an author represented by Emily Keyes of the L. Perkins Agency. She is currently revising her second novel.

Meet Our Authors

Jack Canfield is the co-creator of the *Chicken Soup for the Soul* series, which *Time* magazine has called "the publishing phenomenon of the decade." Jack is also the co-author of many other bestselling books.

Jack is the CEO of the Canfield Training Group in Santa Barbara, California, and founder of the Foundation for Self-Esteem in Culver City, California. He has conducted intensive personal and professional development seminars on the principles of success for more than a million people in twenty-three countries, has spoken to hundreds of thousands of people at more than 1,000 corporations, universities, professional conferences and conventions, and has been seen by millions more on national television shows.

Jack has received many awards and honors, including three honorary doctorates and a Guinness World Records Certificate for having seven books from the *Chicken Soup for the Soul* series appearing on the New York Times bestseller list on May 24, 1998.

You can reach Jack at www.jackcanfield.com.

Mark Victor Hansen is the co-founder of Chicken Soup for the Soul, along with Jack Canfield. He is a sought-after keynote speaker, bestselling author, and marketing maven. Mark's powerful messages of possibility, opportunity, and action have created powerful change in thousands of organizations and millions of individuals worldwide.

Mark is a prolific writer with many bestselling books in addition to the *Chicken Soup for the Soul* series. Mark has had a profound influence in the field of human potential through his library of audios, videos, and articles in the areas of big thinking, sales achievement, wealth building, publishing success, and personal and professional development. He is also the founder of the MEGA Seminar Series.

Mark has received numerous awards that honor his entrepreneurial spirit, philanthropic heart, and business acumen. He is a lifetime member of the Horatio Alger Association of Distinguished Americans.

You can reach Mark at www.markvictorhansen.com.

Amy Newmark is Chicken Soup for the Soul's publisher and editor-in-chief, after a thirty-year career as a writer, speaker, financial analyst, and business executive in the worlds of finance and telecommunications. Amy is a *magna cum laude* graduate of Harvard College, where she majored in Portuguese, minored in French, and traveled extensively. She and her husband have four grown children.

After a long career writing books on telecommunications, voluminous financial reports, business plans, and corporate press releases, Chicken Soup for the Soul is a breath of fresh air for Amy. She has fallen in love with Chicken Soup for the Soul and its life-changing books, and really enjoys putting these books together for Chicken Soup for the Soul's wonderful readers. She has co-authored more than five dozen *Chicken Soup for the Soul* books and has edited another three dozen.

You can reach Amy with any questions or comments through webmaster@chickensoupforthesoul.com and you can follow her on Twitter @amynewmark.

Susan M. Heim is a longstanding author and editor, specializing in parenting, women's and Christian issues. After the birth of her twin boys in 2003, Susan left her desk job as a Senior Editor at a publishing company and has never looked back. Being a work-at-home mother allows her to follow her two greatest passions: parenting and writing.

Susan's published books include *Chicken Soup for the Soul: Finding My Faith; Chicken Soup for the Soul: Here Comes the Bride; Chicken Soup for the Soul: Devotional Stories for Tough Times; Chicken Soup for* the Soul: New Moms; Chicken Soup for the Soul: Devotional Stories for Mothers; Chicken Soup for the Soul: Family Matters; Chicken Soup for the Soul: Devotional Stories for Women; Chicken Soup for the Soul: All in the Family; Chicken Soup for the Soul: Twins and More; Boosting Your Baby's Brain Power; It's Twins! Parent-to-Parent Advice from Infancy Through Adolescence; Oh, Baby! 7 Ways a Baby Will Change Your Life the First Year; and, Twice the Love: Stories of Inspiration for Families with Twins, Multiples and Singletons.

Susan's articles and stories have appeared in many books, websites, and magazines, including TWINS Magazine and Angels on Earth. She writes a parenting blog at http://SusanHeimOnParenting.com and a writing blog at http://SusanHeimOnWriting.com. She is also the founder of TwinsTalk, a website with tips, advice and stories about raising twins and multiples, at www.twinstalk.com.

Susan and her husband Mike are the parents of four sons, who are in elementary school and college! You can reach Susan at susan@susanheim.com and visit her website at www.susanheim.com. Join her on Twitter and Facebook by searching for ParentingAuthor.

Thank You

Nobody has more experience with rejection than writers, so we felt especially pained that we had to turn away so many wonderful stories for this book due to our limit of 101 stories per book. We read every submission however, and even those that didn't make it in were instrumental in helping us shape the book.

We owe a special thanks to our editor Madeline Clapps, who helped us narrow down the thousands of submissions to a few hundred finalists, and by the way, she complained the whole time that there were too many good stories. D'ette Corona, VP and assistant publisher, worked with all the contributors and helped to edit the stories. And editors Barbara LoMonaco and Kristiana Glavin Pastir performed their normal masterful proofreading jobs while making sure we got to the printer on time.

We owe a very special thanks to our Creative Director and book producer, Brian Taylor at Pneuma Books, for his brilliant vision for our covers and interiors.

Share with Us

We all have had Chicken Soup for the Soul moments in our lives. If you would like to share your story or poem with millions of people around the world, go to chickensoup.com and click on "Submit Your Story." You may be able to help another reader, and become a published author at the same time. Some of our past contributors have launched writing and speaking careers from the publication of their stories in our books!

Our submission volume has been increasing steadily—the quality and quantity of your submissions has been fabulous. We only accept story submissions via our website. They are no longer accepted via mail or fax.

To contact us regarding other matters, please send us an e-mail through webmaster@chickensoupforthesoul.com, or fax or write us at:

Chicken Soup for the Soul
P.O. Box 700
Cos Cob, CT 06807-0700
Fax: 203-861-7194

One more note from your friends at Chicken Soup for the Soul: Occasionally, we receive an unsolicited book manuscript from one of our readers, and we would like to respectfully inform you that we do not accept unsolicited manuscripts and we must discard the ones that appear.

www.chickensoup.com